Assessment and examination in the secondary school

The Education Reform Act has established assessment as the measure by which the implementation of the National Curriculum and school success will be judged. Current initiatives assume, for the first time, the possibility of a new partnership between curriculum and assessment.

This book is designed to provide a practical understanding of recent examination and assessment developments at secondary level, and will be particularly useful to students and practising teachers. It examines the introduction of the GCSE, the use of profiling, equal opportunities issues, examinations at 16+, and the assessment of school-leavers for training and employment. It also includes a brief historical account of the development of secondary education. The fairness and appropriateness of examination results are always a matter of public concern, and the final chapters, particularly, extend these issues by looking at the ways in which variety of experience and learning style are relevant to assessment practices.

The editors

Richard Riding is Director of the Examination and Assessment Research Unit at the School of Education, University of Birmingham. He has written extensively on educational psychology.
Sue Butterfield is Research Fellow at the School of Education, University of Birmingham.

Assessment and examination in the secondary school

A practical guide for teachers and trainers

Edited by Richard Riding
and Sue Butterfield

London and New York

First published 1990
by Routledge
11 New Fetter Lane, London EC4P 4EE

Simultaneously published in the USA and Canada
by Routledge
a division of Routledge, Chapman and Hall, Inc.
29 West 35th Street, New York, NY 10001

Printed and bound in Great Britain by
Biddles Ltd, Guildford and King's Lynn

British Library Cataloguing in Publication Data

Assessment and examination in the secondary school : a
practical guide for teachers and trainers.
1. Great Britain. Secondary schools. Students. Assessment
I. Riding, Richard, *1939–* II. Butterfield, Sue, *1948–*
373.12'64

ISBN 0-415-03108-7
ISBN 0-415-03109-5 pbk

Library of Congress Cataloging in Publication Data

Assessment and examination in the secondary school : a practical guide
for teachers and trainers / edited by Richard Riding and Sue
Butterfield.
p. cm.
ISBN 0-415-03108-7. – ISBN 0-415-03109-5 (pbk.)
1. Curriculum-based assessment – Great Britain. 2. Education,
Secondary – Great Britain – Curricula – Evaluation. 3. General
Certificate of Education Examination. I. Riding, R.J.
II. Butterfield, Sue, 1948–
LB3060.32.C74A85 1990
373.19'0941–dc20 89-27432
CIP

CONTENTS

LIST OF FIGURES

LIST OF TABLES

CONTRIBUTORS

Bill Brown, Deputy Secretary, West Midlands Examinations Board.

Christopher Buckle, Lecturer, Examinations and Assessment Research Unit, School of Education, University of Birmingham.

Sue Butterfield, Research Fellow, Examinations and Assessment Research Unit, School of Education, University of Birmingham.

Mary Jones, Careers Officer, Wolverhampton.

Ian McGuff, Staff Development Tutor, Sandwell LEA.

Merlin Rangel, Psychologist, Birmingham Careers Service.

Richard Riding, Director, Examinations and Assessment Research Unit and Reader in Educational Psychology, School of Education, University of Birmingham.

Brian Roby, Modular Curriculum Adviser, Hereford and Worcester, LEA.

PREFACE

Amongst much repetition of the assurance that the relationship of assessment to curriculum is one of servant to master, it might in fact appear that *assessment* has made a further bid for power. This is an important time, because the debate about assessment has been opened, the criteria of assessment are a matter of national discussion, and in the process, the objectives of teaching and learning are being defined and redefined. 'Master' and 'servant' are no longer appropriate ways to think of the relationship of curriculum to assessment. Current assessment initiatives are predicated upon the belief that curriculum and assessment can enter into a new partnership.

This book explores current developments in assessment from a number of perspectives. Its starting point is the introduction of the General Certificate of Secondary Education, which is discussed in terms of its origins, its objectives design, and its organization at examining group level. The school context of the examinations at 16-plus is changing too. Major curricular developments are associated with vocational education, and profiles are being introduced in order to record a greater range of achievement than examination results. The place of examination results and other achievements in recruitment is illustrated by a survey of the practices of employers.

The fairness and appropriateness of examination results are always a matter of public concern. The final two chapters of this book, particularly, extend these issues by looking at the ways in which variety of experience and learning style are relevant to assessment practices.

The book is designed to provide a practical understanding of recent examination and assessment developments for teachers, student teachers and general readers. It is not intended that the lists of references and bibliographies are exhaustive, but they are designed to give starting points for further reading.

LIST OF ABBREVIATIONS

AS	Advanced Supplementary Level
BTEC	Business and Technician Education Council
CGLI	City and Guilds of London Institute
CPVE	Certificate of Pre-vocational Education
DES	Department of Education and Science
GCSE	General Certificate of Secondary Education
LEA	Local Education Authority
LMF	Leicestershire Modular Framework
NVQ	National Vocational Qualifications
RSA	Royal Society of Arts
SEAC	School Examinations and Assessment Council
TGAT	Task Group on Assessment and Testing
TVEI	Technical and Vocational Education Initiative

Chapter One

THE DEVELOPMENT OF SECONDARY ASSESSMENT AND EXAMINATIONS

Sue Butterfield

This chapter will indicate some of the sources of dissatisfaction with public examinations in England and Wales at secondary school level, prior to the introduction of the General Certificate of Secondary Education (GCSE) and explore the extent to which the new examination system is achieving its aims. The GCSE's place in a developing context of assessment purposes and procedures is outlined.

SECONDARY SCHOOL EXAMINATIONS: WHAT DO WE ASK?

> 'Bitzer,' said Thomas Gradgrind; 'Your definition of a horse.'
>
> 'Quadruped. Graminivorous. Forty teeth, namely twenty-four grinders, four eye-teeth, and twelve incisive. Sheds coat in the spring; in marshy countries, sheds hoofs, too. Hoofs hard, but requiring to be shod with iron. Age known by marks in mouth.' Thus (and much more) Bitzer.
>
> 'Now girl number twenty,' said Mr Gradgrind. 'You know what a horse is.'
>
> Charles Dickens, *Hard Times*

> 'An Army marches on its stomach' (Napoleon). Illustrate and examine.
>
> Sellar and Yeatman, *1066 and All That*

What society asks of its examination systems is reflected in a number of ways in what those systems ask of their candidates. The development of our examination systems at 16-plus and 18-plus dates from the formalization of assessment in the nineteenth century. Nineteenth-century urban expansion and social legislation led to a rapid growth in local government and an increasing requirement for officers and clerical workers. The enlarged British Empire demanded an administration, and the Civil Service expanded accordingly. The greatly increased recruitment need made earlier systems of informal recommendation inadequate and inefficient. In the 1850s Civil Service entrance examinations were introduced, followed in the 1870s by recruitment examinations for military colleges. Some professions were introducing examinations of their own, aware of the improvement in status that could follow from a more rigorous entrance test.

The grammar schools were attracted by the development of written examinations away from the system of 'Locals' (inspection visits by a University Fellow). In 1858 the universities of Oxford and Cambridge introduced examinations to be taken in schools, and from 1877 issued certificates. The prestigious, university-controlled system of school examinations had been born; its power developed apace. The University of London issued School Leaving Certificates, and developed matriculation examinations for university entrance. The matriculation examinations also served as entry qualifications to local government posts.

Oral examining, the previously accepted method of conferring university degrees, was now called into question, and came to be regarded only as a suitable way of examining the basic accomplishments of the elementary schools. There, the art of oral examining was far from well developed and the requirements of inspection visits did little to invigorate the curriculum — strategic seating of the brighter pupils could do much to improve the apparent performance of all.

Technical and vocationally oriented examinations, such as the City and Guilds of London Institute examinations dating from 1878, or the Ordinary and Higher National Certificates introduced in the 1920s, recognized the increasing specialism of industrial recruitment, but had limited impact upon the conceptions of school curricula.

In 1917 the Board of Education introduced the School Certificate, and in 1922 the Higher School Certificate. One essential feature of the School Certificate examinations was the grouping of subjects. Candidates for the First level — sixteen-year-old grammar school pupils — would obtain a certificate by achieving a pass level in five subjects, to include one from each of the three groups: humanities; languages; sciences and mathematics. Practical and aesthetic subjects constituted a fourth group of unequal status with the others. The Board of Education, through the School Certificate and the regulations covering schools in receipt of grants, exercised control over what it considered to be its broad and balanced curriculum.

Interestingly, any diminution of the curriculum's academic content was more likely to be allowed in the case of girls:

> For older girls (over 15 years of age) Natural Science may be wholly or partially dropped, and Mathematics may be confined to Arithmetic, in order to make room for a fuller course in a combination of Domestic Subjects.
>
> (Board of Education 1923)

From the same publication comes the view that 'It is obvious that the greater staying power of boys probably gives them an advantage in studying difficult subjects such as Mathematics.'

So 'difficult subjects', academic subjects, and subjects with written outcomes came to acquire status over other areas of the curriculum, and written examinations certified achievement in those subjects. Seen by many as the only convenient assessment instrument in a mass examination context, by others as the only rigorous method of testing ability and accomplishment, and justified by its availability to checking and second opinion, the written examination gained considerable acceptance and power.

The General Certificate of Education introduced in 1951 to replace the School Certificate was a response to a recommendation of the Secondary Schools Examinations Council of 1943, that subjects should be individually certificated. (The recommendation that external examinations be replaced by internal certificates proved less acceptable.)

The benefit of the introduction of GCE O levels was greater opportunity for flexibility in the curriculum, and the possibility of some certification even if all-round educational progress was uneven. Its pass standard was, however, set at the previous credit level, to satisfy critics of the new system, and the inevitable consequence was a considerable failure rate in a system which *could* have given improved opportunities for certification. In practice, the notion of a large core curriculum in the grammar schools persisted, with considerable academic emphasis, and limited accommodation of either the special talents of the few or the academic limitations of some of the pupils whom the 11-plus examination selected for grammar school places.

The Beloe Report of 1960 recommended that beyond the 20 per cent of the secondary school population for whom the GCE provided certification, there would be the possibility of certificating a further percentage with other public examinations. A further 20 per cent, it envisaged, might take four or more subjects in a new examination system, and another 20 per cent again might take a smaller number of subjects.

The birth of the Certificate of Secondary Education was not a cause of universal rejoicing: 'The education service has accepted, though with mixed feelings, the inevitability of the Certificate of Secondary Education.' These are the opening words of the Secondary Schools Examination Council (1963), in the year when the first candidates began preparing for the new examinations to be held in 1965. The somewhat despondent mood recorded here was occasioned by regret and anxiety at the 'formalizing effect' of examinations. As CSE examinations developed, many teachers continued to feel that the influence of GCE over the newer system was too great, and that the excessively academic curriculum, unsuitable for many grammar school pupils, had now spread its tentacles more widely into other secondary schools.

Among the most positive effects of the development of CSE was its emphasis upon teacher involvement in public assessments, especially in the development of Mode 3 syllabuses. These syllabuses, devised by schools and groups of schools to meet their pupils' needs, allowed teachers to give curricular considerations the central place in assessment. Coursework assessment challenged the omnipotence of timed written examinations.

However, there was at best a system which paid little attention to the educational achievements, or needs, of 35 to 40 per cent of the school population. CSE, despite innovative features, existed in the shadow of GCE, and its introduction created a dual system. Some of the problems which inhered in GCE were to remain, and new problems were created by the existence of two systems.

A dual system

The sections below look at some of the problems of the GCE/CSE examinations which have dominated thinking about assessment throughout the school years. The first two sections refer to difficulties which are directly the result of a dual system, the other sections with problems which inhered in both systems, mainly for historical reasons.

Organizational difficulties

The development of a dual system of examinations was already present within the context of selection, and de-selection, at 11-plus. The Education Act of 1944 had enshrined the notion of three kinds of secondary pupil to be identified for grammar, technical or secondary modern school education. The two systems of examinations seemed a not wholly illogical extension of different styles of education for pupils in different kinds of schools, though in practice, of course, the logic broke down. The Newsom Report of 1963 did much to expose not only the inequality between grammar and secondary modern schools, but also the inequality among secondary modern schools, where opportunity to stay on into a fifth year and gain certification was far from guaranteed. Moreover, the Newsom Report, like many other studies, drew attention to the fact that a significant proportion of secondary modern school pupils out-performed grammar school contemporaries. The selection procedures at 11-plus not only created social and educational divisions, they did so on the basis of 'intelligence' and other tests which could not measure or predict motivation, future development, or aptitude in the more specialized secondary curriculum.

The raising of the school leaving age complemented the introduction of CSE examinations. The widespread reorganization along comprehensive lines in the 1970s, however, exposed increasingly the weaknesses of the dual system of examinations. Teachers, pupils, and parents were very aware of difficult and often premature choices to be made in preparing candidates for one examination or another. Smaller comprehensive schools — particularly those with four-form entry or less — would find it difficult to offer optional examination subjects for both examinations: the numbers of candidates involved would often not justify two teaching groups. So candidates had sometimes to be prepared for two different examinations with very different syllabus content and possibly different styles of examining, within the same teaching group. Schools often found it difficult to explain and justify entry policies to pupils and parents. Examination centres — schools and colleges — had to meet the administrative and other requirements of at least two examining boards.

The demand for comparability

Understandably, there were demands from many quarters that the comparability of the two systems be established. The principle that CSE was not an inherently easier examination, but rather a different examination with the capacity to discriminate in a different part of the ability range, was not easy to establish. The comparability of a grade 1 CSE with an O level grade C *or above* was not felt to be recognized by all employers. The use of coursework in CSE was felt by opponents to be a soft option but less has been said of that kind since the introduction of GCSE.

Even across examination boards comparability is hard to establish — across different examination systems it is inevitably more difficult. The technique used in the studies conducted by the Schools Council of the 1968 and 1973 examinations was to measure ability of candidates on reference tests against which examination performance could be compared. The nature of such reference tests will always, however, be open to question, as being nearer to one style of examination than another, as being incapable of repeated use over time, or on the fundamental assumptions enshrined in the notion of 'ability'.

In the past, it has been rare for public examination syllabuses to state objectives. Typically, examination syllabuses have consisted of indications of content only, so that while it was stated that students would prepare for the examination by studying, for example, British history from 1066 to 1485, the qualities and achievements to be assessed were unstated. This fact rendered comparability additionally problematic. By what criteria could a performance on one examination be said to be weaker or stronger than a performance on another?

The Schools Council study of 1973 (Willmott 1977), concluded that 'subject grading standards *appeared* to have fallen from 1968 to 1973' (my italics), and acknowledged that a number of factors could account for that apparent fall. It 'could simply result from the fact that teachers are better at their job in 1973 than they were in 1968, thus producing a situation where subject grades have improved while reference test scores have been unaffected.' This possibility was offered, however, without conviction. The spectre of falling standards had entered public mythology.

The emphasis on recall

If some feared that CSE was detracting from the rigorous standards of public examinations, many others were lamenting that in spite of its brave intentions to certificate different kinds of achievement, the CSE was being dominated by the GCE. Far from being a curricular advance for the vast majority of students, the introduction of CSE examinations was turning the curriculum of whole comprehensive schools into a slightly diluted grammar school experience. Both systems, it has been argued, relied far too heavily on recall, and the backwash effect of both systems was to create transmission teaching. In this model, the teacher/transmitter talks, dictates or writes on the board, (or in a highly sophisticated version of the same, hands out duplicated notes), and the pupil/receivers write, recall and repeat the transmission. Emphasis is on recall of a simple, explicit, factual kind. The pupil develops (if successful) speed in writing and ability in recall. The popularity of mnemonics serves to demonstrate how context-free and meaningless some facts were felt to be.

Examination of recall is relatively unproblematic for examiners and can give teachers the impression that they are getting immediate feedback on the effectiveness of their teaching. In the common transmission-lesson, recall-homework, repetition-test model, however, the criteria of acceptability are not defined. The teacher/transmitter is likely to see a range of scores from 10 out of 10 to 0 out of 10 as proof of an eternal order of things, rather than an indication that for some of the students the teaching is wholly ineffective. If a number of students score 5 out of 10 does the teacher consider the possibility that the teaching may be only 50 per cent effective?

Timed examinations

Ability to work at speed has a certain status in assessment, and is certainly easier to assess than other qualities. Like recall, its tenacity in assessment models derives from its apparent ease of use rather than from its educational justifications. Putting a tight time limit on a test is the best way of ensuring that some candidates do not finish. That will help to spread the marks out and suggest that the examination is discriminating between candidates. However, if the discrimination is wholly or partially on grounds of speed, the examination may not be fulfilling its objectives. Since examination syllabuses have not traditionally stated objectives, this has been a difficult case to argue. The development of syllabuses with explicit objectives allows teachers to challenge and reform assumptions about the importance of working at speed. If it is not an assessment objective, then there can be little justification for a tight limit on the time allowed.

Timed examinations will probably always have some place in assessment, for they ensure standard conditions for candidates. Their use, however, has been felt unduly to dominate public examinations and their status has persisted even where their validity has been questioned. CSE schemes which did not have timed elements found it the hardest to win public credibility. Yet timed examinations cannot measure many of the qualities, skills, and processes which our students are developing, need to develop, and need to identify as valuable. The Cockcroft Report of 1982 challenged the exclusive use of the timed, pen and paper examination in what might have been considered its strongest bastion — mathematics.

> Examinations in mathematics which consist only of timed written papers cannot, by their nature, assess ability to undertake practical and investigational work or ability to carry out work of an extended nature. They cannot assess skills of mental computation or ability to discuss mathematics nor, other than in very limited ways, qualities of perseverance and inventiveness. Work and qualities of this kind can only be assessed in the classroom and such assessment needs to be made over an extended period.
>
> (Department of Education and Science 1982)

Question style

The codes of examination questions — 'illustrate', 'discuss', 'compare', 'contrast', are part of a private language to which only school can initiate. The words have special meanings in the ritual of 'essay' answers. The history of School Certificate and GCE as entry examinations to universities and to the professions, established essay-writing skills as the most desirable communication skills. Learning to structure the answer to an unstructured question has occupied much teacher and student time. Again, as long as CSE had to compete for credibility with GCE it was bound by many of its traditions and methods. The 16-plus examinations introduced as pilot schemes in the 1970s to test the feasibility of a single examination system often pioneered new approaches for a wide ability range — structured questions, objective questions and coursework projects — but the entries were not considered to have proved the applicability of common undifferentiated examinations at the extremes of the examinable range (Department of Education and Science 1978).

Lack of vocational relevance

GCE and CSE examinations inevitably, in view of the university entrance/matriculation model which they served, paid limited attention to skills which might be of use to those entering work at 16 or 18. Leaving school to take an apprenticeship or employment has all too readily been seen as dropping out of school rather than as the culmination of a successful school career. Thus the realistic aspirations and career plans of the huge majority of students have been subordinated to the academic route of a tiny minority. In the name of freeing young people from a merely utilitarian education, and clinging to horrific images of child mineworkers, teachers have until recent years proved very resistant to vocational education.

Norm-referencing

A commonly held view is that public examination results are determined in such a way that a fixed proportion of candidates are awarded each grade irrespective of the standard of performance. Such a system is known as norm-referencing, and is so called because it realies upon the notion of a normal distribution of marks. The system is further explained and examined by Christopher Buckle in chapter two.

Examiners do indeed pay attention to distributions of marks, and use the distribution to judge whether their examination was unduly difficult or easy. Public examination grades have not, however, generally been awarded on the basis simply of a distribution. In the great majority of syllabuses the borderlines between grades are decided by the connoisseurship of experienced examiners and teachers as subject panels. This referencing of grades according to panel-judgement has been described as limen referencing (Christie and Forrest 1981).

However, it remains the case that an acceptance, an expectation, has developed that examination standards can be looked at in terms of proportions achieving certain grades.

This is another way in which failure has been built into the system. The targeting of GCE at 20 per cent of the population and CSE at a further 40 per cent placed both examinations too firmly within the notion of norm-referencing. Criterion-referencing can have limited meaning in a system which dictates the award of an overall aggregated grade (Cresswell 1987), despite the desirability of a profile of examination performance (Harrison 1983).

PURPOSES OF ASSESSMENT

Before looking at the main new initiatives, it might be useful to reflect on some of the purposes of assessment, to consider which purposes are, or can be, addressed by the GCSE and by other assessment systems.

There are a number of ways of looking at the purposes of assessment, and the answers we give when asking 'why assess?' will depend very much on the perspective or discipline that underlies the question. A sociologist might see assessment primarily in terms of social management, an anthropologist in terms of social ritual. The perspective also alters greatly over time; giving *An Historian's View of Examinations*, Norman Morris classified the uses that examinations can be put to: 'a means of maintaining standards ... an incentive to effort ... an administrative device and ... a tool of social engineering' (Wiseman 1961). Later writers might share many of these views while being more likely to stress some of the benefits that can also derive from an assessment system, even operating within the constraints of public examinations.

Motivation

A commonly held view, and one of great significance to the teacher, is that assessment motivates students. One viewpoint is that competition between students will spur them to greater efforts; another is that students will gain confidence and direction from feedback on their achievements. These two models have very different implications for classroom management. The first implies league tables where achievement (and absence of achievement) are sufficiently public for students to be said to be in competition. The problem here is that while coming 'top of the class' may be very encouraging for the 'winner' and the near aspirants, there is very limited encouragement in such a model for the rest.

The second model requires a more individual approach, so that any student has information about performance on a given assignment, and progress can be recorded on an ipsative basis; that is, by reference to the student's own past performance. The success of this model depends upon the teacher having clear objectives and upon the student knowing what these are. The criteria for assessment need to be understood if the assessment process itself is to be motivating. English compositions, for example, are generally marked on a very wide basis of 'impressions'. Unless the teacher helps the learners to identify and understand something of this impressionistic approach, it may take several years, or for ever, for learners to begin to identify the criteria. The student who scores, over ten composition assignments, five As, two Bs, and three Cs will be in a good position to meet the criteria in future pieces of work, having plenty of evidence as to what 'worked' and what did not. The student who scores ten Es, however, will not be any the wiser. Assessment as part of the learning process may be called formative.

Diagnosis

Formative assessment, which takes place during a course, should ideally identify areas in which students need additional support. Such assessment may be called diagnostic. Sometimes it may take the form of commercially available test materials designed to highlight particular strengths or weaknesses in basic skill areas. The teacher, too, is making continual diagnostic assessments of groups or individuals. This assessment is often informal and often impressionistic. There can be gains, as suggested above, in making the criteria more explicit, so that assessment is part of 'a "system" of diagnosis and consequently the outcome of the assessment is not an end in itself, but a guide to remedial action if required' (Black and Devine 1986).

Certification

This purpose of assessment is most usually linked, outside the context of academic education, with a criterion-referenced model. In swimming or musical achievement certificates are awarded for fixed levels of achievement. Examination certificates have been linked to partially norm-referenced systems, and so 'certification' does not necessarily keep the more everyday meaning of the recording of an event or fixed level of achievement. The GCSE examination pledges itself to certificate what candidates 'know, understand and can do'; in other words, to a more criteria-based model than previous examinations.

Selection

A very powerful influence is exerted over all other kinds and purposes of assessment by its use in selection. The fact that career and higher education opportunities are finite and fewer than the numbers of school leavers means that examinations at 16-plus must regulate demand. This fact militates against the use of assessment to motivate and certificate achievement, for it dictates that only a proportion must achieve any particular level, as represented by a grade. The most efficient way to control proportions is by norm-referencing.

Selection is too generally experienced as de-selection. While the expansion of opportunities is one answer to this, the development of planned and progressive educational routes may also help to give all students a greater sense of control, understanding and achievement in their school careers, and limit the extent to which academic success eclipses all other.

THE CURRENT ANSWERS

The General Certificate of Secondary Education

The need for a single system has been strongly felt since the introduction of CSE. Work by the Schools Council, and the Waddell Committee reporting in 1978, established the feasibility of a single system. The Cockcroft Report, *Mathematics Counts* (Department of Education and Science 1982), was influential in shaping the way all assessment in the new General Certificate of Secondary Education examinations would be conceived and conducted.

The common system of examining at 16-plus was, despite many years of related research and development, announced amidst counter-predictions in the press and with a very tight time-scale for implementation. The announcement of its introduction was made in the House of Commons on 20 June

1984, and the first courses began in September 1986.

The features of the new examination system were signalled by Sir Keith Joseph in public speeches in the first half of 1984. In a speech at the North of England Conference, Sheffield, 6 January 1984, he said the following. 'I conclude that it is a realistic objective to try to bring 80 to 90 per cent of all pupils at least to the level now associated with the CSE grade 4: i.e. at least to the level now expected and achieved by pupils of average ability in individual subjects ...' There would be, he implied, 'standards of competence' not offered by the existing system, though his use of the term 'objectives' in this speech referred to the objective of raising standards rather than to educational objectives as such. The 'curriculum should be relevant to the real world'; there 'should be 'differentiation within the curriculum for variations in the abilities and aptitudes of students.' 'We should move towards a greater degree of criterion-referencing in these examinations and away from norm-referencing.' In a speech to the Assistant Masters and Mistresses Conference, Bournemouth, 16 April 1984; he stated that the central objectives of the examination system itself, 'enhancing standards, motivation and esteem', were to be achieved through the use of grade related criteria: 'to define more precisely for each subject, the skills, competencies, understanding and areas of knowledge which a candidate must have covered, and the minimum level of attainment he [sic] must demonstrate in each of them if he is to be awarded a particular grade.'

Following its official introduction in June, the new examination system was to be in operation for the summer 1988 examinations, and the first candidates would therefore embark upon their courses in September 1986. A training programme began with the appointment by examining groups of 'subject experts' (Phase 1). The phased training for teachers began in January 1986 (Phase 2), to be followed by school-based in-service training (Phase 3) in July 1986, and syllabus-related training (Phase 4) in September 1986, to run concurrently with teaching for the examinations.

In March 1985, the National Criteria documents (Department of Education and Science/Welsh Office 1985) were published, providing the general criteria which were to govern the examination system, the subject-specific criteria which were to govern syllabuses in twenty subjects, and the subjects for which those were to be a template, as in the case of French which was also to provide the criteria for other modern languages.

The general National Criteria lay down the principle of the

grading on a seven-point scale: A, B, C, D, E, F, and G. 'Grades A, B, and C will be linked to the standards of the previous O level grades A, B, and C; grades D, E, F and G will be similarly linked to CSE grades 2, 3, 4 and 5.' (Department of Education and Science/Welsh Office 1985, para. 7).

> The standards required in the GCSE examinations will be not less exacting than those required in the previous GCE O level and CSE examinations. O level and CSE, taken together, were originally designed for the upper 60 per cent of the ability range by subject. GCSE is not to be limited in that way.
>
> (Para. 9)

If this appears to be self-contradictory, the problem is to be resolved by the grade criteria which 'are being developed ...' (para. 9). Draft grade criteria in key curriculum areas were subsequently rejected after a research study to link them to grades, and at the time of writing, examining groups have explored the possibility of using performance matrices in relation to individual syllabuses.

The new examinations are required to provide both certification of achievement for school leavers at 16 and 'to serve as a basis for further study ...' (para. 11). Candidates across the ability range must be 'given opportunities to demonstrate their knowledge, abilities and achievements: *that is, to show what they know, understand and can do*' (my emphasis).

Syllabuses must follow certain patterns. The general aims of the course of study must be stated, such aims here defined as 'the educational purposes of following a course in the subject ...' (para. 21.b). 'The assessment objectives (including a statement of the abilities to be tested)' are recommended to follow (para. 21.c), but are not there further defined. The parentheses prompt a question as to what else the assessment objectives were anticipated to cover, in addition to or as an umbrella for, the statement of the abilities to be tested. In the annex to the document, 'Glossary of terms for a single system of examining at 16-plus', this definition is given.

> **Assessment objectives**
> The term *assessment objectives* is used to describe the skills/abilities which are measured and recorded for assessment purposes within a particular subject examina-

tion. Such *assessment objectives* should be expressed in terms of the observable and measurable behaviour which the achievement of the educational *aims* of a course in the subject is intended to bring about.

The new examinations were to have certain distinctive features in their assessment, particularly related to the assessment objectives: 'the scheme of assessment must reflect the assessment objectives ...' (para. 19.e.ii); 'the principle of fitness for purpose must be observed' (para. 19.e); and accordingly, since the examinations are to be designed not only to test recall, but also understanding and skills, 'the scheme of assessment should normally offer an appropriate combination of board-assessed components and centre-assessed course work' (para. 19.e.iv).

Other principles which should govern all syllabuses and assessments would be the avoidance of 'political, ethnic, gender and other forms of bias' (para. 19.h); the bearing in mind of 'linguistic and cultural diversity' (para. 19.i); the use of 'clear, precise and intelligible' language in all parts of question papers (para. 19.j); and 'Awareness of economic, political, social, and environmental factors relevant to the subject should be encouraged wherever appropriate' (para. 19.k).

There are also requirements relating to the processes of moderation, to the inclusion of grade descriptions and so on, but the requirements outlined above are those which have particular relevance to matters addressed in this book, and give an indication of the *range* of examining features which the National Criteria specify. Some of the requirements are problematic in terms of *how* they are to be translated into syllabuses, and how they are to be monitored.

The assessment objectives are arguably a central feature of the new examining system. It is the attention of the assessment objectives to skills and processes which determines the need for a coursework element, and which marks the greatest departure from the emphasis upon recall of knowledge and upon timed, written examinations. The assessment objectives, however, were not, at the inception, seen to be the means by which the candidates were to be assessed, but rather as guiding principles in devising suitable syllabuses and assessment procedures. The grade criteria were to provide the yardsticks for assessment and it is still uncertain that such criteria can be satisfactorily prescribed or deduced.

The emphasis upon understanding, skills and processes is in contrast, for many subject areas, to the knowledge/content base or product assessment of previous public examinations. Candidates would be examined on their ability to:

> 'select, use and communicate information and conclusions effectively.'
> 'analyse an idea, theme, subject or concept and to select, research and communicate relevant information and to make and evaluate in a continuum.'
> 'select, analyse, interpret and apply data.'
> 'distinguish between evidence and opinion, make reasoned judgements and communicate them in an accurate and logical manner.'
> 'translate information from one form to another.'
> 'justify judgements and choices in the light of evidence.'
> (Department of Education and Science/ Welsh Office 1985)

Interestingly, similar objectives can be drawn from a range of subjects. Those above are selected from (in order) geography, art and design, economics, business studies, physics, and home economics. One of the immediate implications of the introduction of GCSE is that the common interests of different subject departments are underlined. Further, the assessment instruments needed to assess processes and skills, many of them by their very nature providing evidence that is ephemeral or can take place only in the context of an extended programme of work, cannot only be written examinations. The introduction of coursework needs, as many schools realized, a whole school policy, to build up library and other resources, and to ensure that major coursework projects do not coincide across subjects. More fundamentally, research and study skills need a whole-school approach.

The emphasis in the National Criteria assessment objectives upon communication and evaluative judgement by students is very important. These are areas where further development is needed to ensure that all forms of communication are encouraged and that the context and purposes of judgement are fully established for the candidates.

There are other aspects of the assessment objectives that need further exploration. In some subject areas the aims and assessment objectives are expressed in identical terms, and in few areas could the assessment objectives be said to state 'observable and measurable behaviour', as the National General Criteria defined their purpose. Where they are expressed in terms of observable behaviours, they may not marry well with the aims. The GCSE objectives in modern languages (as in the National Criteria for French) offer an example of the conflict that arises between aims and objectives. The aims include:

> To offer insights into the culture and civilization of French-speaking countries. (National Criteria French 2.3)
> To develop an awareness of the nature of language and language learning. (2.4)
> To provide enjoyment and intellectual stimulation. (2.5)

The assessment objectives, however, read rather differently; for example *Basic Reading*:

> Candidates should be expected, within a limited range of clearly defined topic areas, to demonstrate understanding of public notices and signs (e.g. menus, timetables, advertisements) and the ability to extract relevant information from such texts as simple brochures, guides, letters ... (3.1.2)

It is less than clear how the teacher bridges the gap between the aims and the assessment objectives. It is a risk in all human activity, that what is assessed, measured and rewarded will eclipse wider aims. Most modern language teachers using GCSE have found it a stimulus to their students: the quality of their courses — how far the aims as well as objectives are satisfied — will depend upon their own powers and enthusiasm.

If not all assessment objectives are as clear-cut as the modern language objectives, problems have frequently been turned to advantage. Home economics teachers, faced with a somewhat daunting interpretive challenge in their list of assessment objectives, have shared their own processes of interpretation with students, giving students a greater sense of ownership and understanding of their courses.

The GCSE was to enable greater comparability, since the proliferation of subject titles would be controlled, and since National Criteria would govern very closely the aims, assessment objectives and style of examining. It should now be possible to require that a grade in a subject with one examining group, or under one syllabus, should be held against another example of the same grade, and that against the assessment objectives it would be possible to state whether the two were comparable.

It is unlikely, however, that comparability has in fact been facilitated, at least so far as scientific studies are concerned. The assessment objectives are of course expressed in words, are not precise in their meanings, and have so far defied all attempts to derive from them precise, operational grade criteria. However, what GCSE and its method of introduction have stimulated is a considerable raising of teachers' awareness of assessment issues, and a gathering together of teachers on an unprecedented scale, initially through a 'cascade' training system.

The cascade training depends in theory upon a downward transmission. Examining groups appointed 'subject experts' who then trained teachers. Where it was not considered practical for all subject teachers within a school or college centre to attend a training meeting, those who did attend would 'cascade' down to their colleagues the information and skills acquired. The sessions with trainers were characteristically of one day's duration. The industrial/commercial model of the cascade begged the question of whether such a short period of training would be used in an industrial setting to prepare personnel for such a complex task as introducing new subject curricula, and in many cases radically different styles of teaching and assessments of young people. The practical aspect of the problem was that, however thin the preparation was felt to be for those who did attend, the onward transmission of training to colleagues was often totally unprovided for in terms of time and resources.

The very notion of downward transmission, inherent in the cascade model, militates against the teaching and learning styles of the GCSE examinations. However, teachers and trainers (who usually are also teachers themselves) have characteristically used sessions for more experiential learning and sharing of ideas. Therefore the 'training' sessions have evolved, from the unsatisfactory picture described by Hilary Radnor in *The Impact of the Introduction of GCSE at School and LEA Level* (Radnor 1987) during the introductory phase, into sessions which do far more to acknowledge the central professional role of teachers in introducing the new examination system.

It is in the process of discussion, shared learning and sharing of experience, that teachers have negotiated, defined and turned into practical assessment instruments the generally worded assessment objectives. These are living objectives, but their continued existence and meaning depend upon the continuation of the discussion groups countrywide that have given them life. These groups, either as Phase 4 training meetings, or as cluster groups organized by Local Education Authority Advisers or by teachers themselves, often involve teachers across related syllabuses, and characteristically are area-based rather than syllabus-based. So, teachers working to different syllabuses and to different examining groups are in regular discussion, comparing work, exchanging ideas, and standardizing their assessments. Such a process has considerable potential in establishing comparability of standards in examinations.

GCSE has also been given the daunting task of raising standards. Past comparability studies have tended to see relative improvement in marks as a falling of standards, and so there could well be a conflict, in terms of public confidence, between the wish to enlarge the target group and the wish to raise standards. This will remain a controversial area, particularly since historically it has been difficult to prove the worth of a qualification unless there is a high degree of failure. The GCSE Modern Language examinations have perhaps gone further than any others in setting realistic, achievable targets for students, and giving reward for specified achievements. Positive marking, which can be an elusive concept in some subject areas, is most clearly applied in modern languages where candidates are awarded marks for what is right, or communicates effectively, and not penalised for mistakes. Yet the main worry in the first round of the examinations was that the results might be too good. There are endless problems ahead if criteria for achievement are set, and then questioned on the grounds that too many students meet them.

The organizational difficulties of the dual system are theoretically simplified by a single system, though there can be few school or college examination secretaries who would support that view while adapting to change. Since schools and even departments are free to choose their examining groups (a freedom not all Local Education Authorities endorse) the network of relationships is not necessarily simplified. Because of the number and variety of examination components within a single examination, simply filling in entries has become a more difficult task. The change in the nature of examinations has undoubtedly put extra burdens of all sorts on teachers, and while the adaptation has in some respects been professionally enlarging, in others it has highlighted shortages of accommodation and furniture in many schools, and lack of clerical support for the great majority of teachers. The storage of coursework items and the proliferating paperwork are likely to remain problems for most teaching departments long after the teaching and assessment associated with coursework are smoothly integrated into classroom practice.

Strategies at department and school level are needed to minimize the difficulties. Examining groups are keeping their syllabuses under review and the tendency following the introduction of the new system is for coursework requirements to be trimmed. Examiners need to consider further how best to moderate teacher assessment without requiring undue storage of evidence. Again, the most promising route looks like inter-school moderation, which does not have to take place only at the end of a course. The Graded Assessment in Science Project (GASP) offers the opportunity to build to a GCSE through graded steps, and this kind of model has, among other advantages, some organizational possibilities, especially in subjects which at present have cumbersome coursework requirements.

It is in its effect upon styles of examining, and by the effect — the 'backwash' effect — that examining has upon teaching, that GCSE can claim its major achievement. The teaching process has become less a transmission and more an interaction between student and teacher and between students. The teacher is a facilitator or enabler of learning, and one of a number of resources, in an educational model which asks students to take greater responsibility for their learning and thereby to develop the independence and confidence needed for lifelong learning. The student becomes central in this learning model and interacts with a variety of resources. 'The GCSE is a better examination in terms of its curricular and educational aims than those that preceded it' (Her Majesty's Inspectors 1988).

The backwash effect of examinations has long been lamented, in that recall examinations led to limited learning programmes and styles. Now this effect has been used to beneficial purpose. However, there is still much work to be done if the good effects are not to be diluted over time. The assessment of *processes* is not easy. Much of the process work is obscured or overshadowed by impressive finished products when final assessment and moderation are carried out in, for example, art and design. Only full teacher involvement at all stages of assessment and moderation will safeguard the notion of process. Some of the timed examinations, set to examine very broad and open syllabuses in terms of content, nevertheless asked very specific content questions in 1988. The backwash effect of this could have teachers cramming students — over the whole ability range — with facts, on an even wider content basis than before. Some 1988 examinations, set across the ability range, depended partly upon unstructured essay questions. Again, the effect of this in the classroom has to be considered. Do the majority of candidates benefit from the long (possibly never-ending) training necessary to enable them to write creditable essay answers in examination conditions?

The vocational relevance of GCSE is intended to be

stronger in two main ways than that of its predecessors. Firstly it is intended that 'end users', that is employers, trainers, colleges etc., of GCSE qualifications, by the descriptions that can be given to grades, will have more information than before about the meaning of a grade, in terms of knowledge, understanding and skills associated with that grade. This at least was the intention in the establishment of GCSE. In any full sense this intention looks unlikely to be realized. Very general descriptions of grades do exist in syllabuses and provide a broad framework for awards. However, the search for grade criteria was abandoned in 1985, for a number of reasons, not least that the criteria associated with any grade were so numerous as to make assessment totally impractical. In the absence of examples of work at particular grades and the connoisseurship of 'subject experts', the grade descriptions, or the putative grade criteria, can have very limited meaning. What should not be underestimated, however, is the significance of the search. As part of the establishment of GCSE, examining groups have been involved in a communication exercise with industry. Schools, colleges and Local Authorities have, in GCSE aims and assessment objectives, something much more tangible than before with which to open a dialogue with end-users about educational achievement. The terms of the conversation exist. Within the existing framework, end-users can suggest their own desired adaptations.

Secondly, GCSE syllabuses must wherever possible address 'economic, political, social and environmental factors' (Department of Education and Science 1985) so that subjects are not studied in isolation from the 'real world'. In science subjects, for example, industrial processes and everyday applications of scientific principles must be included in the examinations. This is proving quite a difficult area to examine, since it is by definition very broad, and it is sometimes a matter of chance whether a candidate has a particular piece of general knowledge. Also, candidates are likely to become anecdotal and personal when asked everyday questions, or invited to speculate. With the development and extension of GCSE approaches the ability of students to bring 'education' and 'life' closer together should improve. That is, after all, one of the aims of the exercise.

Has GCSE done anything to reduce the 'built-in failure' associated all too often with the examining systems? It was to be designed to certificate 90 per cent, or more, of students. That clearly would be an unrealistic aim in subjects which have a long history of being very specialized, or of interesting and motivating a very small proportion of the school population, such as Latin or Greek. However, in subjects that are to form the basis of the National Curriculum, it would be regrettable if that aim were too readily abandoned.

It is not easy to find centres or teachers who have actually been able substantially to alter their entry practice because of the new system. Initial fears have been that the *increased* volume of writing apparently required in some subjects (home economics and geography in particular), and the cross-curricular burden of coursework might actually reduce entry possibilities for some candidates. As the examination works through its early years these fears are likely to subside. Much unnecessarily lengthy coursework has been produced in the first year of the examination. Training, syllabuses, and individual schools can address the problem now it has emerged. Forward planning is recognized as essential if teachers and students are not to be deluged by coursework in the last few months before the examination.

The development of inter-school moderation has considerable potential in removing some of the anxieties attached to postal moderation and in reflecting other changes in assessment practice. The national testing as conceived in the Task Group Report (Department of Education and Science 1988a) was to depend upon group moderation of teacher assessments, and though this point remains unsettled, it is difficult, at the time of writing, to see how even some of the standard assessment tasks will be moderated unless by groups of experienced teachers. Profiling and records of achievement depend upon an 'ongoing', formative conception of assessment. Group standardization and moderation does not have to be terminal, end-of-course assessment involving the much publicized over-burdening of teachers and students towards the end of their GCSE course.

The GCSE in its present form may not, because of other changes in assessment following rapidly in its wake, have a very long future, but that is not because it is a bad examination, and certainly not because teachers have failed to make it work. It has solved more of the problems of past public examinations than could realistically have been expected. It has been the flagship of change, and it will have carried out its work well if it soon appears outmoded.

GCSE and other assessments

Graded objectives

The development of graded objectives in mathematics, science, and modern languages is now well advanced. Defining specific learning targets for students, in terms of what they will actually *do* helps to focus the attention of teacher and learner upon progress and learning difficulties. Short-term and achievable goals have beneficial effects in motivating students. An essential feature of graded objectives, in contrast to a modular scheme of assessment, is the *progression* in levels of difficulty. Emphasizing the achievement of targets removes part of the very powerful effect that thinking in terms of ages has upon notions of educational progress. If we can think less in terms of *ages*, and more in terms of *stages*, then individual needs and capabilities are made central to the process of education, and not made subordinate to the organizational features of the school.

Arguments against the use of graded objectives are that the use of predetermined targets limits the recognition of unexpected or accidental learning, the 'emergent' objectives, that can develop as part of the learning and teaching process. Predetermined objectives may be felt to be unambitious, ignoring qualities and achievements which are not readily stated. Goals that are necessarily short-term may be very different from the general aims of a course of study. Further experience and evaluation of graded assessment projects will be needed in order to keep such matters under review.

The graded objectives movement is another educational initiative which is helping to focus attention upon targets, helping teachers to define their purposes and explore their methods — and helping learners to see achievement. The principles are capable of use in GCSE, as the Graded Assessment in Science Project is demonstrating.

Profiles and records of achievement

The Technical and Vocational Education Initiative (TVEI) and the Certificate of Pre-Vocational Education (CPVE) have done much to address the argument that the wide range of skills involved in successful employment have been overlooked in formal education and the system of examining at 16 and after. Vocational education has had far-reaching consequences throughout the curriculum in the way teachers think about assessment. The challenge is to show students that qualities such as perseverance, independence, initiative, practical abilities, and social skills are valued and can be developed. In order to give recognition to the full range of educational experiences and achievements, and in order to give students helpful grounds for self-assessment, profiles are used. 'A profile is a method of displaying the results of an assessment; it is not a method of assessment. It is essentially derived from a separation of the whole of an assessment into main parts or components' (Further Education Unit 1987).

Profiling has been developed to a considerable extent in the CPVE, but is not of course confined to vocationally framed courses. Simple profiles have been used whenever teachers have recorded assessments, not chronologically, but grouped under headings, according to different types of work within their subject. This helps to draw attention to strengths and weaknesses within an individual student's work, and can therefore serve a diagnostic purpose. It also helps, of course, to give the student a 'profile' of the subject so that s/he is not just studying 'geography' or 'chemistry', but can begin to share the teacher's view of what studying such subjects consists of.

As part of the profile, more detailed components can be singled out, providing objectives, graded objectives, or, as they will be called after the introduction of the National Curriculum, attainment targets. While it would be distorting to suggest that there are not significant differences in the kinds of profiles mentioned here, the principles are not wholly dissimilar. The usefulness of a profile approach to recording assessment is in the invitation to teacher and learner to identify and share explicit goals. It is an approach which ideally teachers should explore and develop for themselves, in order to become articulate in the discussion of national testing, which is bound to depend heavily for its development upon the expertise of classroom teachers.

Records of achievement represent the use of profiling to build up as wide a picture of a young person's time at school as possible. The purposes of these records are:

1 Recognition of achievement.
2 Motivation and personal development.
3 To stimulate a reconsideration of the curriculum.
4 To give school leavers 'A document of record'.

(Department of Education and Science 1984)

By 1990 all Local Education Authorities must ensure that

procedures are in place for the records, and by 1995 all those leaving state schools must have a record to take with them.

Records of achievement can claim to address all the educational aims of assessment. Moreover, they have an enormous role to play in reshaping the way we think about the teacher/student relationship since a fundamental principle is that the student makes self-assessments. They also provide a constructive alternative to the end of term report, and a rationalization of record-keeping. The final Records of Achievement National Steering Committee (RANSC) Report (Department of Education and Science 1989) places records of achievement as 'the cornerstone of schools' assessment arrangements, bringing together in one policy continuous assessment by teachers, self-assessment by pupils, public examination results and, in the future, reported assessments under the national curriculum'. The record is a document which can be a source of pride to its owner — the student — and its contents will, at best, reflect a new involvement by students in learning as a co-operative enterprise, and in assessment as a step towards the future, not simply as a summation of the past.

Taking the document to prospective employers or to colleges is seen by some teachers as a possible problem. Records of achievement have to depend upon subjective judgements and are designed to concentrate upon positive achievement. Will they have credibility? Those schools who are furthest in developing records see rather differently. The student who has a record of achievement and who has grown within the context of recording achievement, will be well placed to represent her/himself to an employer or other interviewer. It is not the document that such a student will have to take to the interview, but the skills of self-evaluation and the sense of purpose which have been developed *with* the document.

Concern lingers among users however, about the extent to which the record is capable of external validation. The RANSC interim report on records of achievement (Department of Education and Science 1987) points out that 'the national curriculum proposals for external moderation of school-based assessments call into question whether further separate accreditation or validation of this aspect of the record will be required.' Again the emphasis is on school-based assessments moderated by schools working as groups, the recommended basis of moderation for part of the national assessments, for the accreditation of the records of achievement, and with surely a more significant part to play in GCSE. The rationalization of moderation for all these schemes, under a system giving schools direct involvement, would give additional coherence. Further issues associated with profiles and records of achievement are discussed by Ian McGuff in chapter four.

National testing

The development of a National Curriculum has arisen from concerns that breadth and balance are not achieved in the curricula followed by all pupils in state schools. While the principle that there should be entitlement to such breadth and balance is uncontroversial, analyses of what constitutes breadth and balance differ considerably. There are fears that the large prescribed core of subjects will not meet the needs of either the most or the least able — in short, that more flexibility is needed. In many schools the provision prescribed is a marked change from what has proved practical for them in the past. Modern language provision, for example, will have to increase considerably in most schools, and it appears unlikely that the availability of suitably qualified teachers will match the need.

There are many aspects of the National Curriculum proposals, however, which have significant potential advantages for teachers. The principle that a school must have 'clear aims and objectives' and 'comprehensible language for communicating ... achievements to pupils, parents and teachers, and to the wider community' (Department of Education and Science 1988a) is a necessary feature of support for the work of individual teachers, but has not been followed by all schools in the past.

In the development of objectives, or attainment targets, the National Curriculum and National Testing proposals go much further than work on GCSE has yet done in defining levels of achievement. Unlike GCSE, results will be reported, for some purposes at least, in the profile components, so that students, teachers and parents have more detailed, more diagnostic, information about progress. One of the problems in the search for satisfactory grade-related criteria in GCSE is that the final reported assessment of the public examination system is a single grade, which militates against the notion of precise descriptions of performance.

The GCSE assessment objectives are strikingly different in some respects from emphases emerging with the publication of proposed National Curriculum attainment targets; and the model of progress used by the Task Group on Assessment and

Testing raises its own questions in relation to GCSE (*see* Figure 1.1).

Figure 1.1 Sequence of pupil achievement of levels between ages 7 and 16

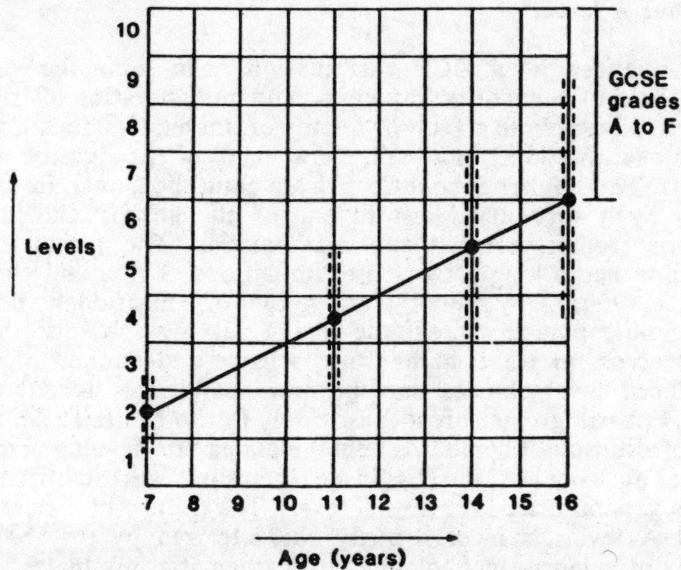

Note The bold line gives the expected results for pupils at the ages specified. The dotted lines represent a rough speculation about the limits within which about 80 per cent of the pupils may be found to lie.

Source: National Curriculum: Task Group on Assessment and Testing, A Report, Department of Education and Science 1988.

The level achieved in Figure 1.1 by the majority of 14-year-olds is not apparently appropriate to their producing GCSE coursework, to be summationally assessed at the end of their two-year course at the age of 16. In *Three Supplementary Reports* (Department of Education and Science 1988b) there is some modification of the Task Group's position in assigning equivalence to GCSE, 'once the criteria and levels have been settled, the actual equivalence between the national assessment of the profile components and the GCSE grades will be a matter of empirical performance.'

A very important development in GCSE, as well as others resulting from the National Curriculum, would be the increased emphasis on staged assessments. If the task group model of progress and its putative relationship to GCSE is accepted, then the final assessment of two years' GCSE coursework must be reconsidered.

Whither A levels?

The advanced level GCE examination is to some the last stronghold of the world they knew, and any alteration of it is thought adversely to affect the quality of university education. As an examination it does still show many of the signs of its origins. The Higher School Certificate could be gained in the 1920s by a specialized test in one of the groups: classics; modern studies; science and mathematics. The legacy of grouping had a long effect on examinations at 18+, and well into the 1960s many schools were neither organizationally nor philosophically adaptable to the idea of 'mixing' subjects in A levels across arts and humanities, science and mathematics. Advanced level choices may be more ambitious than they were, but still greater breadth is widely felt to be desirable. A fear of dilution of standards nonetheless haunts development.

In February 1987 the Higginson Committee was established with a general brief to review A levels. The context of concern about A levels is most strongly characterized by the short supply of science, technology, and mathematics graduates. A level science entries have been in decline over recent years, affected by the attraction of the Business and Technician Education Council (BTEC) courses and further threatened by falling rolls. Lack of industrial relevance has been criticized by employers. Of A level courses generally, the criticism has been of over-specialization, and narrowness.

The report of the Higginson Committee recommended that five, rather than three, advanced level subjects be taken, the courses not diluted but made more rigorous. Factual content and memorization could be reduced, and skills of analysis given greater emphasis. The Government rejected the proposal: reduction in the content of A level syllabuses was resisted, and it was felt that schools had enough reforms other than this to deal with. The Department of Education and Science expressed optimism that the recently introduced Advanced/Supplementary levels would increasingly redress the narrowness of the typical A level package.

Schools and colleges have broadened A level programmes over the years. Liberal or general studies courses have an established place, and examinations at ordinary, intermediate, or advanced levels have existed to certificate these. However, the introduction of advanced/supplementary levels seeks to give greater structure and recognition to curricular breadth by introducing the notion of a half A level (two A/S levels equalling one A level). This would in theory allow a typical A level student to take, say, two full A levels and two A/S levels, giving a coverage of four instead of the present three subjects.

The potential of A/S levels is not yet entirely clear. They may cater more effectively than A levels for the sixth former who has general abilities and immediate vocational goals. The prestige of being on an advanced rather than a vocational course is strongly felt by some students who none the less have less aptitude for the specialization of A level, and only limited commitment to its goals. The Higginson Committee saw the usefulness of A/S levels in supporting and complementing A level studies. The issue for schools and colleges at the moment is whether the A/S levels might be used to allow students to explore areas well outside the usual A level course, or to ensure breadth within the established range. These philosophical uncertainties are not easy to master amidst the practical difficulties of introducing the new examinations.

Generally, schools have no spare resources with which to staff or equip additional classes, and A/S courses are in most subject areas too different from A level courses to make integration of lessons straightforward. However, some pioneering work is in hand on modular experiments, involving adaptation of A level syllabuses so that, by a combination of compulsory and optional modules, an A/S level can be gained by studying half the modules necessary for an A level. Examining boards are generally showing a flexible approach in supporting such schemes, and there is some scope for schools to meet their own educational and organizational needs while mapping possible wider developments for examining at 18-plus.

Some schools and colleges see A/S levels as necessarily eroding the general studies programme, and thus narrowing the sixth form curriculum. Others feel that A level groups are already fully subscribed. Some A/S courses are heavy in content, and in practice account for more than half an A level in terms of workload. While some schools are mapping change for themselves, others feel that a change in A levels is likely, and while waiting for it to happen, are unwilling to commit energy and resources to reshaping the provision.

The introduction of GCSE, and the different styles of teaching and learning established, are being felt in A level courses. There are different possible responses to this. Bridging or foundation courses may be needed to prepare students embarking on A level courses. Alternatively, A level courses themselves can change. In some subjects it is possible to find coursework options to replace some parts of the written examination, and the extent to which teachers and students opt for such syllabuses will dictate the pace and the nature of change. The reality that most A level teaching groups are less than suited to transmission teaching might get fuller recognition in the light of GCSE. A level examination is set to change, but its change may be more evolutionary than was recently thought.

REFERENCES AND BIBLIOGRAPHY

Black, H.D. and Devine, M.C. (1986) *Assessment Purposes: a study of the relationship between diagnostic assessment and summative assessment for certification*, Edinburgh: Scottish Council for Research in Education.

Board of Education (1923) *Report of the Consultative Committee: differentiation of the curriculum for boys and girls respectively in secondary schools*, London: HMSO.

Broadfoot, P. (ed.) (1984) *Selection, Certification and Control: social issues in educational assessment*, Lewes: Falmer Press.

Broadfoot, P. (ed.) (1986) *Profiles and Records of Achievement: a review of issues and practice*, London: Holt, Rinehart & Winston.

Burgess, T. and Adams, E. (eds) (1980) *Outcomes of Education*, London: Macmillan Educational.

Christie, T. and Forrest, G.M. (1981) *Defining Public Examination Standards*, London: Macmillan.

Cresswell, M.J. (1987) 'Describing examination performance: grade criteria in public examinations', *Educational Studies* 13: 3.

Department of Education and Science (1978) *School Examinations: Report of the Steering Committee established to consider proposals for replacing the GCE O level and CSE examinations by a common system of examining* (Waddell Report), London: HMSO.

Department of Education and Science (1979) *Aspects of Secondary Education in England: a survey by HM Inspectors of Schools*, London: HMSO.

Department of Education and Science (1982) *Mathematics Counts: Report of the Committee of Enquiry into the teaching of Mathematics in schools* (Cockcroft Report), London: HMSO.

Department of Education and Science (1984) *Records of Achievement: a statement of policy*, London: HMSO.

Department of Education and Science/Welsh Office, (1985) *General Certificate of Secondary Education: the national criteria*, London: HMSO.

Department of Education and Science (1987) *Records of Achievement: an interim report from the National Steering Committee*, London: HMSO.

Department of Education and Science/Welsh Office (1988) *A Report from the National Curriculum Task Group on Assessment and Testing*, London: HMSO.

Department of Education and Science (1988a) *National Curriculum: Task Group on Assessment and Testing, A Report*, London: DES.

Department of Education and Science (1988b) *Three Supplementary Reports*, London: DES.

Department of Education and Science (1989) *Records of Achievement: a report from the National Steering Committee*, London: HMSO.

French, S., Slater, J.B., Vassiloglou, M., and Willmott, A.S. (1988) 'The role of descriptive and normative techniques in examination assessment', *British Journal of Educational Psychology* Monograph Series No. 3: *New Developments in Educational Assessment*, Edinburgh: Scottish Academic Press.

Further Education Unit (1987) *Profiles in Context*, York: Longman.

Harrison, A. (1982) *Review of Graded Tests: Schools Council Examinations Bulletin 41*, London: Methuen Educational.

Harrison, A. (1983) *Profile Reporting of Examination Results: Schools Council Examinations Bulletin 43*, London: Methuen Educational.

Her Majesty's Inspectors (1988) *The Introduction of the General Certificate of Secondary Education in Schools, 1986–1988*, London: DES.

Radnor, H. (1987) *The Impact of the Introduction of GCSE at LEA and School Level*, Slough: National Foundation for Educational Research.

Willmott, A.S. (1977) *CSE and GCE Grading Standards: the 1973 comparability study, schools council research studies*, London: Macmillan Education.

Wiseman, S. (ed.) (1961) *Examinations and English Education*, Manchester: Manchester University Press.

Chapter Two

THE TYPES, PURPOSES AND EFFECTS OF ASSESSMENT

Christopher Buckle

The General Certificate of Secondary Education was introduced after many years of discussion about the nature and purpose of secondary education in this country. It had been argued that with an increasing number of young people continuing their education after the age of sixteen the traditional examinations no longer merited such an important place in the education system. While this may not have been the case there was wide agreement that the nature of the skills which could be tested by traditional examinations was restricted and did not properly reflect the actual learning outcomes of the courses. It was also argued that many of the skills which were not adequately tested by such a system were those skills considered to be of particular value after the individual had completed that part of their formal education.

Three important questions should be asked about examinations. These are:

1 To what extent does the examination enable students to reveal the variety as well as the level of the knowledge and skills they have acquired?
2 Does the format used to report the results to candidates, teachers, potential employers, etc., ensure that such information is full, detailed, and described in such a way that it is meaningful to them?
3 Do the syllabuses and examination provide an adequate framework for improving the quality of teaching and learning?

These questions raise issues which are related to the types of evaluation and the individual's learning characteristics and learning history. These issues have been developed and discussed in educational literature in recent years. In this chapter the GCSE syllabuses and examinations will be considered in the light of this discussion. A knowledge of this literature and its associated technical terminology on the part of the reader has not been assumed.

POSITIVE ACHIEVEMENT

One of the principal intentions of the GCSE was to devise a form of examining which would enable the positive achievements of all, or nearly all, the candidates to be recognized. Positive achievement refers to the actual attainments of an individual in a subject area. The range and level of attainment will vary between individuals but very few, if any, will have learned nothing in terms of knowledge and skills. The traditional approach to examinations required the possession of a certain set of knowledge and skills before the candidate could pass the examination. Those who did not demonstrate their possession of these failed. However, the level required to pass was high and among those who failed there were doubtless many who possessed a substantial set of attainments which went unrecorded. It might be appropriate to comment, at this point, that the use of grades below the pass level did not alter the fact that in the minds of the vast majority of candidates, their parents, and potential employees, there are in practice only two categories, pass and fail.

If candidates are to be given the opportunity to demonstrate their actual achievements, as opposed to their performance at or above a pre-determined level then the form of the examination will have to be matched to the level and nature of the candidate's attainments. This not only involves testing at differing levels of difficulty, but also of including skills not directly tested in traditional examinations. These aspects are discussed below under differentiation and forms of examining.

The recording of an individual's achievements, whether or not these reach a pre-defined level, has been shown to have important effects on motivation. Part of the success of programmed learning and mastery learning is undoubtedly due to this effect. The importance attached to recording the positive achievements of most of the candidates, rather than that of a smaller percentage who achieve the pass grade, reflects a particular philosophy behind the examination.

An examination may be designed to serve two very different purposes. It can be used to ascertain whether an individual possesses certain knowledge and skills defined by the syllabus for the course. The individual's performance is judged solely in terms of the content of the course. This is known as criterion referenced testing and it provides the opportunity for all those taking the examination to pass. Alternatively the individual's performance may also be judged against that of other individuals, thus introducing an additional comparison. In this case the percentage who are likely to pass will normally be much lower. This is called norm-referenced testing.

The decision about which of these approaches is the most appropriate to decide the relative level of an individual's performance can have a crucial effect on the assessment of an individual's performance. These approaches are discussed in Note 1.

Note 1: norm- and criterion referenced testing

It had frequently been observed that when the pattern of the variations in a characteristic of a naturally occurring object, e.g. length or weight, were plotted as a graph, the shape of the graphs were often similar. If, for example, the size of each apple was plotted against the number of apples having that size for the whole crop a curve similar to that shown in Figure 2.1 was produced.

This type of pattern occurred so frequently that it became known as the normal curve. The argument could be, and was, applied in reverse in circumstances where direct measurement was not possible. This happened in some parts of the mental testing movement in the first half of the twentieth century. Since intelligence or ability cannot be directly observed and measured, tests were devised to produce a pattern of scores similar to Figure 2.1 when a large number of individuals took the test.

The general assumption that ability is normally distributed in this way may be correct but unfortunately it has affected widely held views about attainment. Attainment, unlike ability, can be observed and measured directly. School and public examinations measure attainment but many pupils, teachers, parents, and others concerned with the results of examinations expect a pattern which is similar to the normal distribution. This expectation has done a great deal of harm to the education and career prospects of many pupils.

Norm-referenced assessment basically depends on comparing the performance of an individual with the performances of all the members of the group which is taking part in the assessment. It is useful in situations where the selection of a fixed percentage of the total group is involved. It is administratively convenient since if the tests results fit the normal pattern the number of individuals who will appear in any particular category is known in advance because of the mathematical properties of the normal curve.

Figure 2.1 The normal curve

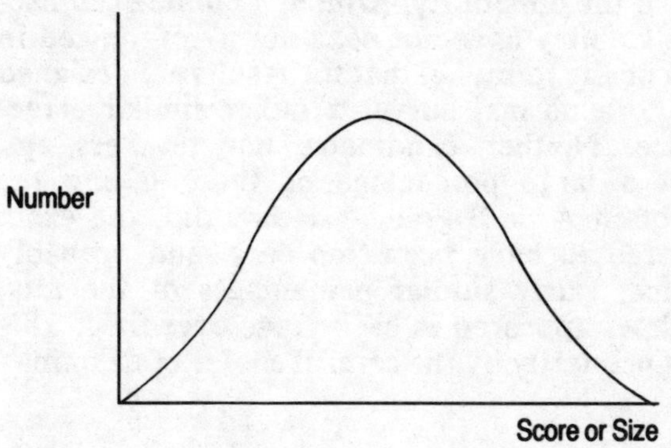

In this situation the *majority* of the individuals can expect to receive a moderate grade *at best*. This philosophy will clearly have an adverse effect on the motivation of a substantial proportion of the students taking a course and can have very serious consequences for their relationships with their teachers. It is argued later in this chapter that a free flow of information between teacher and student about the extremely complex processes taking place when the individual is learning a subject is essential if the highest possible levels of attainment are to be achieved by each student.

An alternative approach is required which enables the achievements of each individual to be recognized. If the syllabus is defined as a set of knowledge and skills which would be possessed by a student who had successfully completed the course then the assessment can be directed towards certifying the particular knowledge and skills which an individual has attained. In this case the student's performance on the assessment tasks is being judged against the set of knowledge and skills, that is the criteria, defined by the syllabus. This approach is called criterion referenced assessment.

In criterion referenced assessment it is essential that the criteria are carefully defined and clearly communicated. It is equally important that the relationship between the assessment items and the criteria have been thoroughly worked out. If this has been done *and* if a large number of the students studying a course have achieved a high level of knowledge and understanding of the subject then the pattern of results will contain a much larger proportion of high grades than would be produced by a norm-referenced pattern. It must be stressed that a criterion referenced approach does not produce or predict high scores from a large proportion of the candidates, but it does allow for the possibility. Although public examinations at 16 in this country have not been norm-referenced in the strict meaning of the term, i.e. that the results are designed to be plotted on to a normal curve, a rather similar effect occurs in practice. Neither candidates nor teachers and employers expect a large percentage of those taking the examination to obtain A or B grades. If they did, the exam would be considered to have been 'too easy' and probably invalid. In practice, fairly similar percentages of the total number of candidates appeared in each grade over time. This has been achieved primarily by the careful choice of examination questions.

The GCSE represents a move in the direction of criterion referenced examining. The *National Criteria* states,

> The standards required in the GCSE examinations will be not less exacting than those required in the previous GCE O-level and CSE examinations. O level and CSE, taken together, were originally designed for the upper 60 per cent of the ability range by subject. GCSE is not to be limited in that way. It will be designed, not for any particular proportion of the ability range, but for all candidates, whatever their ability relative to other candidates, who are able to reach the standards required for the award of particular grades. Grade criteria are being developed for this purpose and will be incorporated into the subject criteria and syllabuses as soon as practicable.
>
> (Department of Education and Science/ Welsh Office 1985)

THE USES OF EXAMINATION RESULTS

The purpose of traditional public examinations was to certify that a candidate had reached a certain standard in the subject. That is to say that the candidate possessed skills of recall, understanding and application of the knowledge in the subject at a level appropriate to the qualification. To discover the details of these skills the syllabus would have to be consulted, but since the time spent examining the student is often one per cent or less of the time s/he has spent studying the course only a small sample of the skills represented by the syllabus have actually been tested. It may be reasonable to assume that a student's performance on these skills is typical of the performance in the others, but it may not be.

A student's grade in a subject gives limited information about a candidate's knowledge and skills to a teacher or lecturer in another institution, a training officer, or a potential employer. Even if they consulted the syllabus, this usually described skills in fairly general terms. The syllabuses constructed for the GCSE are designed to reduce these problems.

THE DESIGN OF GCSE SYLLABUSES

The General Criteria refers to the term syllabus as 'the complete description of what may be examined in a particular subject and how it will be examined'. The syllabus for each subject includes the aims and where appropriate the assessment objectives which relate to these aims. The assessment schemes detail the types of assessment (see below), and the weighting for the different types of intellectual skills. The procedures by which candidates from a wide range of ability will be given the opportunity to demonstrate positive achievement are also included. This process is known as differentiation.

Differentiation

Basically there are two approaches to differentiation. One involves the setting of assessment tasks at differing levels of difficulty, the other the use of common tasks capable of revealing wide levels of performance. The first is known as differentiation by task and may include more than one set of content in a subject area. The second is called differentiation by outcome.

Both these approaches are reflected in the national criteria. In the areas of mathematics and science the emphasis is on differentiation by syllabus content and task.

> Mathematics: there will normally be at least three levels of assessment. For each of these levels a separate content must be prescribed.

(Department of Education and Science/Welsh Office 1985)

> Science: schemes of assessment involving alternative components for candidates of different levels of ability must normally be used ...

The syllabuses for biology and physics require assessment which involves the use of alternative components for candidates of different levels of ability.

A mixed approach is taken in a number of subject areas, computer studies, geography, history, home economics, religious education and social science. Assessment in these subjects may involve the use of examinations having differentiated questions on papers, a common set of papers which includes an undifferentiated element, and courses that employ assignments which are intended to be appropriate to the individual's level of ability.

The English examination also aims to:

> provide the opportunities for all candidates to demonstrate the full range of these skills and abilities at a level of performance determined either by the nature of the tasks themselves or by the competence of the candidates or both.
>
> (Department of Education and Science/ Welsh Office 1985)

In craft, design, and technology the arguments for the second approach are based on typical teaching practices:

> The majority of pupils following CDT courses are however taught in mixed ability groups and consequently it is appropriate for a common examination to be taken by such candidates.
>
> (Department of Education and Science/ Welsh Office 1985)

A particular problem arises in music, where some candidates will have received substantially more extra-curricular tuition and experience of instrumental work, giving rise to a wide range of attainment amongst students. The needs to ensure the possibility that candidates who have only followed the normal course can attain the highest grade is stressed.

Grade descriptions

The performance of a candidate will be represented by a grade. There is a seven-point scale from A to G for the GCSE. The problem of attaching a meaning to a grade is reduced by the introduction of grade descriptions. While the grade awarded to a particular candidate reflects his or her overall performance in the examination and not his or her performance on particular aspects of it, the grade description is intended to convey the level of knowledge and skills in the subject that an individual obtaining the grade might be expected to possess. Where differentiation is achieved by differing syllabus content and assessment, certain levels of assessment are restricted to a particular range of grades, e.g. French grade E three common-core elements, grade C three common-core elements plus basic writing plus any one additional higher level element.

If the grade descriptions were to be tied exactly to specific assessment objectives, it would be possible to establish grade related criteria. The decision as to whether an individual obtained a particular grade would then depend on his or her performance on those questions which tested the assessment objectives for that grade. For communicating results to potential employers etc., in many cases grade descriptions may be adequate. Where the requirements for a particular job or course are described in detail, however, grade related criteria would be needed. The production of such criteria clearly depends on the accuracy with which it is possible to describe the outcomes of the course in terms of objectives. The techniques for developing objectives from the aims of a course are discussed in Section 2 of the paper.

Forms of assessment

Assessment can take place at the end of a course by final examinations or during the course-continuous assessment. It should be noted that, strictly speaking, the process should be similar and continuous assessment should not provide an unfair advantage to the candidates examined in this way. The main function of course work is to test skills which cannot be easily or reliably tested in a final examination.

Course Work

All the subjects include course work with a minimum of 20 per cent of the overall examination grade being awarded from this component. The candidate's attainments may be measured at various points during the course and the opportunity given for a skill to be tested on more than one occasion. The examination of practical skills in biology (Midland Examining Group, 1986) is an example of this practice, and positive achievement is stressed by the use of the candidate's best performance for the determination of his or her grade.

The nature of course work varies between subjects and extends beyond those with which practical examinations have traditionally been associated. In the criteria for business studies it is stressed that assignments which could be carried out by 'desk top research' and no other form of data gathering should be avoided (Department of Education and Science/Welsh Office 1985). Many of the skills required for the production of successful course work have cross-curricular aspects even though they are acquired and assessed in the context of a particular subject. They include the planning of an activity, the use of systematic procedures to gather and record data, and the choice of the most appropriate forms for the presentation of the data to facilitate comparison and discussion. The candidate's ability to comment on process, and to discuss and draw conclusions from a prepared set of data can be tested, also, in a final examination, but the other skills cannot. Moreover, the information presented as part of an examination question is somewhat artificial in nature and unlikely to be directly related to the experience of the individual candidate. The use of course work, however, can enable such skills to be tested in connection with activities which the candidate has carried out. With less successful work there is, of course, the problem of the degree to which the data that has been gathered can realistically be discussed or commented upon, and it may be impossible to draw conclusions from it.

At the final stage of examining a course this would represent a serious failing in the learning-teaching process. At an earlier point, however, if the student encountered this situation and gained a better understanding of the problem as a result, an important education objective would have been achieved. With suitable guidance the student may also realize the implications for his or her course work in other subjects.

Another important aspect of course work is the

involvement of the teacher in the examining as well as in the teaching. This represents a fundamental change, and although many teachers have worked for examination boards as examiners marking scripts, and have set and marked school examinations, this departure places a major new responsibility on teachers.

Moderation

The deliberate move from uniformity to diversity raises issues of validity and objectivity. It is not basically a question of individual teachers lacking objectivity when marking the work of their own students, although there is always a question of perceptions and implicit rather than explicit meanings in candidates' answers with internal examining at any level of education. The adequate and fair testing of the range of skills used in course work necessitates variety in the assignments themselves. It is clearly essential that the tasks set for different candidates are, within the procedures for differentiation, of equal difficulty. This process is assisted by analysing the skills, describing them in detail and relating each detailed skill to the appropriate assessment objectives. Performance of these skills can also be judged at different levels of attainment. The successful moderation of course work depends on the examiner's experience and knowledge of the type and standard of work that is representative of a particular grade in the subject.

The National Criteria stress that where work is assessed during a course the standard relates to the level of achievement appropriate to the end of that course. The skills valued in a number of subjects are best, and in some cases can only be, acquired through group work. Many of these skills, which involve reconsideration of the individual's understanding and point of view and the communication of his or her ideas about the subject to other people, are among the most important for future use. The omission of such skills from a course, because they are more difficult to examine, would represent a serious educational weakness. The training of teachers and moderators in techniques for awarding grades on these skills to individual candidates is essential if such grades are to be objective and the danger of their exclusion is to be avoided. The use of carefully and clearly defined assessment objectives is essential in this area.

Final examinations

These may consist of written papers and/or aural, oral, and practical examinations. The last three modes of examining also play an important part in the assessment of course work. The final examination provides the opportunity to test such skills under very closely controlled conditions, reducing the problems involved in moderation.

Written papers

The questions on written papers vary in the extent to which the form and content of the candidate's answer is prescribed by the examiner. The question may require a single word to be provided by the candidate. This might be based on the recall of a single piece of factual information which limits the range of possible answers, frequently to one. If a recognition test is used, by giving two or three incorrect and one correct answer complete objectivity in marking is assured. Recognition tests need not, however, be limited to factual information. True/false statements can be used, with conditions attached as necessary, so that the candidate's understanding of question is being tested even though their answer may take the form of ticks in boxes. The question may take the form of an assertion for which a number of reasons are listed and the candidate has to choose the one, or in a more difficult item the combination, which supports the assertion. Questions of this type can enable a number of topics and skills to be tested in a relatively short period of time, ensuring coverage of key aspects of the syllabus.

More extended questions of this type have similarities with structured questions. In this case the answers are provided by the candidate, instead of being provided by the examiner and recognized by the candidate. With a finely structured question the candidate is receiving detailed guidance about the answer required and has the opportunity to accumulate marks as he or she works through the question. This guidance is extremely important since the examination has very strict and brief (1 to 2 hours) time limits. The main problem with this approach is that some candidates may prefer a different structure when dealing with questions in that topic. This is discussed further in Note 4 (page 67). A structured question will not be valid if the failure to successfully complete one part has a serious adverse effect on the remaining parts. This could occur where mathematical computation or the selection of information is involved.

A valuable type of question which can test a range of skills is one in which a set of information in written, numerical, diagrammatic or practical form is provided in the examination paper. Subject areas particularly rich in such materials are geography (using maps and photographs), and business studies. The authors of the National Criteria for business studies consider:

> Data response questions are particularly valuable, if appropriately structured using carefully selected material, in discriminating across the whole range of ability and are a means of introducing motivating material into both teaching and assessment and providing for flexibility and originality.
>
> (Department of Education and Science/ Welsh Office 1985)

This is clearly an appropriate way of testing a number of important skills in depth and context, although the extent to which a single set of information could be equally appropriate for candidates at different levels in the subject is less clear, since level and experience are often related. Despite this difficulty this type of question comes closest to meeting the requirement to relate courses to future employment and meet the needs of candidates of a wide range of ability.

Aural and oral tests

The post-school importance of listening and speaking skills has long been recognized in modern languages, and in more recent years in the examination of English. The GCSE confirms this view. A uniform stimulus situation can be ensured by the use of a cassette recording. The associated questions and candidates' answers for modern languages are in English.

The importance of these skills is increasingly being recognized in other areas of the curriculum. In an era when large numbers of adults are engaged in work which involves communicating by the spoken rather than the written word, and the skills of negotiation and problem-solving are more widely needed, it is essential that such skills are encouraged.

The National Criteria for business studies, computer studies, craft, design, and technology, physics, and science refer to the inclusion of these skills in the examining process. Attention is drawn, however, to the problem of moderation if the skills are to be tested in context and to the consequent resource implications. In view of the importance of these skills in post-school life it would clearly be in the general interest, as well as that of the candidates, for such components to be included in these examinations as a matter of priority.

The major feature of secondary education for the majority of students, their parents, and their teachers has been the examinations at sixteen. In view of the importance attached to the results of such examinations in making decisions about an individual's future education or employment, the influence of the examination system on secondary education is unlikely to decline. However, the education system of which these examinations were such an important part resulted in 40 per cent of the students leaving school without *any* formal recognition of their attainments.

If this situation is to be improved it is not only the syllabuses and teaching methods which need to be reviewed. It is the nature and purpose of the examination process itself which requires reconsideration.

The traditional concepts of examination, in both its denotative and connotative aspects, as held by students and indeed many teachers, is too narrow for this purpose. A more appropriate concept is evaluation.

Note 2: types of evaluation

Bloom and his colleagues proposed a definition of evaluation which contains five key points:

1 Evaluation as a method of acquiring and processing the evidence needed to improve the student's learning and the teaching.
2 Evaluation as including a great variety of evidence beyond the usual final 'paper and pencil' examination.
3 Evaluation as an aid in clarifying the significant goals and objectives of and as a process for determining the extent to which students are developing in these desired ways.
4 Evaluation as a system of quality control in which it may be determined at each step in the teaching-learning process whether the process is effective or not, and if not, what changes must be made to ensure its effectiveness before it is too late.

5 Finally, evaluation as a tool in education practice for ascertaining whether alternative procedures are equally effective or not in achieving a set of educational ends.

(Bloom *et al.* 1971: 7–8)

The term evaluation, used in this way, clearly encompasses more than the public examinations at the end of a course., It includes examinations given during the course which may have an important function in deciding whether a student is encouraged or permitted to continue with the course. The final examinations comprise one category of evaluation known as summative evaluation. Points 1 and 4 refer to another type of evaluation. In this case it takes place during the course of the learning and is intended to identify an *individual's* difficulties when they arise so that help can be offered at the appropriate time. This type of evaluation, which is intimately linked to the teaching–learning process, is called formative evaluation. It informs the teacher and the student about *each other's* progress and assists in forming the student's understanding of the subject. Closely related to formative evaluation is a third type which is designed to discover what the student already knows about the subject so that s/he can be put at an appropriate place in the teaching sequence. This is called evaluation for placement or, more simply, initial evaluation. It must be stressed that initial evaluation is solely concerned with determining the level of the student's previous knowledge and experience to ensure that s/he can obtain the maximum benefit from taking the course. It will frequently reveal gaps in a student's knowledge in areas which the teacher had reasonably assumed that s/he would know. The student must be given the opportunity to remedy these before the course gets very far under way.

These three types of evaluation clearly extend the idea of examining beyond final examination itself, although this is included, and relate to many other procedures carried out by effective teachers in the normal course of their work. Homework frequently set, regularly marked, and the results discussed with students appears very similar to the formative and initial evaluation processes outlined above. Indeed it is not unreasonable to ask whether they differ in more than name. The writer hopes that any reader who is not familiar with the concept will postpone making a decision until he or she has read the remainder of the chapter.

SUMMATIVE EVALUATION AND THE GCSE

Summative evaluation takes place at or towards the end of a course. It covers the whole of the course. The time available for such an evaluation is normally very limited compared with the time spent studying the course. In the case of the GCSE it may be about 1 per cent. For this reason the assessment is aimed at the higher level skills and broader outcomes of the course. It is assumed that the attainment of higher level skills implies the possession of related lower order skills and more specific detailed information.

The higher levels skills, which are relevant to large parts of the syllabus, tend to be less precisely defined in terms of specific details. A candidate who can apply the skill to one area may be less successful in doing so in others. This not only reduces the objectivity of the examination, but it means that summative assessment may not be suitable for providing detailed information about a candidate's knowledge and understanding of the subject.

The GCSE syllabuses describe the intended outcomes of the course in terms of skills and content. Ways in which these can be more closely defined are illustrated by the examples in mathematics, English and physics given below.

The National Criteria for mathematics includes such skills as:

1 Recall, apply and interpret mathematical knowledge in the context of everyday situations;
2 Set out mathematical work, including the solution of problems in a logical and clear form using appropriate symbols and terminology;
3 Organize, interpret and present information accurately in written, tabular, graphical and diagrammatic forms.

(Department of Education and Science/ Welsh Office 1985)

A total of fifteen skills are listed. In addition, attention is drawn to oral, practical and investigational skills which will be required to be assessed from 1991.

The Midland Examining Group's syllabus goes further and specifies the type of question which will mainly be used to test particular skills (see Table 2.1).

Table 2.1 Objectives and question type in mathematics

	National Criteria	*Short answer questions*	*Structured extended answer question*
1	{Recall	/	/
	{Apply		/
	{Interpret	/	/
2			/
3	{Organize		/
	{Interpret	/	/
	{Present		/

Source: General Certificate of Secondary Examination Syllabuses, Midland Examining Group 1988

The content prescribed by the National Criteria includes, in addition to traditional mathematical concepts, topics relating to post-school needs such as:

> Personal and household finance ... wages and salaries ... VAT, the use of tables and charts. Mathematical language used in the media. Simple change of units including foreign currency. Use of drawing instruments. Reading and making scale drawings. Reading, interpreting and drawing simple inferences from tables and statistical diagrams.
>
> (Department of Education and Science/ Welsh Office 1985)

In cases where these topics relate to the individual's previous experience, as opposed to future needs, the possibilities for meaningful lessons to occur (see Note 4, page 67) are greatly increased. The skills represented by the National Criteria in English include the ability to:

1 Understand and convey information;
2 Understand, order and present facts, ideas and opinions;
3 Evaluate information in reading material and in other media, and select what is relevant to specific purposes;

4 Articulate experience and express what is felt and what is imagined;
5 Recognize implicit meaning and attitudes;
6 Show a sense of audience and an awareness of style in both formal and informal situations;
7 Exercise control of appropriate grammatical structures, conventions of paragraphing, sentence structure, punctuation and spelling in their writing;
8 Communicate effectively and appropriately in spoken English.

(Department of Education and Science/ Welsh Office 1985)

The Midland Examining Group offers three schemes, two including an aural examination and course work while the third is composed exclusively of course work. Scheme 1 consists of an aural examination, the examination of directed and continuous writing, and course work. The candidate must submit four pieces of work including personal descriptive or narrative writing, argumentative or informative writing and two further pieces which reveal the candidate's response to the work which he or she has read during the course.

To increase the precision of the nature of the assessment for the benefit of candidates and those who need to interpret results in more detail the Board provides a chart which indicates the relative weighting given to the objectives. The table also contains the percentage given to the different forms of examination.

The National Criteria for physics list three skills:

1 Know and recall: factual information; conventions; requirements for safety; etc.
2 Show understanding of: concepts, theories and models; information presented in various forms; the use, application and implications of physical facts and principles; etc.
3 Show, with reference to familiar and unfamiliar situations, that they can: apply laws and principles; explain phenomena in terms of theories and models; solve problems by designing, conducting and interpreting the results of simple experiments; translate information from one form to another; recognize mistakes; misconception, unreliable data and assumptions; draw conclusions and formulae generalization.

(Department of Education and Science/ Welsh Office 1985)

Table 2.2 Objectives and nature of assessment in English

Objective	*Overall Weighting*	*Paper 1 Aural*	*Paper 2 Section A Directed writing*	*Section B Continuous writing*	*Course work*
1	/	/	/	—	/
2	//	/	/	/	/
3	//	//	//	—	//
4	///	/	—	///	//
5	//	//	/	—	/
6	//	/	//	/	//
7	//	/	/	//	/
8*					
Total	100	20	20	30	30

* Objective 8 will be tested by the oral component which is assessed separately.

Source: General Certificate of Secondary Education Examination Syllabuses, Midland Examining Group 1988

These skills are clearly intended to be used in verbal, visual and practical contexts. They go beyond working from set texts, requiring the learner to become actively involved in the subject.

The core content for all physics is set out under four headings: matter — atomic and microscopic structures; energy — forms, conservation and transfer; interactions — forces; and physical quantities. A fifth aspect relates to the social and economic applications of physics. It is, however, stressed that in assessing this area it is the candidates' knowledge and understanding of the principles of physics which are involved.

It can be seen from these examples that the GCSE syllabuses seek to describe the intended outcomes of a course in ways which will help both the learner studying for the examination and others who have to make judgements on the basis of the results. In all these cases the emphasis is on the skills which should be acquired rather than specific items of content. This reflects the approach to defining learning outcomes in objective terms adopted in Bloom's taxonomy of the cognitive domain (see Note 3, page 57). This is essentially a process- rather than a product-approach which considers learning in terms of intellectual skills. The products of learning are regarded as the effects of the operation of these skills, by the learner, on particular items of content.

The assessment objectives in mathematics and physics contain distinctions between the skill of remembering, in the form of recall or recognition, and those of understanding and application. In English remembering is implicit, rather than explicitly stated. The importance of understanding and application is stressed in all three areas, both by the nature of the assessment objectives and the weightings used in the examinations. There is also emphasis on skills not traditionally associated with the examination of these subjects — the inclusion of practical and investigational skills in mathematics, extended prose in physics, and the use of material in forms other than printed text and oral communication in English.

The relationship between the skills and content in physics is set out in Table 2.3. The importance of experimental work and the applications of the content to social and economic issues is stressed in all sections, at least 15 per cent of the marks being allocated for this purpose, with a bias towards the technological aspects.

The relevance of the courses to the wider social context is explicitly stated in the content for mathematics and the principles to be applied in teaching the content outlined for physics. This aspect is less clearly dealt with in English, although reference is made to the use of newspaper articles and advertisements in the reading component.

Grade descriptions

The GCSE seeks to relate the grades awarded to criteria. As an initial step, descriptions of the performance which might be expected from a candidate awarded grade C or grade F were produced. The use of grade descriptions is illustrated by examples for grade C in English, mathematics and physics given below. It will be noted that English also includes a separate description for oral communication. This is graded from one to five, with one as the highest.

Table 2.3 The assessment of skills and content in physics

Assessment objectives	*Knowledge recall*	*Understanding*	*Processes**	*Marks (at least)*
Content				
1 Matter				15%
2 Energy				15%
3 Interactions				15%
				60%
-				
4 Physical quantities				5%
Extension of or addition to the core				33%
Mark allocations in complete assessment	About 45% (at least 20% to understanding)		Not less than 40% (at least 20% to experimental skills)	100%

*Including experimental skills.

Source: After the National Criteria for physics, Department of Education and Science/Welsh Office 1985.

English

The relevant assessment objectives will be found on page 47. Extracts from the descriptions relating to performance at grades C and 4 are given below. The numerical prefix identifies the assessment objective on which the description is based.

Grade C The candidate can be expected to have demonstrated competence in:

1 Understanding and conveying information both at a straightforward and at a more complex level;
2 Understanding facts, ideas and opinions, and ordering and presenting them with a degree of clarity and accuracy;
3 Evaluating material and selecting what is relevant for specific purposes;
4 Describing and reflecting upon experience and expressing effectively what is felt and what is imagined;
5 Recognizing the more obvious implicit meanings and attitudes;
6 Showing a sense of audience and an awareness of uses of language appropriate in different situations;
7 Writing in paragraphs, using sentences of varied kinds and exercising care over punctuation and spelling.

The following grade descriptions apply to the assessment of performance in oral communication.

Grade 4 The candidate can be expected to have demonstrated competence in:

1 Understanding and conveying straightforward information;
2 Presenting facts, ideas and opinions in an orderly sequence;
3 Selecting and commenting on spoken and written material with some sense of relevance;
4 Describing experience in simple terms and expressing intelligibly what is felt and what is imagined;
5 Recognizing statements of opinion and attitude;
6 Using some variation in speech style according to situation and audience;
7* Speaking audibly and intelligibly with some sense of appropriate tone, intonation and pace.

(*Assessment objective 8.)

Mathematics

Assessment objectives:

1 Recall, apply and interpret mathematical knowledge in the context of everyday situations;
2 Set out mathematical work, including the solution of problems in a logical and clear form using appropriate symbols and terminology;
3 Organize, interpret and present information accurately in written, tabular, graphical and diagrammatic form;
4 Perform calculations by suitable methods;
5 Use an electronic calculator;
6 Understand systems of measurement in everyday use and make use of them in the solution of problems;
7 Estimate, approximate and work to degrees of accuracy appropriate to the context;
8 Use mathematical and other instruments to measure and to draw to an acceptable degree of accuracy;
9 Recognize patterns and structures in a variety of situations, and form generalizations;
10 Interpret, transform and make appropriate use of mathematical statements expressed in words or symbols;
11 Recognize and use spatial relationships in two and three dimensions, particularly in solving problems;
12 Analyse a problem, select a suitable strategy and apply an appropriate technique to obtain its solution;
13 Apply combinations of mathematical skills and techniques in problem solving;
14 Make logical deductions from given mathematical data;
15 Respond to a problem relating to a relatively unstructured situation by translating it into an appropriately structured form.

Grade C examples Extracts from the descriptions relating to performance at grade C are given below. The numerical prefix identifies the assessment objective on which the description is based.

3 Construct a pie chart from simple data. Plot the graph of a linear function;
4 Apply the four rules of number to integers and vulgar and decimal fractions without a calculator. Calculate percentage change;
5 Perform calculations involving several operations,

including negative numbers;

7 Give a reasonable approximation to a calculator calculation involving the four rules;

8 Use a scale drawing to solve a two-dimensional problem;

9 Recognize and in simple cases formulate, rules for generating a pattern or sequence;

10 Solve simple linear equations. Transform simple formulae. Substitute numbers in a formula and evaluate the remaining term.

Physics

Assessment objectives:

1 Know and recall:
   facts, vocabulary, conventions, physical quantities, and units in which they are measured, requirements for safety, names and uses of common measuring instruments;

2 Show understanding of:
   2.1 definitions and laws;
   2.2 concepts, theories and models;
   2.3 information presented in various forms
   2.4 the use, applications and implications of physical facts and principles;
   2.5 safety procedures;

3 Show, with reference to familiar and unfamiliar situations, that they can:
   3.1 use given formulae;
   3.2 apply laws and principles;
   3.3 explain phenomena in terms of theories and models;
   3.4 solve problems by designing, conducting and interpreting the results of simple experiments;
   3.5 translate information from one form to another;
   3.6 extract and evaluate information from that which is given;
   3.7 present information in a precise and logical form;
   3.8 recognize mistakes, misconceptions, unreliable data and assumptions;
   3.9 draw conclusions and formulate generalizations.

Grade description Extracts from the descriptions relating to performance at grade C are given below. The numerical prefix identifies the assessment objective on which the description is based.

A typical candidate for the award of a minimum grade C might know and have been able to recall:

1 The total current flowing into a junction equals the total current flowing out of the junction.

A typical candidate for the award of a minimum grade C might understand:

2.1 The basic relationship underlying Ohm's law.
2.2 How to use a theoretical circuit diagram.
2.3 Some of the principles underlying the safety procedures adopted.

A typical candidate for the award of a minimum grade C is likely to have been able to:

3.1 Apply the principle of conservation of energy to the operation of an immersion heater (including simple calculations).
3.2 Undertake an investigation of the relationship between electric energy used and the rise in temperature produced.
3.3 Determine the velocity from a displacement-time graph.
3.4 Offer reasons for discrepancy between expected and actual results when water is heated and the temperature change is measured.

Objectives and the GCSE

The National Criteria reveal the strong influence of some form of objective approach in all the subject areas. Every one contains a section headed assessment objectives, since this is a requirement of the General Criteria. A study of the examples in English, mathematics and physics given above shows that the grade description is more precise than the assessment objective. The increase in the degree of precision, however, varies widely between English and the other two subjects. The first assessment objective in English provides an example. The requirement to understand and convey information is elaborated by reference to a straightforward and a more complex level. It is assumed that the reader will be familiar with the nature of these levels and the principles by which they are determined. This assumption is sound in the case of the experienced teacher, although even here genuine differences of view might arise: but in the case of the student or others using the information the situation is altogether less clear. The first assessment objective listed in mathematics, again a broad statement, is interpreted with a degree of precision which enables students and others as well as teachers to be clear about its meaning. It is pointed out that these grade descriptions are examples based on the core content for the subject and other examples could have been used equally well. The essential point is that the degree of precision is relatively independent of the example which is chosen, while in the case of English the use of examples was considered to be inappropriate. In mathematics there is a description of a skill, or a set of skills, listed in the assessment objectives applied to a particular area of the course content. In English the skills listed in the assessment objectives are described in a little more detail. It must be stressed that this is not a criticism of the authors of these objectives; the differences reflect the nature of each subject and the degree to which educational objectives in the present state of our knowledge can be usefully applied to them. This issue is considered further in Note 3 (page 57).

The grade descriptions for physics illustrate another important aspect of educational objectives in summative evaluation. They are divided into three groups. The first group refers to what a candidate might know and have been able to recall. The second refers to understanding and the third to what the candidate is likely to have been able to do. These can be regarded as levels of attainment in which achievement at the highest level depends on the candidate's knowledge and understanding of associated information and ideas. For example, description 3.2, 'Undertake an investigation of the relationship between electric energy used and the rise in temperature produced' is related to 2.1, an understanding of the 'basic relationship underlying Ohm's law', which involves description 1, knowledge that the 'total current flowing into a junction equals the total current flowing out of the junction.'

Some advantages of the GCSE

An answer to two of the questions raised at the start of the chapter can now be considered.

Question 1 To what extent does the examination enable students to reveal the variety as well as the level of the knowledge and skills they have acquired?

It is clear from the examples described above that the GCSE does go a long way towards providing a more satisfactory answer to this question than was the case with more traditional, mainly written-paper, examinations.

Question 2 Does the form used to report the results to candidates, teachers, potential employers, etc., ensure that such information is full, detailed and, described in such a way that it is meaningful to them?

The practice of presenting a course in term of assessment objectives, combined with grade descriptions, provides a greater amount of less subjective information about the meaning of an individual's results. The inclusion of a substantial proportion of content which is relevant to commerce and industry is helpful to employers and also assists them further in attaching meaning to the results in subjects relevant to their work. The emphasis on criterion referenced assessment is useful in cases where employers are concerned with the knowledge and skills which a candidate possesses rather than with a comparison between that candidate's performance and some less clearly defined norm. The success of these factors, however, depends on the extent to which the syllabuses and the candidate's performance can be described in objective terms.

A great deal of work, in theory and practice, has been carried out in the field of educational objectives in the last forty years. Two major contributions of particular relevance to the GCSE are discussed, briefly, in Note 3.

Note 3: objectives

Among the views expressed by the practitioners and theorists on the application of objectives to education, two have been very influential. These are Robert Mager's work on the preparation of instructional objectives (Mager 1962) and the ideas of Benjamin Bloom and his colleagues (Bloom 1956). Although both are concerned with bringing increased precision to the description of the outcome of a course they represent different approaches to achieving this.

A major influence on the development and use of objectives came from the behaviourist school of psychology. This concentrates on *observable* behaviour. The best-known exponent of this school, Professor Skinner, also invented programmed learning. With the behaviourist model the outcomes of the course are described in terms of the activities or actions which a student will be able to perform on successful completion of the course. Objectives of this type are not concerned with assumptions about the nature of the mental processes which the student will have to employ to enable him or her to carry out these actions.

Mager lists three criteria which behavioural objectives should possess:

1 The actual behaviour which it is intended that the student will engage in should be identified and named.
2 The important conditions under which the behaviour will be exhibited should be clearly specified.
3 The criteria for an acceptable performance must be clearly stated.

(Mager 1962)

An example of this type of objective might be the correct addition of three two-digit numbers. The conditions under which the addition had to be performed would be given. Where a number of examples were involved the acceptable level of performance, e.g. 7 out of 10, would be included. This approach is concerned with the answer rather than the processes by which the students learned and used the skills which enabled them to produce it. The application of this approach results in a set of precise descriptions of learning outcomes and the conditions under which they will be required to be demonstrated. It can have the advantage of helping students, and even perhaps occasionally teachers, to be clear about the intended outcomes of the course and whether they have been achieved. Objective questions of various types are based on it. Although they allow a range of subject content to be examined in a relatively short time such questions appear best suited to, or at least most easily devised for, recall and the lower levels of understanding.

The approach has been criticized on a number of grounds:

1 It represents a narrow view of the learning process and the aims of a course.
2 There is the danger of a highly prescriptive approach to the teaching and examining of a course.
3 It focuses on the outcomes rather than the process of learning.
4 It generates a wealth of detail which can overwhelm the students, making it difficult for them to distinguish between key ideas and points of detail, i.e. the well-known problem of failing to see the wood for the trees.

The third point can be partially met, with suitable topics, by analysing the learning process which the students are expected to employ, breaking these down into very small steps and testing each one. This technique is used in programmed learning. The fourth criticism depends on the management and presentation of the course, and if this is carefully done the worst effects should be avoided. The first two points are inherent in a behaviourist approach and many teachers are reluctant to use objectives in any form for this reason, which is unfortunate as they can bring real benefits when used with care.

There is in any event an alternative view offered by Bloom and his colleagues, whose work was aimed at helping to improve communication between examiners about their assumptions and intentions when setting questions. They divided educational activities into three domains: the affective or attitudinal/emotional; the cognitive or intellectual; and the psychomotor. The most widely used has been that for the cognitive domain. It is assumed that the skills in a domain constitute a taxonomy. A taxonomy is an arrangement in which the higher order members include features of the lower orders. In the case of the cognitive domain higher order skills such as applying ideas are assumed to include lower order ones of understanding and recalling them. Thus students who can perform the higher level skills may be assumed to possess the lower order ones without the need for explicit testing.

The main levels of Bloom's taxonomy of the cognitive domain are outlined below.

Knowledge

This is concerned with remembering facts, procedures and principles in a particular subject area.

Intellectual skills

1 Comprehension:
This is the lowest level of understanding and includes translation into the student's own words, or from one form to another, and interpretation limited to particular cases.

2 Application:
Solving problems which are new to the student. It involves the reordering of ideas within the topic and the use of ideas from other areas.

3 Analysis:
Identifying the main ideas, including unstated assumptions, and making clear the relationship:
(a) between the ideas themselves,
(b) between the ideas and the evidence or conclusions.

4 Synthesis:
The expression of the student's own ideas, interpretations, conclusions, in the form of an essay, a project report or a plan.

5 Evaluation:
Making judgements using the student's own criteria, or those which are given.

There are two basic differences between objectives based on Bloom's taxonomy and those derived from strict behaviourist principles:

1 The taxonomy emphasizes the skills and processes involved in the course.
2 These objectives are less precise, and hence less prescriptive.

The term 'educational objectives' is more appropriate for objectives derived using Bloom's taxonomy.

A typical example of the general approach from a course in biology is outlined below.

1 Recall basic biological facts and principles.
2 Recall a wide range of biological facts and principles.
3 Understand simple safety precautions in laboratory work.
4 Understand simple safety precautions in laboratory work and explain the principles underlying them.
5 Make simple observations from a variety of sources (e.g. photographs, drawings, graphs).
6 Make accurate and detailed observations from a variety of sources (e.g. photographs, drawings, graphs).

Teachers of biology will no doubt find the examples familiar. They are extracted from the F and C grade descriptions in the National Criteria. The actual content is not specified since the objectives apply to a wide range of content. The implementation of the distinctions between the F grade and C grade objectives, e.g. basic versus wide range in objectives 1 and 2, is left to the experience of the teachers and examiners.

FORMATIVE EVALUATION IN THE GCSE

Summative evaluation is used to determine the extent to which a candidate has achieved the intended outcomes of a course. Formative evaluation is designed to enable the individual to attain the highest level of achievement of which he or she is capable.

Formative evaluation has to take place during the course since the information which it provides is used to modify the learning and teaching *before* summative evaluation occurs. It is essentially a dialogue between the learner and the teacher about the current state of the learner's knowledge and understanding of the course, and the ways in which it has been achieved. The term 'formative' draws attention to the fact that the student's knowledge and understanding are still being formed.

The type and content of the summative evaluation of a GCSE course is decided by the examination board, but the responsibility for formative evaluation lies with the teacher taking the course. For the majority of students the degree to which they succeed in the examinations depends to a large extent on the quality of formative evaluation which is available to them. Its purpose is to help students relate new information and ideas to their existing knowledge and experience.

Initial evaluation

This involves finding out what the students already know about the topic and the ways in which this knowledge was acquired. Initial evaluation is the name sometimes used to describe the aspect of the overall process.

Figure 2.2 Initial evaluation

Existing knowledge	→	New learning	→	Learning outcomes
Initial evaluation	→	Formative evaluation	→	Summative evaluation

At the start of a course there is a danger that the teacher makes assumptions about the background knowledge and experience of the students without very much information about the extent to which all of these assumptions are true for the whole of the group. The pressure to cover the syllabus in a limited time is a major contributory factor. The purpose of initial evaluation is to test in detail assumptions about those aspects of previous work which are essential to the understanding of the current course. This goes further than testing the ability to recall and understand the content. It should include tests of the assumptions which the student has about the uses of this knowledge and the contexts in which it was acquired. If the student has substantial gaps in his or her knowledge this means s/he does not have the opportunity to relate the new learning to a stable knowledge base. Such a student is unlikely to make much progress with the subject until the gaps have been identified and appropriate steps taken to remedy the situation. There is also the danger that the teacher or the student will assume that his or her lack of progress in the subject is caused by a much higher level of ignorance or interest than is actually the case. These points are discussed in Note 4 (page 67).

Initial evaluation is *not*, and should never be, used to exclude a student from a course. If after taking the initial evaluation the *student* (not the teacher) feels that there are too many gaps in his or her knowledge and that s/he would prefer to postpone the course then careful counselling is required. In the case of GCSE courses where postponement would usually mean a delay of at least a year, the opportunity to make up the required knowledge may be the better alternative.

Objectives in formative evaluation

Objectives are staging posts along the route to attainment of the overall outcomes of the course. They provide points at which the learners can check their position and review the progress which they have made. If learning is to be successful it needs to be approached with confidence. This confidence is based on previous successes. The use of objectives can play an important part in this process. They can also provide a clear route through the next part of the course. Unfortunately, for many individuals studying can be more like a mystery tour than a carefully planned expedition. It should be stressed, however, that the objectives approach must not be so rigid that unexpected outcomes are excluded. It is often unanticipated events during learning which sharpen the individual's appreciation and enhance understanding of the subject.

If objectives are to be used in this way the teacher needs to produce a map of the course in terms of the content, skills and learning experiences which will be involved (see Figure 2.3). This map contains the assessment objectives for the course, the objectives which provide the knowledge base for the attainment of the assessment objectives, and the assumptions about the students also expressed as objectives.

Figure 2.3 Objectives in formative evaluation

Objectives students are assumed to know and understand ⟶ Objectives on attainment route ⟶ Assessment objectives

In practice this exercise is more easily carried out if the assessment objectives are used as the starting point. It should be noted however that such a product-oriented approach would *not* be suitable for the overall design of a course. It should only be used *after* the assessment objectives have been established. The purpose of the exercise is to determine optimum learning routes, not a single route. As far as possible, the way and order in which he or she tackles the objectives should be left to the student. Some objectives do, however, appear to exhibit a hierarchical structure, in which case the lower levels would normally be dealt with first. This point applied both to skills and content.

In developing objectives for formative evaluation the use of a grid showing the relationship between content and skills has been proposed, see Table 2.4. It is very important to note that a similar approach could be used with the assessment objectives in designing the *summative evaluation* of the course. However, there are two essential differences:

1 The number of objectives covered by a summative grid would be very large and extremely confusing, not to say

daunting, for the student.

2 The *purpose* of the grid is different when formative evaluation is involved:
   (i) it only represents the part of the course, say one term's work, which is being followed currently by the students;
   (ii) the objectives which are represented are those which will assist the student in attaining the assessment objectives.

Table 2.4 Formative evaluation of skills and content

Intellectual skills	*Skill A*	*Skill B*	*Skill C (etc.)*
Content areas:			
Topic 1			
Topic 2			
Topic 3			
(etc.)			

Source: Handbook on Formative and Summative Evaluation of Student Learning, Bloom *et al.* 1971

The term 'enabling objectives' has been suggested (Davies 1976) to distinguish them from the course outcomes or terminal objectives.

Assessment objectives are concerned with the knowledge and skills which a student who has successfully completed the course will possess. Formative objectives are concerned with the learning processes which are involved in this outcome. Towards the end of the course, formative evaluation may consist mainly of checking whether particular assessment objectives have been achieved, but during the course the emphasis should be on testing those objectives which contribute towards the students' knowledge and understanding of, as well as their ability to use, the skills and ideas represented by the assessment objectives. These are the objectives which would appear in Table 2.4 when it was completed for a particular content area.

The skills tested in the final examination will, in many areas, be composed of subordinate skills which must be mastered if the final skill is to be attained. As has already been pointed out, the learning map should include both content and skills.

Progression in a subject is often more closely related to the acquisition of new skills rather than coverage of further content at the same level. This can be illustrated by a practical skill in science.

Skill: To observe and measure.

Component Skills:

(a) Reading a scale on a ruler or instrument.
(b) Reading a scale accurately.
(c) Relating the readings to the quantities being measured.
(d) Making *qualitative* estimates which are accurate enough to decide whether the reading is sensible; e.g. judging a length by eye so that the learner knows whether 9 mm or 9 cm is a sensible answer.
(e) Taking a number of measurements to help to check the results.
(f) Systematic recording of the results.
(g) Including the correct units in the results.

Higher level skills include:

(h) Choosing the most suitable measuring instrument.
(i) Investigating results which are inconsistent with the general pattern.

The student has to use these skills in a variety of contexts and this will be facilitated and the understanding of the skills made deeper if they are learned in that way.

The objective grid is shown in Table 2.5. The topics A, B, C, D, etc., should not only be drawn from different parts of one syllabus, but from all of the science syllabuses, biology, chemistry and physics. This would ensure the use of a range of measuring instruments, rulers, balances, watches, thermometers, electrical meters, etc., with a wide variety of contents. It would also help the student in understanding the principles of observing and measuring which are common to these situations. It is necessary to plan a course in this way if the students are to see these connections. All too frequently learning takes place in isolation so the students can only perform the skill in the context in which it was learned (see Note 4, page 67).

Table 2.5 Formative evaluation of measuring skills

	General objective — observing and measuring								
Skills	*a*	*b*	*c*	*d*	*e*	*f*	*g*	*h*	*i*
Content									
Topic A									
Topic B									
Topic C									
Topic D									
(etc.)									

The skills listed here also involve the understanding and use of number skills. If the student is weak or lacking in these then difficulties will arise in learning the skills relating to observing and measuring. This should be taken into account in the initial evaluation. Where difficulties do arise they should be remedied before the student tackles the new work. If the defects are not too severe the problem may be overcome by building work on number skills into the teaching programme for observing and measuring. This approach, combined with some additional help, can avoid excluding students from the programme which their peers have just embarked upon. It has already been stressed that the function of initial evaluation is to assist the learning process, and identifying some members of the group as being unsuited to proceed with new work could have exactly the opposite effect in their case.

Many of the skills listed above can be applied at different levels. The criteria for accuracy in (b) can vary from getting more than half the readings correct within the nearest whole number to using subdivisions, estimating readings between divisions on the scale, and repeating readings to reduce inherent errors of measurements. This factor can be utilized to enable a mixed ability group to engage in work on common topics. Higher level skills can also be included, providing activities for students who attain the other objectives more rapidly.

It does, however, require a great deal of time and effort on the part of the teacher to design the teaching-learning programme. The example on page 65 also involves teachers from different subjects working together to design such a programme. This gives an opportunity for teachers to share their knowledge, expertise and experience of the ways students learn their subject. It can also ensure that skills are not taught on different occasions in isolation in the, usually vain, hope that the students will perform the necessary integration for themselves. The use of the grid serves to make explicit the connections. Once the skill has been firmly established in the mind of the student it leaves the teacher free to reallocate the time that would have been spent on it to other aspects of the topic.

It is clear that breaking down a subject into objectives at this level of detail provides the signposts for each stage of the journey through the course. If the learners are successful in attaining the majority of these detailed objectives it is very probable that they will also be successful in attaining the broader assessment objectives. The obvious question would then be whether the development of such grids and their use in the course would guarantee a high level of success for the majority of the students. While genuine improvements would undoubtedly occur, the grids only refer to two aspects of the teaching-learning processes involved in a course — the content, and intellectual skills. There are other factors which play a key part in determining the learning outcomes. These factors can be grouped together under the general title of the individual's learning history. They are described in the final note.

Note 4: The individual's learning history

Bloom (1976) has coined the term 'learning history' to describe the amalgam of factors which influence an individual's learning. It includes affective, cognitive, and psychometer components. School learning has laid great emphasis on the cognitive or intellectual component. The acquisition of knowledge and skills, however, does not occur in isolation. It also involves the expenditure of a great deal of effort over a long period of time. Such a prospect is not immediately appealing to the majority of learners. If they are to engage in such activity they must believe that there is a good chance of a successful outcome. Education has, however, been described as the only major area of human activity which is undertaken in the confident expectation of failure for a substantial proportion of the participants. If this is the case then the prospects of a successful outcome for many learners are anything but good. This lack of success does not begin at the age of 16 for most of these pupils but can be traced back to the early days of their schooling. The nature of the problems which can arise at this stage are discussed by Professor Donaldson in her book *Children's Minds* (Donaldson 1978). She draws attention to the problems which arise from differences of expectations and perceptions between pupil and teacher. Such problems can easily form the basis for a history of failure in school learning. In some cases this may affect all the subjects which are studied at the later stages of education, while for others it may only apply to certain subjects.

There may also be a distinct contrast between an individual's attitude and attainments outside and inside the school. Such variations are often explained by the use of the term 'ability', which may relate to a specific subject or be used as a more general term. The difficulty with this approach is the danger that ability is regarded as a factor which is, to a large extent, outside the influence of the teacher or the learner. However, it is frequently observed that a student may work better and attain higher levels of performance with one teacher rather than another, despite the fact that both are successful and dedicated members of the profession. The student will often explain his or her preference in terms of a more interesting presentation and above all that they find the subject easier to understand. Explanations of this type draw attention to two of the key factors in Ausubel's (1978) model of meaningful learning.

Meaningful learning

Ausubel suggests that if new information and ideas are to be understood, rather than merely memorized, they must be related to the learner's existing knowledge and ideas. Ausubel considers that three conditions must be fulfilled if meaningful learning is to occur.

1 The new learning material must be inherently meaningful. Although Ausubel's original model was concerned with contracting the nature of the materials, often lists of nonsense syllabus, used in research on learning with that of the present in the classroom situation, it does raise an issue about the information sometimes given to students. The presentation of complex definitions, a large number of technical terms, symbols and equations, in rapid succession without proper explanation could produce a similar effect to that of being

asked to learn nonsense syllables, even for the reasonably knowledgeable student.

2 The student must possess the ideas to which the new learning materials can be related. The use of initial evaluation is clearly essential if this is to be ensured before the new topic is introduced. The situation is not, however, straightforward, as different learners may prefer to express these ideas in different ways. This point is discussed further under 'Learning style', page 71.

3 The student must intend to learn the new material in a meaningful fashion. Even if the conditions in (1) and (2) are met there is still the possibility that the student will concentrate on memorizing the material in a rote manner. The student's learning history may contain many examples of assessment which place greater emphasis on verbatim recall than explanations which are the student's own words. Courses with assessment of this nature are unlikely to spark much interest in the student. The other principal reason for verbatim learning lies in the apparent security which it provides. For students who have a history of indifferent performances in the subject the temptation is particularly great and almost certain to maintain their performance at its previous level. This is because rote or verbatim learning provides a *wholly inadequate basis for further learning*. Meaningful learning consists of establishing patterns of ideas and information in the mind of the learner. When the student encounters new ideas or information s/he asks how s/he can relate these to the pattern in his or her mind. In doing so s/he will alter the pattern to a greater or lesser extent, depending on how easily the new information and ideas can be fitted into it. For much of the time the changes will be fairly small, adding new examples to an existing idea or seeing that an idea can be used in circumstances in which it had not previously been encountered.

Occasionally a more substantial change occurs, and the learner's pattern is reformed. Learning a new idea reveals ways of relating existing ideas and information in a manner which had not previously been considered, or was indeed possible without the new idea. Such points in the learning process are not only important in developing understanding but have a powerful motivational effect. The student becomes genuinely excited when such 'insights' occur. Her understanding of the subject has undergone a change, the outcome of which is not only easy to remember but also forms an enhanced basis for further learning. The basis is enhanced in two respects:

1 The new pattern can be used in the learning of a wider range of information and ideas.
2 Selecting and remembering the appropriate ideas for use in solving problems is made easier.

By contrast, verbatim or rote learning lacks pattern and organization. At best, the pattern is learned from the textbook or teachers' notes without a proper appreciation of its nature and power to help understanding and recall. With meaningful learning the pattern of ideas is the property of the individual student. It reflects the way in which s/he has learned the ideas and the particular examples which help to make these ideas meaningful for him or her. These patterns will not be identical for all the students who have learned the material in a meaningful fashion. Indeed there will be some way in which each student's pattern of information and ideas is unique.

Ausubel (1978) makes a distinction between logical meaning, the formal and generally accepted meaning presented in textbooks etc., and psychological meaning which also includes the ways in which the individual learned the logical meaning. The logical meaning of the content is common to all the students who have understood the contents of the course. The psychological meaning will, however, vary to some degree between such students. This variation reflects the differences in the way in which students learn, or at any rate, in these aspects of learning which involve understanding.

Ausubel's theory is mainly concerned with the way secondary school pupils, i.e. age 12 and over, learn from text. The bulk of secondary school learning and examining is still text-based, despite the changes introduced by the GCSE, so his ideas are relevant for the great majority of secondary students.

The role of experience

Mention has already been made earlier in this note of Professor Donaldson's work with young children (Donaldson 1976). They come to school with a set of expectations which are based on their experience. If the teacher is unaware of this experience s/he cannot take advantage of it to help the child to learn. If the child is placed in situations which contradict his or her experience, this can have serious negative effects on the child's learning. The confusion which arises may not only cause emotional strain, making learning a misery rather than an enjoyable activity, but the child's confidence may also be damaged, causing long-term problems. There is evidence from a number of sources that, not only with young children, experience plays a very important part in developing understanding. More details of some of this work can be found in a set of highly readable articles in a recent book edited by Professor Entwistle (Entwistle 1985).

The course work requirement in the GCSE provides an opportunity for the students to obtain experiences not normally available on traditional courses. Experience of this kind is only likely to promote understanding of the key ideas in a subject if the course work is carefully integrated with the rest of the teaching. The most important thing is for the teacher to be aware of the experiences that a student has had, (a) on the course itself, (b) on courses in other subjects, and (c) outside school, which are likely to help promote his or her understanding of the subject.

Formative evaluation of a large group, e.g. a class, is unlikely to be of much value. Small group or individual discussion is required but if the teacher sets an outline agenda for such discussions it is very important that the students help to develop it. The existence of such an agenda enables the students to prepare for the discussion. This preparation gives them time to think about the experiences which they see as relevant in addition to identifying the points which they are finding difficult. In this way the time spent in discussion can be used most effectively and efficiently.

Learning style

Entwistle (1981) and Riding (1983) have shown that many students have a preferred style of learning. The issue is complicated, but one style which has clearly emerged relates to the way in which an individual stores information and ideas in his or her memory. Some learners show a preference for visual forms of representation, while others predominantly think in terms of words. An interesting example of a person who thinks in visual terms is Seymour Papert, Professor of Education and Mathematics at Massachusetts Institute of Technology. He invented LOGO, the computer language for use by young children, and in his book *Mindstorms* (Papert 1980) he tells how from an early age he thought of mathematical problems as a set of cogs and wheels. His book also contains good examples of how children's mathematical understanding can be developed by relating the ideas to their everyday experience.

It is not only the student who has a preferred style of learning; the teacher has one as well. This means that the teacher will be predisposed to present and explain information and ideas in a way which accords with his style. It is not just the delivery of his or her teaching but the choice of textbooks and other supporting materials, visual aids, slides, videos, etc., which will be affected. A teacher with a strong preference for a verbal style may make little or no use of such aids. Even the most dedicated teacher may be unknowingly placing a number of their students at a serious disadvantage. Formative evaluation, however thorough, if based on the teacher's preferred style may fail to reveal this problem.

Summary

The individual's learning history is composed of a number of factors, each of which has an important bearing on his or her achievement at the end of the course. These factors can be divided into three groups:

1 The affective or emotional factors. These determine the student's attitude to and expectations of the course. The student's self-concept is a very important factor. Traditional systems and attitudes which divide students into above average, average and below average have a negative effect on the learning of the latter groups. Students who have repeatedly been told that they are only average may see no point in attempting to improve their performance. While it is not suggested that individuals should attempt work which is clearly too far beyond their current levels of performance, it is nevertheless true that traditional views on ability have been more hindrance than help to the majority of students.

It is equally important that students' experiences and views are treated not only as a valid but also as an invaluable contribution to learning about the subject. Interest, even in the most modest degree, is usually an essential condition for understanding a topic.

2 The cognitive or intellectual factors. An important distinction here lies in the differences between meaningful and verbatim or rote learning. In meaningful learning the new information and ideas are related to the existing pattern of ideas and information in the student's mind. It is this pattern which provides a secure basis for further learning. The pattern has been created by the student in his or her mind with the help of the teacher and text books, etc. This means that the

student is able to think about his or her experiences inside and outside school in terms of this pattern of ideas. The student who learns in this way is better equipped to use ideas in problem-solving situations.

If students are to learn meaningfully they must believe in their ability to do so and that such learning will be rewarded, not penalized, by the criteria used for assessment.

3 The preferred learning style of an individual can have a major effect on their performance. One learning style relates to the presentation of information and ideas in visual rather than verbal form. There is a danger that a teacher will concentrate, almost exclusively, on presenting the course in line with his or her preferred learning style. This practice can put students who have a different preferred learning style at a real disadvantage.

The most important aspect of adopting a learning history approach lies in its effects on the beliefs which the teacher holds. The emphasis changes from one of largely externally imposed limitations to finding ways of enabling students to fulfil their potential. This is not an argument that every student should be able to achieve an A grade in every subject of the GCSE, but that their level of attainment and appreciation of their courses could be enhanced, in many cases to a substantial degree.

CONCLUSION

At the beginning of the chapter three questions were posed, viz:

1 To what extent does the examination enable students to reveal the variety as well as the level of the knowledge and skills they have acquired?
2 Does the form used to report the results to candidates, teachers, potential employers, etc., ensure that such information is full, detailed and described in such a way that it is meaningful to them?
3 Do the syllabus and examinations provide an adequate framework for improving the quality of teaching and learning?

Answers to the first two questions have already been suggested on page 57, where it was argued that the GCSE represents a useful step forward, especially with regard to question (2). The principal purpose here is to discuss question (3), but question (1) will also be considered in the light of the note on learning history.

In question (3) the emphasis shifts from the examining to the teaching-learning process. The responsibility for carrying out the activity is also changed from the examiners to the teachers. The examination boards and the examiners have much less control over the situation, but they are still responsible for determining the syllabus and the form and content of the examinations. It is the teachers who play the key role of mediating between their student's knowledge, experience and learning practices and the demands of the examiners.

This distinction is clearly reflected in the differences between formative and summative evaluation. The former is a dynamic, interactive, and individual activity varying in content and approach between students but always aimed at the determination of their learning needs. It is not normally concerned with making comparisons between students but with ascertaining the individual's approach to and perceptions of the learning task in hand. The topics have to be analysed in ways which provide a realistic basis for this information to be obtained. If the student faces too many difficulties with a topic s/he will even become unsure about points which they actually do understand. The nature of such an analysis varies between subjects and there are not simple prescriptions which can be applied on a general basis. Objectives which emphasize observable behaviour (see Note 3, page 57), are of greatest value for topics which are 'closed' in nature and have a clear and generally agreed structure, e.g. rules of arithmetic, grammar or spelling.

There is a great danger of assuming that the inclusion of behaviourial objectives is, of itself, sufficient to improve the teaching-learning process. They can be of real benefit but only when used in the correct manner and circumstances. Even here the objectives provide no more than a framework of outcomes which help to structure and guide the learning process. In such circumstances their use offers the opportunity for the encouragement provided by the regular achievement of short term goals. It enables these goals to be set in the context of longer-term goals culminating in the examination. The student is aware of this structure, so s/he can see where these achievements are leading. If, however, the emphasis is on short-term goals attained in isolation the course is likely to produce short-term satisfaction.

If formative evaluation is to be fully successful, however, it needs to take into account the factors involved in the individual student's learning history. This shows that the teaching-learning situation is much more complex than has previously been recognized. In particular it is suggested that the explanation of lower levels of attainment by students in terms of an abstruse property known as ability is not merely unhelpful and probably unfair to the student but is actually counter-productive to improving the quality of the teaching. This does not mean that all students should be expected to attain the same levels of performance in all subjects. It is concerned with finding ways of helping students to improve their performance, not with providing reasons why they cannot expect to do so. The arguments presented here do not exclude the use of differentiated examinations in subjects where these appear to be necessary.

It has already been stated in answer to question (1), on page 57, that the type of summative evaluation which the GCSE represents is a real improvement over much traditional examining. The emphasis on positive achievement, understanding, and application as opposed to merely recalling information and ideas fits well with a number of the issues raised in Note 4. There is a recognition of the importance of variety in the mode of presentation of examination questions to allow, for example, for students with a preferred learning style which is visual. A more explicit statement of this issue can be found in paragraph 47 of the National Curriculum TGAT Report.

> Standard assessments need not only be in written form. Indeed, the wide variety of possibilities can be explored by analysing any one task in terms of three aspects or modes, which can be defined as follows:
> — the presentation mode — the method of delivery of the questions (oral, written, pictorial, video, computer, practical demonstration);
> — the operation mode — the expected method of working (mental only, written, practical, oral);
> — the response mode — pupils may answer in various ways (e.g. choosing one option in a multiple-choice question, writing a short prescribed response, open-ended writing, oral, practical procedure observed, practical outcome or product, computer input).
>
> (Department of Education and Science/ Welsh office 1988)

It is, however, in the teaching-learning part of the whole process that the main impact will have to be made if students are to benefit from such changes at this stage of their education. There must be some doubt whether the training which teachers have received in the past has properly equipped them to deal with this challenge. Before the current and potential benefits of the introduction of the GCSE can be fully realized by the majority of the students, appropriate changes in both initial and in-service training courses will be required to help teachers to reflect on these issues and incorporate them into their daily work.

The main beneficiaries of such training will, however, be the students who will remain, as they have always been, dependent on the support and encouragement of their teachers if they are to achieve their true potential.

REFERENCES AND BIBLIOGRAPHY

Ausubel, D.P., Novak, J.S., and Haneslan, H. (1978) *Educational Psychology: a cognitive view*, New York: Holt, Rinehart and Winston.

Bloom, B.S. (ed.) (1956) *Taxonomy of Educational Objectives, Handbook 1: cognitive domain*, New York: McKay.

Bloom, B.S., Hastings, J.T. and Madaus, G.F. (1971) *Handbook on Formative and Summative Evaluation of Student Learning*, New York: McGraw Hill.

Bloom, B.S. (1976) *Human Characteristics and School Learning*, New York: McGraw Hill.

Davies, I.K. (1976) *Objectives in Curriculum Design*, New York: McGraw Hill.

Department of Education and Science/Welsh Office (1985) *General Certificate of Secondary Education: the national criteria*, London: HMSO.

Department of Education and Science/Welsh Office (1988) *A Report from the National Curriculum Task Group on Assessment and Testing*, London: HMSO.

Donaldson, M. (1978) *Children's Minds*, London: Fontana.

Entwistle, N. (1981) *Styles of Learning and Teaching*, Chichester: John Wiley.

Entwistle, N. (ed.) (1985) *New Directions in Educational Psychology*, Lewes: Falmer Press.

Mager, R.F. (1962) *Preparing Instructional Objectives*, Palo Alto, California: Fearson.

Midland Examining Group (1986) *Biology.*

Midland Examining Group (1988) *General Certificate of Secondary Education examination syllabuses.*

Papert, S. (1980) *Mindstorms: children, computers and*

powerful ideas, New York: Basic Books.

Riding, R.J. (1983) 'Adapting instruction for the learner', in K. Wheldall and R. Riding (eds) *Psychological Aspects of Learning and Teaching*, London: Croom Helm.

Chapter Three

THE ADMINISTRATION OF GCSE: AN OUTLINE

Bill Brown

INTRODUCTION

School examinations are part of the English way of life. They have become established to the point that their need is seldom questioned. And if there was any doubt about their immediate future, this uncertainty seemed to have disappeared with the introduction of the General Certificate of Secondary Education in 1988 and the proposal to test pupils at the ages of 7, 11 and 14 also.

However, although examinations are generally accepted and regarded as important, there is considerable ignorance of what is involved, even among teachers. Naturally enough, interest is primarily in the outcome — the results — rather than in the examining process. And yet there is high expectation of this process; it must produce complete and accurate results on time. It is an expectation that the examination boards often have difficulty in fulfilling. They tend therefore to go quietly about their private business.

It would be far better if there was a greater awareness, particularly among teachers, of what examining entails, its capability, and its limits. For examining will only improve and develop along appropriate lines if knowledge and understanding of its procedures and standards extend well beyond those who work directly for the examining boards. This is in everyone's interest, not least the boards themselves.

This chapter looks at the formation of the examining groups and how they operate, and then takes a board's-eye view of examining from the production of a GCSE syllabus through to the issue of results. But first it is necessary to look at the modern context in which this activity takes place, for there are a number of radical changes occurring in education (of which the GCSE is one) that all interact, and this has significance for everyone concerned.

BACKGROUND

Examining is at its most comfortable when it becomes repetitive, tried and tested, familiar and predictable. It rests easily within an education system in which the imperative to conservatism is strong and where there is a natural concern for the maintenance of standards which change might undermine.

It was therefore something of a surprise, even to those who had worked for many years towards this goal (feasibility studies using joint GCE O level and CSE examinations had been carried out since the early 1970s), when in June 1984 the introduction of the General Certificate of Secondary Education was announced.

For the new examination to be accepted, however, it had to set out to preserve standards and maintain good examining practice. Because of this, though its design had novel features, such as its differentiated approach to assessment, there was no difficulty in recognizing the GCSE as a development of the traditional type of examination. The maintenance of the standards of the GCE O level in the award of grades A, B, and C at GCSE and of CSE grades 2, 3, 4, and 5 in the award of GCSE grades D, E, F, and G provided a bridge of continuity.

But the normality of its appearance belied the true significance of the GCSE; its importance lay not only in the substantial improvement that it brought to the domain of examining, but also in its role and relationship to other major educational developments. For, together with the proposals for a national curriculum, testing pupils at the ages of 7, 11, and 14, and the opportunity for local school management, the GCSE formed part of a national strategy for education, with the twin objectives of raising standards and making education more publicly accountable. And although in 1988 the outcome of these changes was uncertain, history will almost certainly show that in combination they were among the most radical and significant of the twentieth century.

If it was to perform effectively within this modern context, the GCSE had to be clearly specified and its operation controlled. Hence the introduction of National Criteria and the establishment of the Secondary Examinations Council.

A further consequence of the determination of its role was that if the GCSE was to be used to improve standards and report educational achievement, it could not be allowed to have the same uncertain and uneasy relationship to the curriculum as the GCE O level and CSE examinations had had.

It is of major importance that in this latter regard the GCSE recognized and formalized, in a way that previous examinations had failed to do, the essential interrelationship of assessment, the curriculum and teaching. From this recognition flowed a reappraisal of course aims, subject content, assessment objectives, and the training of teachers for their role in the assessment process. In addition, and importantly, it brought about a review of the working relationship of examination boards and the schools and colleges they serve, albeit largely as a consequence of the other changes.

Examining was no longer independent or the private preserve of the boards; its activities had been rationalized and rules drawn up in the form of National Criteria that would require examining to play a specific role within the context of a national plan for education.

GCSE ADMINISTRATION

The formation of the examining groups

Under the terms of the National Criteria (General Criteria Part 1) the task of organizing and administering the GCSE was given to examining groups formed by the association of GCE and CSE boards. Four groups were established in England: the London and East Anglia Group; the Midland Examining Group; the Northern Examining Association and the Southern Examining Group. Each group was required to have among its constituent board at least one GCE and one CSE board so that the standards of the GCE O level and CSE examinations would be maintained in the provision of GCSE syllabuses and in the award of the equivalent GCSE grades. Although all of these groups were regionally based, they were free to operate nationally (General Criteria Part 1).

The composition of the four groups based on England and the names and addresses of all of the boards is given on page 99.

The Northern Ireland Board and the Welsh Board had previously administered both GCE O level and the CSE examinations and assumed responsibility for the conduct of the GCSE in their respective countries. Scotland maintained its own individual examination system.

Each of the groups had to formalize the association of its member boards and regulate the group's activities. The outcome of this was dependent upon a variety of circumstances, of which the most influential by far was the short time that the groups were given to organize their administration of the GCSE. Subsequently, various internal and external pressures upon the groups induced changes in the way they have operated.

In these circumstances it is difficult to foresee the final situation of the groups or to identify for the purpose of illustration a typical group. What follows, therefore, is a description of the working arrangements of one group, the Midland Examining Group. However, because the nature of the GCSE work undertaken is common to all, many of the features described can be assumed to be the same as those of other groups.

The constitution of the Midland Examining Group identifies its member boards: the University of Cambridge Local Examinations Syndicate; the Oxford and Cambridge School Examinations Board; Southern Universities Joint Board for School Examinations (three GCE boards), and the East Midland Regional Examinations Board and West Midlands Examinations Board (both CSE boards at the time of the group's formation). The constitution also sets out its committee structure: Council; a Joint Management Committee; an Examinations Committee and a Finance and General Purposes Committee. Each of these committees has a particular function and among their membership are an equal number of GCE board and CSE board representatives.

The Council provides a forum for the discussion of matters which relate the GCSE to the needs of education and the world of work, and has among its membership representatives of teacher associations, independent schools, further education, universities, and commerce and industry. The Joint Management Committee is the policy-making body and directs the activities of the examining group. The Examinations Committee is responsible for the conduct of the Midland Examining Group's examinations, and for this purpose sets up subject panels which are responsible for the provision of syllabus and the assessment of candidates' performances. (A description of the work of subject panels is given on page 85.) The Finance and General Purposes Committee ensures that financial and administrative arrangements are carried out in accordance with the group's policy.

The constitution also preserves the links with the local education authorities from within the Midland Examining Group's East Midland and West Midland geographical areas that were established for the purposes of the CSE. Chief education officers from among these local education authorities contribute to the membership of each of the group's committees.

The 'Instruments of Government' of the Midland Examining Group (these are published with the constitution) give the standing orders for the Midland Examining Group committees; they state the principles upon which the work of the group will be allocated among its member boards, and identify the functions of the board's administrations, the committees and subject panels.

Administrative arrangements

Work undertaken by the groups in connection with the GCSE falls into two broad categories: that which concerns the conduct of examinations in particular subjects, and that which relates to general examination administration. The first category includes the writing of syllabuses, the setting of question papers, the appointment of examiners, and the assessment of candidates' performances. The second category includes the collecting of examination entries and the issue of results.

The basis of the allocation of all of the work among the constituent boards of a group depends upon the way in which the group is organized. The Midland Examining Group has chosen a federal arrangement under which each of the boards has a share of both types of work. Under this arrangement all of the subjects that the Midland Examining Group examines are allocated among its member boards and each board undertakes specific responsibilities as a 'conducting board' of the examinations that relate to those subjects which it has been given.

The general responsibilities requiring direct communication with the Group's examination centres are shared on a geographical basis. Thereby the East and West Midlands boards act as 'home boards' to the schools and colleges in their respective regions, and the GCE boards serve as home boards to those centres outside that geographical area. There is an exception to this general rule, that permits a school in the East or West Midlands that has an established relationship with another Midland Examining Group board to use that board as its home board for GCSE purposes.

When acting on behalf of the group as a home board, each constituent board assumes responsibility for the provision of examinations to the particular schools and colleges it serves. This includes the collection of all examination entries and marks awarded to candidates for teacher-assessed work, and the supply of syllabuses, question papers, stationery, course work mark sheets and other materials required for those examinations. In addition, each home board acts as the group's correspondent with those schools and colleges (usually referred to as 'examination centres').

The principal advantage of adopting this type of federal arrangement was that it enabled the group to function quickly without the disruption and financial outlay that would have arisen if a more integrated form of organization had been adopted, and it encouraged the development of the working relationships established with schools and colleges for the purposes of the GCE and CSE.

The Midland Examining Group maintained the form of organization it originally adopted but set out to eliminate unnecessary differences in which individual member boards operate without imposing unreasonable restrictions on their ability to maximize use of their resources and respond to the needs of the schools and colleges they serve. Other groups have chosen a more integrated operational arrangement under which certain functions, such as the collection and processing of entries, have been centralized thereby eliminating those problems that tend to arise when a number of units are involved in a single process. In this situation care must be taken to ensure that any central service meets the general need and does not create a bottleneck when working at peak level.

It is in the nature of the groups' accountability that they must regularly review the way in which they work, not only to ensure domestic efficiency but also to respond to any directives from the Department of Education and Science (DES) and the School Examinations and Assessment Council (SEAC), GCSE developments, and the needs of schools and colleges.

Income and expenditure

The income of the group is largely derived from the examination fees received from the local authorities. The fees charged to schools are controlled by the twin influences of local education authority representation on examining group committees, and GCSE market forces. There are therefore natural pressures that restrict GCSE entry fees and operating costs.

Communication between a group and its centres

It is in the nature of the GCSE and other forms of reporting that require a significant input by teachers, such as records of achievement, to depend for their success upon a close working relationship between the examination boards and schools and colleges. This demands the use of efficient systems of communication. It is not simply a matter of dealing effectively with increased volumes and frequency of data transmission; communication systems must help to make the assessment process more flexible and responsive to the individual and diverse needs of schools and colleges.

Acting in its capacity as home board, the West Midlands Examinations Board set out to provide for those centres for which it was responsible to the Midland Examining Group, a system of communication which would significantly improve its service. With the co-operation of the eleven local education authorities in its region, the board developed a direct electronic communication link with the centres it serves.

MEGLINK, as it is called, connects schools' microcomputers to the board's central computer by means of the public telephone system. The service has five facilities: electronic mail; data transfer; databases; typesetting and printing; and conferencing. The first of these enables a prompt exchange of mail and the ordering of syllabuses, question papers and other materials. Data transfer allows examination entries to be submitted by centres directly to the board (the information may perhaps have been abstracted by a school from its administrative system), and at the end of the process, the examination results are transferred by the board quickly and efficiently to centres. Thd databases give the syllabus provisions, past question papers and other examination information.

The typesetting and printing, and the conferencing facilities, are being developed so that, in the first case, it will be possible, for example, for a school which has, through reference to the database, identified questions suitable for use in an internal examination, to have a question paper set and printed by the board. (This facility could be used for the production of a Mode 3 question paper.) Conferencing will provide teachers who have a common curriculum interest with the means to correspond electronically on a range of topics.

To stress the importance that the board attaches to the use of MEGLINK, it provided modems (equipment needed to connect the computers by telephone), introductory training, communications software and operating manuals, free of charge to participating centres. Furthermore, for the 1989 GCSE examinations it offered to pay a fee of one pound for each subject entry to each centre which submitted its entries through MEGLINK and made regular use of electronic mail.

There will, of course, continue to be a call for traditional forms of communication, but in this field modern technology offers tremendous scope for the development of close working relationships and significant improvements to the assessment process.

Subject panels

Because they are at the sharp end of the examination activity, the role of the subject panels is crucial to the success for the GCSE. It is within the subject panels that the views and wishes of the classroom teachers are related to and reflected by the examining process. And notwithstanding the constraints imposed on their activities by National Criteria, it is the subject panels that bear the prime responsibility of ensuring that examining is happily married to the curriculum and to teaching.

Those teachers who serve on the panels act in two capacities. As individuals they bring personal expertise and experience to those activities that require the identification and application of standards in their subject. In this connection they do not have a representative function. On the other hand as individuals and collectively, members endeavour to represent the views of their colleagues when, for example, syllabuses are being designed.

Each of the subject panels of the Midland Examining Group has a membership of fourteen people. When the panels were first formed, half were chosen because of their previous involvement with the GCE O level examination and half because of their experience of the CSE. This enabled the examining group to carry over equivalent standards to the GCSE as required by the National Criteria. (As GCSE standards become established and free-standing it will become unnecessary to refer to their previous equivalence.)

A subject panel has two main areas of responsibility: it must produce syllabuses which conform to National Criteria and generally meet the needs of schools, and it must oversee the examinations in the subjects for which it is responsible. In carrying out each of these activities the panel is responsible for the maintenance of standards in the subjects.

For those examinations within its purview a subject panel must see that suitable syllabuses and question papers are devised and assessments made of candidates' performances. The production of syllabuses normally involves all of the members so that there is a wide representation of views, whereas the moderation of question papers and the assessments are normally carried out by subcommittees appointed for the purpose.

There is also an input by those people (usually teachers) who have been appointed to undertake specific examining tasks. They include chief examiners and chief coursework moderators, who become members of the moderation and assessment subcommittees.

A senior member of the administrative staff of a board acts as servicing officer to each subject panel. There are three principal parts to the servicing officer's role: he or she must organize meetings and record and implement decisions, advise on assessment techniques and other practical aspects of examining, particularly in the subject concerned, and give information and guidance on the policies and practices of the group. In this latter connection it is the not inconsiderable task of the servicing officer to help a subject panel to follow its chosen and perhaps individual path within an agreed group system which seeks to provide schools with a cohesive examination service.

GCSE syllabuses

Prior to the introduction of the GCSE, syllabuses were produced without having to conform to a nationally agreed specification. This resulted not only in a wide diversity of syllabuses within a subject area but also in a lack of coherence within and across subjects. GCSE examination criteria rationalized and significantly improved the examination provision.

Although subject-specific criteria created a tight framework within which those subject panels responsible for the twenty subjects covered by the criteria had to work, there was nevertheless considerable scope for the design of the GCSE syllabuses, and groups sought the views and wishes of all interested parties, including of course teachers, in the production of their syllabuses.

The GCSE 1988 syllabuses and specimen question papers were approved by the (then) Secondary Examinations Council but the process of rationalization and co-ordination of syllabus provision did not end there. Syllabus approval by the SEAC was subsequently extended to all subjects in all modes of the GCSE examination and consideration is being given to a reduction in the number of syllabuses available.

A syllabus is, of course, a teacher's main reference source when he or she is looking for a suitable assessment provision or is preparing candidates for examination. For these reasons a syllabus must, under the rules of the GCSE, state its educational aims, give the assessment objectives, their relative importance and where they feature in the examination components, and specify the examination's subject content.

A syllabus also provides the basis of an agreement between the examining group issuing it and each centre which enters candidates. There is no formal agreement for the provision of an examination until candidates are entered, but many months earlier teachers commit themselves and their pupils to a particular syllabus and usually the group offering it has to supply information and course work materials in advance of its receiving entries.

Though provisional entry information is sought by the groups, centres are not obliged to give it. Furthermore, in the early years the groups were not always certain of the schools and colleges to which the request for information should be addressed.

When an examination is established, the syllabus tends to be followed from year to year by a core of schools and a group's register of centres becomes more reliable in the identification of those schools and colleges that are likely to take its examinations. Nevertheless, the GCSE is not best served by an arrangement that fails to formalize the relationship between the schools and colleges committed to an examination and the group providing it until well after the course has begun. It would help the groups to provide a more efficient service if the centres taking examinations were required to identify themselves at the outset of the course.

The marking and moderation of coursework

Coursework and all other work which is marked by a candidate's teacher has its requirements stated in the relevant syllabus and in documents provided by the group about the marking and submission of work and marks for moderation. When the work has been produced and marked, the group has a responsibility to check that in type and quantity the work meets the syllabus requirements and the teacher has consistently applied appropriate criteria to the marking. This job is undertaken by a moderator who has been appointed and briefed for the task.

If the work is ephemeral or bulky, it is normally necessary for moderation to be carried out at the examination centre submitting it. Usually, however, coursework takes a written form that makes it suitable for postal moderation. In both situations, because of the size of most entries, moderation is normally based on a sample of what has been produced and marked by the centre. The sample is chosen to represent both the work and the marking.

Upon receipt, the moderator checks that the sample submitted is in accordance with the group's specification and then goes on to consider the suitability of the work. In this connection most subjects offer centres and candidates a choice, and though the type of work and the assessment criteria are specified, it is not normal for the content and length to be prescribed.

If more than one teacher at a school has marked and the group requires all the candidates to be treated for moderation purposes as though they were a single unit (i.e. only one set of mark adjustments is contemplated), the moderator checks that the marking has been brought to a common standard within the centre. When this proves not to be the case the sample is returned and another sample submitted after the marking has been standardized.

Provided that the work is suitable and the marking is found to be consistent, the moderator will be concerned only with the marking standard. Since the sample will have been selected to cover the whole of the ability range at the centre, the moderator should have sufficient evidence to decide whether the criteria have been uniformly applied across the range of marks awarded. But if the sample is inadequate for this or any other reason, a further sample is sought.

It may be that in the moderator's judgement the marking is of an appropriate standard at the higher level but rather severe in the middle or at the lower end, in which case only those marks will be adjusted. In other circumstances, the moderator may decide that all of the marks require adjustment, though not necessarily by the same amount across the mark range. Whatever the conclusion the moderator will inform the group, on a form provided for the purpose, of the adjustments, if any, that are required in order to bring the marking of a centre in line with the group's standard. And where the change is significant, if not in all cases, the reason is recorded on the form.

All moderators are supervised by a chief coursework moderator whose job it is to ensure that they are applying appropriate standards. A sample of each moderator's judgements is checked and, if necessary, the moderation is reviewed and revised. When adjustments are made, it is normally the policy of the groups not to change the order of merit of the candidates.

In 1988 there was no common practice adopted by the groups for the notification to schools of the outcome of moderation. Schools were normally told of the amount of any change but the reasons were not generally given. There was little time to make suitable arrangements to provide feedback on the moderation of coursework in the first year of GCSE, but many schools sought this information and groups acknowledge that this is a request that they must address in future years.

It was clear when teachers received notice that their marks had been changed that a significant number misunderstood the process of moderation. Some regarded any adjustment to their marks as an implied criticism of their professional competence. Though teachers are expected to be able to apply the specified marking criteria consistently, it is unreasonable and unnecessary to expect that they will mark to a standard that corresponds exactly to that agreed by the group.

Teachers must recognize that marks are the means of distinguishing levels of performance; they have no absolute value across subjects or, with a few exceptions, from year to year. Provided that the marking is consistent and moderation is successfully carried out, each mark will represent a particular level of performance on course work for a certain examination. It will be for the assessors to decide the mark that represents the minimum performance required for the award of each component grade. (A description of the assessment process is given on page 92–7.)

Question paper preparation and external marking

The process of producing a question paper begins perhaps eighteen months prior to its use in an examination. At the outset the appropriate chief examiner, who has been appointed on the grounds of his or her educational qualifications and teaching and examining experience, is given a specification for the preparation of a draft question paper. The servicing officer for the subject provides: a copy of the syllabus; information about the candidates who will sit the examination (the target group); instruction on the type, number and format of the questions to be set (accompanied by past or specimen question papers and mark schemes); advice on the wording of the instructions and questions so that they may be intelligible to the candidates; and, of course, instructions for the submission of the draft paper and mark scheme.

(The importance of wording a question so that it is free from ambiguity may be brought home to an unsuspecting chief examiner for whom a candidate is lying in wait. The woodwork chief examiner who drew a spokeshave and posed the question, 'Name this tool' did not expect the response of one candidate, 'I name this tool Norman'.)

Upon receipt by the servicing officer, the draft question paper and associated mark scheme are sent to those people appointed to act as moderators of the papers. They will normally be teachers and members of the moderation and assessment subcommittee of the subject panel. The moderators' responsibility is to ensure that the specification given to the chief examiner has been met. Particular care is taken to ensure: that all of the questions are within the scope of the syllabus and that there are no significant parts of the syllabus not represented in the questions; that the appropriate assessment objectives are being tested and their relative importance maintained; and that the mark scheme is sufficiently detailed to show clearly the answers that are expected and will reward positive achievement. (The production of mark schemes is one of the areas of examining that have been improved by the GCSE. Detailed mark schemes are now produced to a much tighter specification than tended to be the case previously, and the preparation of mark schemes and question papers is acknowledged to be a conjoint activity.)

All of the papers that comprise a particular examination follow this procedure and when each has been individually moderated, the moderators take an overview to ensure that collectively they form a cohesive set and that unnecessary overlap is avoided.

The mark scheme prepared by the chief examiner, and moderated with the question paper to which it relates, provides the basis of external marking by (assistant) examiners. The examiners are given a copy of the question paper and the marking scheme in advance of their receiving scripts from schools. When the scripts arrive, the examiners are required to do some preliminary marking prior to their attendance at a briefing meeting at which the application of the mark scheme is considered and discussed in the light of the initial marking experience. The mark scheme is then reviewed and, if necessary, revised.

Within two days of the briefing meeting having been held, each examiner must submit to the chief examiner (or if the examination has a large entry, to a team leader appointed to assist with the supervision of the markers) some 10 to 20 marked scripts. This first sample of the examiner's mark is supplied according to a specification by the chief examiner covering, where possible, a range of questions, topics, and levels of response. The initial check seeks to establish each examiner's basic professional competence in applying the mark scheme and recording marks. If the chief examiner is dissatisfied with the first sample, a second sample is requested.

Towards the end of, or upon completion of, the marking, at least one further and larger check of each examiner's marking is carried out. This check has a dual purpose: it seeks to confirm that the examiner has consistently applied the mark scheme, and it provides evidence upon which the chief examiner judges the examiner's standard of marking.

The chief examiner therefore appraises each examiner's marking and decides whether a change to the marks is needed in order to adjust for any severity or leniency. The process is the same as that described for the moderation of course work (see page 87-9). Occasionally an examiner's marking will be found to be unreliable, in which case it is re-marked. When the marking has been completed, the chief examiner (or the team leader) reports on the marking of each assistant examiner. The report is used if there is any investigation of an examiner's marking.

Mark processing

Marks are normally recorded from the scripts or course work documentation on to a summary mark sheet which is the medium for entering them into the computer system. These mark sheets bear the appropriate subject and component references and are printed with the candidates' numbers upon them. This information will have been taken from the computer's examination entry files.

The marks are then either keyed (punched) or optically read into the computer; the latter method requires the marks to be encoded in pencil on the mark sheet so that the appropriate boxes for hundreds, tens and units are completed. At this stage the marks are referred to as 'raw'. If necessary, they are then 'scaled', which converts the marks to the scale set out in the syllabus (it is often necessary to use a larger scale for marking purposes), and 'moderated', which adjusts for severity or leniency in marking.

Candidates' answers to multiple choice questions are also optically read by the scanning device, the responses compared to the correct answers which have been fed into the computer, and an overall mark obtained.

When the marks of all of the examination components have been entered, a variety of data are produced in preparation for the assessments. These include statistical information on the marking of each examiner which is used to identify and check marking variances.

Assessment procedures

Before looking in detail at the way assessments are carried out, it is helpful to look at the task in outline and the difficulties that are faced.

The process of assessment has a number of steps, and each step has a prime objective. At the beginning, candidates are set tasks which have been designed to enable them to show their true level of attainment in the subject. Each candidate's achievement is expressed as a mark obtained on each of the examination components. The objective is to put the candidates in an order of merit that represents their relative attainment on each component.

Each candidate's marks are then added together and an overall order of merit obtained for the subject option taken. A minimum mark is determined for the award of each grade. The grades awarded should represent comparable levels of performance to those that lead to the award of the same grades in the other options of the subject and should be consistent with those awarded in previous years (in 1988 this meant maintaining the standards of equivalent GCE and CSE grades).

There are a number of difficulties that have to be overcome if these objectives are to be achieved. First of all it has to be acknowledged that since all parts of the operation are heavily dependent upon human skill, judgement and accuracy, they are prone to error. Much time and effort has therefore to be put into identifying and eliminating mistakes. A further problem is that since it is not usually possible at any stage to look closely at the performance of all the candidates, much reliance has to be placed on the evidence provided by a sample. For example, views of the marking of course work and scripts are based on samples, as indeed are judgements taken at the assessment meeting. If decisions are to be securely based, the samples must represent the whole.

There is an additional complication. Prior to the assessment meeting an examination is conducted in a number of self-contained parts (components) which for assessment purposes have to be combined. The marking and moderation of each of these components is normally the responsibility of three people; two chief examiners, and a chief coursework moderator, each of whom looks after one or two components but not all. No one is therefore in a position to report from first-hand, detailed knowledge of candidates' performances on all components.

The overall assessment is therefore reached by the separate assessment of each component. In acknowledgement of errors which if undetected would result in incorrect grades being awarded, a variety of checks are carried out to identify and eliminate these errors.

Prior to the assessment meeting, the chief examiners (there are normally two, and they usually look after different components) receive a report from each assistant examiner (the markers) on the performance of the candidates the examiner marked. This information helps the chief examiner to compile two reports to the subject panel's assessment subcommittee: the first is a confidential report which includes recommended minimum marks for the award of grades on each externally assessed component; the other is a detailed 'report to centres', which will be published.

In addition to the mark recommendations, the confidential report also contains information about how the papers functioned and any difficulties that were encountered, with particular reference to any examiner whose marking requires further checking. General information about candidates' responses to the examination questions is given in the report to centres. Similar reports and recommendations are submitted by the chief course work moderator.

Having processed the marks, the board responsible for the assessment meeting produces distributions of candidates by component and overall, a summary of the grades that have been forecast by the centres (each centre is requested to provide by the beginning of May of the examination year a forecast of the grades its candidates are expected to attain), and, if the syllabus was examined in the previous year, comparative statistics.

The servicing officer tests the mark recommendations by applying them to the appropriate mark distributions and then compares the outcome across the components. Occasionally this produces an apparent anomaly when component grades are compared, and it therefore becomes necessary to review the recommendation by taking a further look at candidates' work.

In preparation for the assessment meeting, samples of candidates' work are chosen to represent the chief examiner's and chief coursework moderator's suggested minimum marks for each grade boundary, and for levels of performance above and below those marks. Each range of marks covers all of the candidates who might reasonably be expected to come within the scope of the grade boundary under consideration and the sample is selected from the work of candidates from a number of centres and from the marking of a number of examiners.

The servicing officer convenes the assessment subcommittee meeting and sends with the notice to the members copies of the question papers and the mark schemes, the reports by the chief examiners and chief coursework moderator, and the grading procedures to be followed.

Additional material and information are made available when the assessment meeting is held. These include for each option: a summary of the grades forecast by centres; distributions of marks by component and overall; the chosen samples of candidates' work; any relevant comments by centres about the examination; and, if the syllabus option was examined in the previous year, comparative statistics, and exemplar scripts and coursework for that year.

At the meeting, the members of the assessment subcommittee begin the process of determining the awards by considering the chief examiner's and chief coursework moderator's reports, and any comments by centres about the examination. If necessary, the comments are taken into account when performances are being assessed.

The meeting will then go on to determine the notional grades for each examination component. (The grades are notional because normally they have no status other than as a means of determining the overall grades. A few syllabuses, for example those for some science subjects, do require a qualifying performance on the basic components in order to give candidates access to the highest grades.) Members assess the levels of attainment evidenced by the candidates' work in the samples provided. At each grade boundary, the work that represents the chief examiner's or the chief coursework moderator's recommendation is looked at first, and higher or lower levels of performance are considered as necessary. Finally, the bottom marks for the attainment of component grades are fixed.

Two methods are used to calculate each overall grade boundary from the decisions reached on performances on the components. The first is the simple aggregation of the minimum marks; the second, the weighted average of the percentages of candidates obtaining notional grades on the components. (The percentage of candidates in each component grade is derived from the application of the minimum marks to the candidate distribution for the component.)

The percentages of candidates in the same grade (or range of grades, see example below) are then combined in a way which reflects the weighting of the components, and the outcome is compared to that resulting from the simple aggregation of component marks. The lower mark is chosen as the grade boundary, because this always favours the candidates.

Example

A three-component subject option has the following weightings:

Paper 1	30%
Paper 2	50%
Coursework	20%

Suppose grades A, B, and C combined are achieved by 32.75 per cent, 34.60 per cent and 41.44 per cent (the percentages should not be rounded to the nearest whole number for these calculations, because rounding errors may be introduced) of the candidates in each of the above components respectively, the cumulative percentage of candidates achieving Grades A, B and C in the subject option will be:

$$\frac{30 \times 32.75 + 50 \times 34.60 \times 20 \times 41.44}{100} = 35.41\%$$

If the minimum scaled marks for the award of grade C on the components were 21:34:14 respectively, the simple aggregate would be 69. By the application of this mark the percentage of candidates achieving grades A to C would be read from the overall distribution of candidates. If this gave, say, 34.23 per cent of candidates in grades A to C, the weighted average

(35.41 per cent) would be used to determine the minimum aggregate mark for grade C, and the nearest cumulative percentage to 35.41 per cent would be chosen.

When all the grades for each of the subject options have been provisionally fixed, they are compared across the options, with the forecast grades, and, if appropriate, with the results in the previous year. Sometimes this overview reveals an apparent anomaly that requires one or more of the assessment subcommittee's decisions to be reviewed by a further scrutiny of the evidence.

Grade review

The provisional awards that are determined by the application of the agreed grade boundaries to the overall distribution of marks are reviewed during the first few days following the assessment meeting. The time taken on the grade review depends upon the number of cases that are referred to it. The number is usually proportionate to the size of the entry.

The prime purpose of the grade review is to investigate the awards to candidates who have been identified as most at risk of receiving an inappropriate grade if any error in the process of assessment were not corrected. Such candidates are identified as having a provisional result that is significantly below their forecast grade, or are shown as giving a very different performance on two or more components, indicating a possible error in marking or in the recording of marks, or are just below a grade boundary, or have had work marked by an examiner whose marking is subject to a further check. In many cases a candidate will appear in more than one of these categories and this will attract the immediate attention of the reviewers.

While the grade review is being carried out, the board staff are completing clerical checks of the recording of marks. The marks are checked from the scripts and course work mark sheets against the computer records. Any marks that are missing are pursued.

A summary of the recommended grades for all subjects in all three modes of examination is submitted for approval by the assessment subcommittee of the group's examinations committee. The meeting to which the provisional results are referred will satisfy itself that in each case the group's assessment procedures have been followed, and if there is a significant difference between the recommended awards and the summary of grades forecast by centres in any subject or subject option, this has been investigated and the awards reviewed. The group's assessment subcommittee will also ensure that appropriate procedures have been applied to the assessment of any special cases, such as handicapped candidates, and will itself consider any matters for which there is no precedent.

The issue of provisional grades

When the group's assessment subcommittee approves the awards, it authorizes their issue to candidates. At this point the results are 'provisional' and are described as such when they are notified to participating schools and colleges.

The awards are confirmed by a meeting of the group's joint management committee some six weeks after their publication. In the meantime, centres are able to submit result enquiries if they consider one or more of the awards to their candidates may be incorrect.

There are four enquiry services available to centres: a clerical check of scripts and records; a re-mark by examiners of all externally assessed components (this includes a clerical check, but a report is not provided); an individual candidate report by examiners on the candidate's performances on externally assessed components (this includes the first two services but is limited to four candidates in any subject); a group report, which is a general report on the work of between five and twenty candidates in any subject (the aim of this report is to indicate the candidates' general approaches and to illustrate strengths and weaknesses but not to provide individual reassessments). These checks normally attract a fee payable with the application, but the fee is refunded if an error is discovered which leads to a change in the provisional grade awarded.

The issue of provisional results and the availability of a result enquiry service clearly acknowledges the possibility of errors in the awards. The vast majority of the awards will, of course, be correct when the provisional results are issued, but the need to include schools' consideration of the awards as part of the final checking process is not freely acknowledged. Indeed, the urgent demand for provisional grades for employment and further and higher education purposes appears to deny the need for any opportunity to reconsider an award. This is a pity, because it represents a failure to recognize the joint involvement of both school and group, and their shared responsibility for the production of soundly based assessments.

BIBLIOGRAPHY

Broadfoot, P.M. (1979) *Assessment, Schools and Society*, London: Methuen.

Department of Education and Science (1982) *Examinations at 16+: a statement of policy*, London: HMSO.

Examiner, The (1986) *MEGLINK* Issue no. 25, March, The West Midlands Examinations Board.

GCSE General Criteria (1985) London: HMSO.

Good, F. and Cresswell, M. (1988) *Examinations: a commentary*, London: George Allen & Unwin.

Good, F. and Cresswell, M. (1988) *Grading the GCSE:* SEC.

Nuttall, D.L. (1986) *Assessing Educational Achievement*, London: Falmer Press.

Stronghorn, R. and Wrigley, J. (eds) (1985) *Values and Evaluation in Education*, London: Harper & Row.

Secondary Examinations Council (1985) *The Development of Grade Criteria For GCSE*, London: SEC.

Secondary Examinations Council (1985) *Working Paper No. 2: course work assessment in GCSE*, London: SEC.

Secondary Examinations Council (1986) *Working Paper No. 3: policy and practice in school-based assessment*, London: SEC.

APPENDIX A
EXTRACT FROM GENERAL NATIONAL CRITERIA

GCSE: Examining Groups in England and Wales

	Group and constituent boards	*CSE boards constituent local education authorities*	*Address for enquiries*
	Northern Group		
GCE:	Joint Matriculation Board		Manchester M15 6EU
CSE:	Associated Lancashire Schools Examining Board	Bolton, Manchester, Oldham, Rochdale, Salford	12 Harter Street Manchester M60 7LH
	North Regional Examinations Board	Cleveland (part), Cumbria (part), Durham, Gateshead, Newcastle-upon-Tyne, Northumberland, South Tyneside, Sunderland	Wheatfield Road Westerhope Newcastle-upon-Tyne NE5 5JZ
	North West Regional Examinations Board	Bury, Cheshire, Cumbria (part), Knowsley, Lancashire, Liverpool, St Helens, Sefton, Stockport, Tameside, Trafford, Wigan, Wirral, Isle of Man	Orbit House Albert Street Eccles Manchester M30 0WL

	The Yorkshire and Humberside Regional Examinations Board	Barnsley, Bradford, Calderdale, Cleveland (part), Humberside, Kirklees, Leeds, North Yorkshire, Wakefield, Sheffield, Rotherham, Doncaster	31–33 Springfield Avenue Harrogate HG1 2HW
	Midland Group		
GCE:	University of Cambridge Local Examinations Syndicate		Syndicate Buildings 1 Hills Road Cambridge CB1 2EU
	Oxford and Cambridge Schools Examination Board		Elsfield Way Oxford OX2 8EP and Brook House 10 Trumpington Street Cambridge CB2 1QB
	Southern Universities' Joint Board for School Examinations		Cotham Road Bristol BS6 6DD
CSE:	East Midlands Regional Examinations Board	Cambridgeshire, Derbyshire, Leicestershire, Lincolnshire, Northamptonshire, Nottinghamshire	Robins Wood House Robins Wood Road Aspley Nottingham NG8 3NH

	Group and constituent boards	*CSE boards constituent local education authorities*	*Address for enquiries*
	The West Midlands Examinations Board	Birmingham, Coventry, Dudley, Hereford and Worcester, Sandwell, Shropshire, Solihull, Staffordshire, Walsall, Warwickshire, Wolverhampton	Norfolk House Smallbrook, Queensway Birmingham 5 4NJ
	London & East Anglia Group		
GCE:	University of London School Examinations Board		London University Stewart House 32 Russell Square London WC1B 5DN
CSE:	East Anglian Examinations Board	Barking, Barnet (part), Bedfordshire, Essex, Havering, Hertfordshire, Norfolk, Redbridge, Suffolk, Waltham Forest	'The Lindens' Lexden Road Colchester CO3 3RL
	London Regional Examining Board	Barnet (part), Bexley, Brent, Bromley, Croydon, Ealing, Enfield, Haringey, Harrow, Hillingdon, Hounslow, ILEA, Kingston upon Thames, Merton, Newham,	Lyon House 104 Wandsworth High St London SW18 4LF

Southern Group

	Board	Area	Address
GCE:	University of Oxford Delegacy of Local Examinations		Ewert Place Summertown Oxford OX2 7BZ
	Associated Examining Board		Wellington House Station Road Aldershot Hants GU11 1BQ
CSE:	Southern Regional Examinations Board	Berkshire, Buckinghamshire, Dorset, Hampshire, Isle of Wight, Oxfordshire, West Sussex (Guernsey and Jersey and schools overseas within the Service Children's Education Authority)	53 London Road Southampton SO9 4YL
	South East Regional Examinations Board	East Sussex, Surrey, Kent	Beloe House 2 & 4 Mount Ephraim Rd Tunbridge Wells TN1 1EU
	South Western Examinations Board	Avon, Cornwall, Devonshire, Gloucestershire, Isles of Scilly, Somerset, Wiltshire	23–29 Marsh Street Bristol BS1 4BP

	Group and constituent boards	*CSE boards constituent local education authorities*	*Address for enquiries*
	Wales		
GCE and CSE	Welsh Joint Education Committee	Clwyd, Dyfed, Gwent, Gwynedd, Mid Glamorgan, Powys, South Glamorgan, West Glamorgan	245 Western Avenue Cardiff CF5 2YX

Chapter Four

PROFILING AND RECORDS OF ACHIEVEMENT

Ian McGuff

The notion that profiles or records of achievement (between which this author makes no distinction) are new developments in education is no longer accurate. The processes of profiling, and the production of summative documents in the form of records of achievement have gone on, in certain schools, for some time, and the Department of Education and Science have been involved in this area since the early 1980s. This contribution will discuss some recent developments in the field of profiling and records of achievement, without claiming to analyse a 'new' phenomenon.

DESIGN AND INTENTIONS

The term 'profiling' is often used in a generalized way by members of the teaching profession to describe a particular approach to assessment and reporting. This approach contains the idea of significant student involvement in the whole process, culminating in some form of 'negotiated' final statement or document. In reality, 'profiling' and 'recording achievement' stand for much more than this. The terms cover an enormously broad range of educational practices and documentary formats, most of which have considerable implications for the nature of teaching and learning. For example, some systems place comparatively tight controls upon what might be said about individuals, while others are based upon extremely loose formats, allowing great freedom of expression to a variety of contributors. Both approaches have their advantages and drawbacks, and in both cases the teachers who have adopted such schemes are highly committed to their own choice. This brief chapter is not the place to go into a detailed analysis of a large number of profiling schemes, but two examples of particular approaches are described, to

Figure 4.1 Progress profile

Profile

Profile No ....

Name of Centre and Course ....

Period covered by this Review From .... To ....

Signed .... (Trainee/Student) Signed .... (Supervisor/Tutor)

PROGRESS IN ABILITIES

Can make sensible replies when spoken to	Can hold conversations and can take messages	Can follow and give simple descriptions and explanations	Can communicate effectively with a range of people in a variety of situations	Can present a logical and effective argument. Can analyse others' arguments
Can read words and short phrases	Can read straightforward messages	Can follow straightforward written instructions and explanations	Can understand a variety of forms of written materials	Can select and judge written materials to support an argument
Can write words and short phrases	Can write straightforward messages	Can write straightforward instructions and explanations	Can write reports describing work done	Can write a critical analysis using a variety of sources
Can use equipment safely to perform simple tasks under guidance	Can use equipment safely to perform a sequence of tasks after demonstration	Can select and use suitable equipment and materials for the job without help	Can set up and use equipment to produce work to standard	Can identify and remedy common faults in equipment
Can count and match objects. Can recognise numbers	Can add and subtract whole numbers to solve problems	Can use × and − to solve whole number problems	Can add, subtract and convert decimals and simple fractions	Can multiply and divide decimals and simple fractions
Can cooperate with others when asked	Can work with other members of the group to achieve common aims	Can understand own position and results of own actions within a group	Can be an active and decisive member of a group	Can adopt a variety of roles in a group
Can follow instructions for simple tasks and carry them out under guidance	Can follow instructions for simple tasks and carry them out independently	Can follow a series of instructions and carry them out independently	Can perform a variety of tasks effectively given minimal guidance	Can assume responsibility for delegated tasks and take initiative
Can identify the sequence of steps in everyday tasks with prompting	Can describe the sequence of steps in a routine task, after demonstration	Can choose from given alternatives the best way of tackling a task	Can modify/extend given plans/outlines to meet changed circumstances	Can create new plans/ routines from scratch
Can cope with everyday activities	Can cope with everyday problems. Seeks help if needed	Can cope with changes in familiar routines	Can cope with unexpected or unusual situations	Can help others to solve problems
Can ask for needed information	Can find needed information with guidance	Can use standard sources of information	Can extract and assemble information from several given sources	Can show initiative in seeking and gathering information from a wide variety of sources
Can help someone to carry out clients' requests	Can carry out clients' requests under supervision	Can carry out clients' requests without supervision	Can anticipate and fulfil clients' needs from existing resources	Can suggest realistic improvement to services for clients
Can recognise everyday signs and symbols	Can make use of simple drawings, maps, timetables	Can make use of basic graphs, charts, codes, technical drawings, with help	Can interpret and use basic graphs, charts and technical drawings unaided	Can construct graphs and extract information to support conclusions
Can estimate answers to tasks involving whole numbers, decimals and simple fractions	Can calculate percentages and averages	Can solve problems involving simple ratios and proportions	Can express a problem in terms of a simple formula and solve it	
Can remember safety instructions	Can explain the need for safety rules	Can spot safety hazards	Can apply safe working practices independently	
Can recognise everyday uses of computers	Can use keyboard to gain access to data	Can enter data into the systems using existing programs	Can identify potential applications for computers	

illustrate the diversity which it is possible to find.

The first is taken from the City & Guilds of London Institute's General Abilities Scheme. It is widely discussed as an example of 'grid style' profiles, and the grid of attainment descriptors (or 'progress profile' to give it the correct title) is shown in Figure 4.1.

The 'basic level' of achievements are described in the vertical column on the left-hand side of the grid. Progress is demonstrated through a series of comments arranged to describe ascending levels of achievement. These go from left to right across the page until one arrives at 'high level' descriptors at the end of each horizontal line.

The grid is used as part of a consultation and review process between the teacher and student. When both parties agree that a particular level has been mastered or demonstrated, the student is given credit for this by the appropriate space under the descriptor being shaded or ticked. As progress develops, the profile in each horizontal line will advance across the page, until hopefully the extreme right-hand side of the grid is reached.

It should be noted that this is only part of the City & Guilds scheme, which consists of many other components, such as log books, etc., not shown here. All systems of profiling or records of achievement tend to have more than one element, and we must be careful not to remove anything from its proper context. Nonetheless this particular part of the City & Guilds scheme is an example of a profiling format which exerts fairly tight control over what is said concerning a student. Five descriptors are predetermined by the authors (City & Guilds) in each achievement area, and the most appropriate one is selected (after due consultation) in relation to each student at a given moment in time. Indeed this is considered to be one of the great strengths of grid type profiles. Unlike the conventional school report, which depends upon a retrospective comment, the student can see what might be said about her/him in the future, as well as what has already been said in the past. It is hoped that this will have a beneficial impact upon student motivation, and teachers who have operated the scheme often refer to the positive feedback which students derive from actually seeing their profiles progress across the grid in each area.

The teacher is also released from the burden of personally having to write individual comments for each student. The descriptors are already provided, and it is hoped that this will enable staff to enter into a more meaningful dialogue with students than would have been the case with traditional report writing. The process of consultation between student and teacher regarding the completion of the 'grid' (or progress profile) is also intended to enhance student involvement in the assessment process, and to develop a sense of ownership for the finally agreed descriptors.

A system which has many elements in common with the City & Guilds approach, but which is also significantly different, is the Midland Record of Achievement. This example has been developed by the West Midlands Examinations Board working in conjunction with a large number of Midland schools. It too consists of more than one component, but its first section, or 'personal record', is an illustration of a much looser format — in terms of what might be said about young people — than is the case with the City & Guilds document cited already.

Figure 4.2 shows the basic layout of the personal record of the Midland Record of Achievement, and you will see that there are no predetermined descriptors of student attainment. Instead, youngsters themselves generate a prose account of their achievements, in consultation with a teacher, under the headings shown. The inclusion of a statement originating with the student is becoming a common feature of many records of achievement schemes (for example, P. Component of the Oxford Certificate of Educational Achievement and the Essex Records of Achievement Project). Many teachers are highly committed to this approach, as they see it as being a most effective method of ensuring greater student involvement in the assessment, and thereby learning, process. Interestingly, the Department of Education and Science do not appear to be as highly committed to student personal statements: 'It seems clear that inclusion of personal accounts by pupils themselves of their activities or experiences ... should be optional' (Department of Education and Science 1984).

Although they advocate an element of consultation with students over what might be included in a summative document, the Department of Education and Science are also anxious to avoid undue pressure being placed upon young people to disclose information, if they do not wish to do so. Policy statements therefore place the responsibility upon the school, rather than the student, to generate summative accounts.

In some ways a student statement is more like the traditional school report than the City & Guilds progress profile or grid. Comments are written by the young person retrospectively and there are no collections of premeditated descriptors to choose from. This clearly increases the variety of statements

Form MRA 1/A

Midland Record of Achievement

SECTION I

The Personal Record

FOR

(1)

PART A

The following statements have been prepared by the student in consultation with a teacher. They record positive achievements which have been attained during full-time education. The statements may be entered in the student's handwriting or in type.

1 **Personal Interests, Experiences and Achievements (3)**

(2)

2 **Attendance and Punctuality (4)**

(2)

3 **School, College and Community Service**

(2)

4 Personal Qualities (8)

....(2)...

....

....

....

....

....

....

....

....

....

....

5 Communication Skills (9)

....(2)...

....

....

....

....

6 Ability to co-operate with others (10)

....(2)...

....

....

....

....

7 Practical and Athletic Skills

....(2)...

....

....

....

....

....

This record was prepared in consultation between a teacher and the student on ....(5)...................

Signature of student ....(6)..............................

Signature of teacher ....(7)..............................

Figure 4.2 Midland record of achievement

which might be made, and it is argued that such schemes promote self-expression and the ability to articulate one's thoughts. They also acknowledge the right of young people, for the first time in some cases, to make a personal contribution to the official documents which they carry away from school.

The two examples of profile formats I have cited raise the issue of control over information and reports. Teachers designing their own profile schemes may like to consider who has control over what is said in the portrayals they are developing. Who are the contributors, and what are the implications for the issue of subjectivity or bias? In report writing it is probable that we can never achieve complete objectivity, since the personal opinions of human beings will inevitably colour the remarks they make on paper. However, one way of limiting the potential damage that may be done by subjectivity or bias is to invite contributions from a variety of sources. It may be that a thorough profiling system is one which includes evidence concerning young people from not only teachers, but students themselves, and also members of the wider community who have been encountered in work experience, part-time jobs, or community service. Statements from less formal contacts and contexts such as neighbours, acquaintances from recreational activities, or parents, may also be appropriate.

The two examples of profiling discussed so far are divergent in some ways, and similar in others. They have been chosen to illustrate the point that although the term 'profiling' is often used as if it applies to a coherent set of educational practices, in reality it does not. There may be numerous subtle, and not so subtle, differences between any two formats, but these differences will significantly influence both the operation and outcome of the scheme. In this case the examples of grids/predetermined comments and discursive student statements were used to represent two of the major approaches to be found, but there are many more variations upon the theme. Educationists embarking upon the design of their own format for recording achievement need a clear vision of the purposes which they seek to emphasize, before selecting the particular methods they intend to use.

Law (1984) has produced one of the most helpful analyses of the distinguishing features of profiles, which sheds much light upon the purposes and intentions lying behind such documentation. He points to three main functions, which represent an attempt to expand and improve upon the approaches characterized by conventional examinations and school reports.

Firstly profiles tend to produce more individualized and idiosyncratic information about young people. If one imagines two school leavers with four GCSE certificates each, it is not beyond the bounds of possibility that those certificates will carry exactly the same grades. Even if they do not, they will say very little about the personality of their owners, or the courses of study which have been followed on the way to final certification. In a variety of ways profiles attempt to get away from this paucity of information. By offering criterion referenced statements on academic accomplishments, they may be offering more helpful details to those engaged in the recruitment process. In many cases, students themselves are actually invited to contribute to their own profiles, by recording information about personal qualities or achievement within and outside school. Inevitably a summative document is produced which cannot possibly be confused with paper-work belonging to another human being. Student personal recording emphasizes this tendency towards individualized or idiosyncratic reports.

Secondly, by their use of criterion referenced statements, profiles and records of achievement make what is expected of students, and what they have accomplished, more manifest and understandable to all those engaged in the educational process. The traditional examination certificate may only offer a grade to describe the performance of the individual. The school report, completed by a subject teacher or pastoral tutor, will contain only a retrospective comment in relation to a recently ended period of study. The profile or record of achievement will generally make use of criterion referenced statements in the form of attainment targets, which are often available to students at the beginning of the educational programme. The teacher therefore becomes more professionally accountable because (a) they have clearly stated the outcomes which their efforts are intended to produce, and (b) the student may now approach them and demand to be given credit for success in a way that was never possible previously when criteria for marking were not clearly stated. Grid profiles or systems based upon selected statements from predetermined banks emphasize this second feature.

Thirdly, profiles and records of achievement seek to break down some of the more artificial barriers which exist in the world of education. For example, they regularly identify and describe cross-curricular skills and achievements which may be common to a number of academic disciplines. They may also provide an opportunity to transcend some of the walls that exist between school and the wider educational environment, through the recording of personal accomplishments in the home or community. Furthermore, we see attempts in individual subject areas to disaggregate assessments into their component parts. Rather than just offering one grade or comment upon a complex subject, various features may be identified and remarked upon under a number of headings. This third tendency is prevalent in virtually all profiling formats, although information regarding out of school interests is obviously best contributed in the form of a student statement.

Law's (1984) analysis of these three aspects of profiles helps to clarify our thinking. The framework which he has established gives us an insight into the likely consequences of particular design features, especially in terms of the kind of documentation which will result. The outcomes for students of being involved in a formative profiling process are discussed in the next section.

Motivation and personal development: the influence of formative processes of recording achievement upon students

One of the original purposes of records of achievement as far as the Department of Education and Science were concerned in 1984 was as follows:

> ii. Motivation and Personal Development. They (records of achievement) should contribute to pupils' personal development and progress by improving their motivation, providing encouragement and increasing their awareness of strengths, weaknesses and opportunities.
>
> (Department of Education and Science 1984)

The effectiveness of profiles or records of achievement in terms of developing students in these areas is an extremely complex issue to evaluate. Impressionistic evidence and favourable opinions offered by enthusiastic teachers are relatively easy to find. On the other hand, hard empirical data is very scarce. This is not surprising if we consider motivation, or a sensitive human condition involved in personal development such as self-confidence, both of which may not be measurable in the usual sense of the word.

Trying to isolate the impact of records of achievement upon motivation or self-confidence is also very difficult because these are extremely dynamic emotional states, subject to considerable fluctuations as the result of the influence of a diverse range of factors.

Inevitably, and despite all the difficulties, an obvious research technique to be utilized in this area is that of discussing the influence of the formative processes of recording achievement with young people and teachers. This has been done extensively by the author in a study of over thirty secondary and special schools in the West Midlands. Numerous other studies have also adopted the same method of interviewing students and teachers (e.g. Balogh 1982, Goacher 1983, Department of Education and Science 1983, Hitchcock 1986) and many of the pilot projects exploring records of achievement with the aid of education support grants have considered student/teacher perceptions in their programmes of evaluation.

As a result of all this work it seems possible to say that recording achievement or profiling has the potential to influence the educational experiences of young people in a number of ways, some of which are discussed below.

Firstly, many teachers and students report that a closer relationship has been developed as the result of the increased elements of consultation that profiling requires. 'She knows me better and now has the right to call me by my first name' was the comment of one 16-year-old about his profiling tutor.

The majority of students demonstrate a very positive attitude to the development of this closer, and in many cases informal, relationship with their teachers. They welcome the opportunity to review their own progress with someone who is able to give them more attention than is usually the case in a conventional classroom setting, and they tend to identify quite strongly with this particular member of staff as the formative process develops.

Whether or not all this has any direct or measurable relevance to the business of improving student motivation or self-esteem is difficult to say. Certainly, the establishment of relationships in which it is possible to discuss one's own progress and achievements would seem to provide the opportunity for greater reflection about personal development, but the outcome of this will be dependent upon the manner in which interviews are conducted; more will be said about this later (see pages 121-6).

It is also possible to find examples of a minority of students who express slight concern over the increased insight which some teachers are gaining into their lives as a result of profiling. This group is in the minority however, and very often their fears are allayed as they come to realize the purposes of being asked to discuss their progress and achievements with a teacher.

Profiling may only pose a threat to the privacy and confidentiality of young people when undue pressure is put upon individuals to disclose sensitive personal information. It is difficult to find any evidence, amongst the reports presently available, that this has actually taken place. This is probably because any attempts to delve into such areas would rarely be appropriate in relation to recording achievement.

The majority of students who have expressed an opinion are very welcoming of the opportunity to contribute to their own record. In nearly all cases this was something that had not happened before the advent of profiling, and youngsters believed that two main advantages are associated with it.

Firstly, there is evidence of a lot of concern about the teacher who might simply form a dislike for an individual student, and show this by writing an unfair or negative comment upon a report. The personal record of achievement may offer students the opportunity to 'write more fairly about our own work and interests' (16-year-old school leaver) and this was seen to be a good thing. Secondly, many students expressed surprise about some of the comments which teachers write on conventional school reports. This was because the youngsters questioned the grounds or evidence upon which these statements were based. This concurs with a finding of Goacher:

> I would like to know from where the information was taken in order to fill in the record. How did my teachers know whether my skill level was satisfactory or not ...
>
> (pupil, Goacher 1983:35)

Again students felt that this was less of a problem in a personal profile or record of achievement where they could offer self-assessments supported by information concerning the context or circumstances in which the achievement had been demonstrated.

What is the outcome of this particular feature of profiling in terms of personal development? A great deal of rhetoric is to be heard nowadays concerning the need to engage young people more actively in the learning process. The student taking greater responsibility for her/his own learning is a frequently used image. These may only be empty phrases if the spirit in which they are uttered is not also extended to the processes of assessment and reporting. Records of achievement may be extremely valuable tools to aid personal development if they require young people to make considered judgements and statements about their own performance at school.

Many profiling systems carry a condition that only positive statements recording the successes of young people should be included in a final document. Being asked to record information concerning positive personal qualities and achievements is also welcomed by the vast majority of students, many of whom said that it is too easy to forget about certain accomplishments, but 'this sort of work helps you to remember all the good things you have done' (pupil).

In relation to the notions of self-confidence and self-esteem, numerous students have mentioned that the greater realization of the depth and diversity of their attainments brought about through records of achievement was an aid to 'feeling good about myself'.

In some cases students do express a concern that they are being asked to boast or 'brag' about their own abilities by virtue of the fact that only positive statements are recorded in a summative document. However, on reflection most of this group agree that provided their summative statements are an honest account of what they know, understand and can do, no harm is done. They all agree that if the document is to serve their best interests in the process of selection/recruitment it is important for it to show them in an accurate but favourable light.

Relatively few reports are made of major disagreements arising between teachers and students concerning the validity of any comments which members of the latter group might want to make. Again the notion of context or circumstance is crucial here. Whenever staff did feel that an unjustified or exaggerated claim was being made by a young person, the question of evidence to support the statement arose. In some instances youngsters were able to cite examples of work or interests from outside the school environment, of which the teacher was not aware, to confirm their own self-assessment. In other cases a lack of realistic evidence resulted in a moderating of the original statement, but in both instances the process of negotiating the final comment is considered to be a valuable experience in terms of personal development.

Many youngsters expressed pleasure that teachers are now giving them credit for experiences entered into outside the school. This may raise the problem of value judgements being made concerning what are, and what are not, worthwhile leisure time pursuits. No such tensions have as yet become widely apparent, but this does not mean that they do not exist, since such issues may not be readily disclosed by either students or teachers. This may be a matter requiring further enquiry and discussion, but once again the findings in this area do point to the possibility of enhanced self-confidence, although no obviously measurable evidence of this was actually displayed.

As a result of work on a personal record of achievement a small number of young people say that they have been forced to question very seriously how they spend their time, how they behave, or how much effort they put into their school work. This questioning is heightened in those schemes where youngsters are themselves required to make a statement about their own achievements and experiences. As a result of an inability to offer information about themselves, or because of a sense of dissatisfaction with their own efforts arrived at through the process of self-assessment, behaviour can be modified or new tasks undertaken. It seems that a greater sense of ownership for the need to alter behaviour was fostered by the requirement to comment upon oneself. Generally, students welcome this development which may be directly related to the issue of increased motivation, or a desire to actually alter previous courses of action.

One potential benefit which is rarely mentioned by students, but which has frequently arisen in conversations with teachers and other adults who interview young people at the age of 16-plus, is the development of confidence in self-expression. Especially in those formative processes which afford reasonable opportunities for consultation/discussion with a teacher, schools may be providing valuable training in interview skills, for example the ability to explain one's achievements in a lucid and unembarrassed manner.

Generally, very few negative or even indifferent reactions to profiling are encountered amongst students. Where they do exist they are usually associated with a lack of understanding concerning the purposes of the whole exercise. This may be due either to a failure to explain and discuss the whole matter at the outset, or to an inadequate tutorial process subsequently.

Second thoughts upon motivation and personal development

The previous section has made some fairly straightforward observations concerning the potential outcomes of recording achievement for students. However, it is possible to argue that records of achievement may also have an important part to play in the breaking down of certain traditional barriers in schools–barriers which have often been identified in the work of educational psychology.

For example, traditional forms of assessment have tended to take place within a role relationship where a judgement is made by someone about someone, for instance the orthodox school report. By making this kind of assessment the teacher may distance, or even alienate, herself/himself from the student, placing the latter in a position of dependence or subordination. The rules are dictated by the school/teacher, and labels are often placed upon the individual referring to levels of competence or motivation: 'good work and progress', 'satisfactory', 'must try harder', etc. This results in 'I-It' transactions (Buber 1958) which 'categorize and objectify' the pupil, and which often have very little to do with the process of education.

In contrast, truly educational and interpersonal transactions may only occur when 'whole persons encounter one another on an equal basis, each with full respect for the array of qualities to be found in the other' (Schmuck and Schmuck 1974). These 'I-Thou' transactions have been ruled out by many of the organizational features of secondary schools in the past, and particularly by common assessment practice.

However, recording achievement may offer an excellent opportunity for teachers to participate in 'I-Thou' situations when they sit down to consult or review the work of individuals with the individual present. This should not be taken to imply a recommendation for the 'cosy huddle' model of education (Dearden 1968). Sentimentality is not involved here, since recording achievement is concerned with the very practical attempt to review the learning experience, in an attempt to promote the competence of the student. The movement within profiling and records of achievement towards inviting the contribution of young people to their own assessments and reports may be seen as something which is orienting schools to the more widespread establishment of 'I-Thou' transactions.

Records of achievement frequently encourage positive approaches to students. Profiling often leads to positive forms of assessment, which seek to emphasize what the young person knows, understands and can do, as opposed to testing with the aim of exposing weaknesses, and thereby undermining self-esteem. Few teachers would argue that there needs to be a diagnostic element within a formative profiling process, which seeks to identify weaknesses as well as strengths in an individual's work, with the aim of helping to improve performance. Nonetheless, in terms of summative or final statements the record is intended to be one of success, and the inclusion of negative comments suggesting failure is rare.

Numerous studies can be found in the literature of behaviourist psychology which identify similar positive approaches to the teaching and learning process, e.g. Wheldall and Merrett (1984) and Cheesman and Watts (1985). Often, the work of such authors has been concerned to help teachers identify the balance of negative to positive comments which they tend to make during the course of their teaching. Frequently this has brought about the realization that some classrooms can be extremely negative environments for many students, where the majority of verbal responses directed at them are critical or even derogatory. The behaviourists argue that rather than modifying the performance of the pupil in the desired way, negative behaviours are simply reinforced by constant attention being focused upon them. The alternative is to place far greater emphasis upon desired reactions by students, through the use of greater elements of positive feedback to the class and individuals. If the balance between negative-to-positive teacher comment can be shifted significantly to favour the latter, a corresponding shift in student behaviour has also been observed.

As a form of assessment, records of achievement are in tune with this positive strategy. Traditional norm referenced examinations and tests have ensured a negative outcome for the majority of the school population. If a system ensures that only a few can succeed through the award of a limited number of high status grades, the possible deleterious consequences for the rest in terms of motivation and self-confidence are considerable. The same may be said of the supposedly criteria-related GCSE examination, which still uses a system of labelling (i.e. letter grades) rather than clearly identifying the achievement of the individual.

Records of achievement, on the other hand, attempt to break out of this framework of negativity in terms of assessment and the way in which assessments are reported. They seek to provide a format in which the positive can be accentuated for all students, without over-reliance upon the drawing of comparisons with other individuals through a grade system. If this positive approach is adopted within the formative process underpinning any summative documentation, the advantages which the behaviourists have observed may also be extended to age groups lower down the school.

Records of achievement may also assist those students who display an inability to plan and dispatch their own work, i.e. a sense of 'learned helplessness' (Seligman 1975). Rotter (1966) originated the concept of 'locus of control'. He and his colleagues discovered that they could distinguish between people who felt that they were very much masters of their own fate, and people who felt that they had very little control over what happened to them. They called the former 'internals' (i.e. their locus of control was within themselves) and the latter 'externals' (i.e. their locus of control was perceived as external to themselves).

Subsequently, there has been considerable research into the differences between internals and externals. In America the Coleman Report (Coleman *et al.* 1966) found that student achievement was more heavily influenced by the student's sense of powerlessness than by any other factors, such as teacher qualifications, parental income, geographical location of school, etc. Students who were able to say 'I am in charge of my life. I can make choices and decisions to get what I want. I feel good about myself' are more likely to achieve success in educational matters than students who say, 'It doesn't make any difference what I do. There's no point in trying because you won't get anywhere unless you're very lucky. Anyway I'm not very good at anything.'

Profiling seeks to combat the attitudes illustrated with these final sentences in two main ways. Firstly, and as already discussed, emphasis upon positive assessment is evidence of the attempt to enhance self esteem and confidence. Secondly, the use of realistic target setting within profiling interviews (and the use of targets which the student has had some part in identifying) seeks to develop the student's sense of being in control of his/her workload.

The technique of students and teachers discussing and agreeing what might be achievable goals during a subsequent period of time is a common feature of profiling systems (e.g. City & Guilds). Even if it is not an integral part of a scheme, it can be easily introduced. However, the practice of target setting in consultation with a teacher is only an introductory phase in seeking to promote the ability of the student to achieve a higher degree of personal responsibility and autonomy. Records of achievement are only able to play a contributory role in the kind of positive processes being discussed. If they are not introduced alongside compatible methods across the whole spectrum of teaching and learning, they will sound a discordant note, and much of their potential will be lost.

PRACTICAL MANAGEMENT AND IN-SERVICE EDUCATION

The practical management of profiling and records of achievement, and the efficient use of time in order to complete the processes which need to be gone through are clearly matters of major concern. At a time when the energies of both teachers and students are being absorbed by the introduction of the new GCSE, other time-consuming initiatives tend to be looked upon with caution, if not suspicion.

Time in relation to records of achievement has become something of a controversial issue, with different groups in the educational world taking opposite views. Many of the teacher associations, not surprisingly, have requested that identified time be set aside within the school day for the completion of the extra work load involved in profiling. Demands have also been made for staffing enhancement, and for extra resources to be made available.

However, the Records of Achievement National Steering Committee Interim Report (1987) took a different view:

> It is proving very difficult to separate out the resources needed to implement and support records of achievement systems from the wider costs of curriculum innovation and provision. Where records of achievement have been successfully introduced, they are not 'bolt on' activities with easily identifiable resource implications; rather, they are an integral part of the school's curriculum and assessment policies. Records of achievement therefore require a re-ordering of educational priorities: the more integral they become to the life of a school, the harder it is to identify specific resource requirements.
>
> (Department of Education and Science 1987)

Some would say that these findings are a fortunate development for a government department already under heavy pressure to increase educational spending. In practice it has been found that there are elements of truth in both viewpoints. For example, good teachers have always exhibited the behaviours which are needed during the formative processes of recording achievement. The carrying out of a dialogue with students about their work and progress, the reinforcement of positive achievements through private and public praise, the use of diagnostic assessment techniques followed by helpful advice as opposed to negative criticism, are already an integral part of effective teaching.

On the other hand, the actual production of summative statements/documents does introduce an extra administrative task into the school year. Depending upon the skills of both teacher and student this can be a more or less time-consuming business, but space does need to be found in an already crowded programme for it to be carried out.

How have the many schools who have already grappled with this problem actually found a solution, bearing in mind that, as yet, the demands for extra resources have not been widely met? The answer must, and does, lie in each school conducting a review or reappraisal of existing practice, with the aim of using available time and resources in the most productive way possible. Obviously the best and most essential of traditional procedures must be maintained, but some refinement and re-organization also usually takes place in order to allow the introduction of records of achievement.

The phrase 'whole-school policy' is rapidly becoming over used, but this is what is necessary here. As well as having some sympathy for the educational principles involved, the staff of individual schools also need to have a sense of ownership for the way the system is going to work in their own establishment. Therefore, consultation between all parties who are likely to be involved is vital. The support of head-teachers, and those able to influence the timetable or daily procedures within the school, are also indispensable. Those schools who have tackled the introduction of records of achievement successfully have done so by involving as many staff as possible in the design of proposals for the operation of their scheme.

All this clearly requires an extended programme of in-service education and meetings, which will need to deal with far more than simply administrative or operational details. It has been found that the introduction of profiling to schools often creates considerable demands amongst teachers for support as far as counselling skills are concerned. The move from subject teacher to records of achievement tutor exposes many uncertainties amongst some staff, who feel that certain elements of the approaches adopted by educational counsellors would be useful to them. The next section explores this theme.

In-service education: counselling and profiling

One of the most commonly expressed requests for in-service support amongst teachers contemplating the introduction of profiling into their schools has been in the area of counselling. Perhaps the correct way to phrase this 'cry for help' (which in many cases is the form that it has taken) would be to pose the question, 'What ingredients of the counselling approach might make our work in the profiling arena more likely to be successful?'

This particular wording is chosen since with profiling we are not quite entering into a 'full-blown' counselling relationship. Some aspects of both types of work may be similar, but others clearly are not. It is the comparable aspects which this section seeks to examine. Furthermore, much of what is said will probably be of most relevance to those schools who would like to allow for one-to-one interview sessions between teacher and student within their profiling framework.

Many counsellors in education (and much counselling literature, e.g. Rogers 1942, Krumboltz 1966, Lewis 1970) agree that one of the main objectives of their work is to assist young people to move toward a position of greater self-reliance. The development of 'enabling skills' and progression from a passive relationship to one where the student is more actively engaged in the resolution of their own problems is often seen as a major goal. For teachers this may have the implication of a shift from a custodial role, concerned largely with the maintenance of discipline and the transmission of information, to a more 'humanistic' approach, where young people are given greater responsibility and a more active part to play in the learning process.

These elements of counselling may also be prevalent in the aims and objectives of a formative profiling process. Those systems which rely upon student self-portrayal in particular, are placing greater responsibility into the hands of youngsters for contributions to their own reports. They are acknowledging the rights and potential of young people to articulate their own achievements, experiences and feelings, and this is an exercise which the secondary education process has rarely entered into in the past. The classic question posed by the counsellor, 'How do you feel about this?', is one which may also frequently be used in the profiling interview.

Profiling is also based upon a perceived need to improve the assessment process by introducing larger elements of the diagnostic approach to the way in which we measure pupil performance. This is one of the intentions which lies behind the advancement of criterion referenced assessment and reporting. The feeling is that if we can develop sentences which actually conjure up pictures of young people accomplishing the outcomes of learning, we may help them to realize

(a) what they have achieved so far, and (b) what they might achieve in the future. This is done with the intention of giving them more information to act upon. For many years the award of grades or percentages has given some notion of a score in relation to other candidates, but little in the way of a clear picture of what levels of performance or standards are associated with these grades. Diagnostic assessment, like counselling, intends ultimately to allow students to identify their own areas of weakness with a view to promoting the awareness which will allow a movement towards positions of strength.

What then are the main approaches and skills, common to both counselling and profiling, which might aid the attainment of these objectives? The first must be a clear identification and understanding by both parties, of the purposes of the interview. This is particularly true in relation to profiling. Nothing is more likely to produce an unsatisfactory dialogue than a lack of definite intent or purpose. This fairly simple observation raises certain crucial questions. Do teachers have a clear picture in their own minds about the purposes of profiling? Are they concerned mainly with the mechanics of producing summative documentation, or do they feel that the formative value of the processes being experienced is more important? What aspects of that formative process is a specific interview working towards? Is the discussion to be about previous achievements and experiences, the affective domain of personal qualities and attitudes, or will it be concerned with dispositions towards future courses of action?

These questions have no 'cut and dried' answers, but it is vital that the teacher has a clear picture of what she or he is about, and that this understanding is communicated to the student. At an even more basic level, have both teacher and student seen the summative documentation that they are working towards? Do they know what information the end product is supposed to contain, and therefore are their conversations relevant? The establishment of goals such as these carries with it the requirement for well-prepared staff development exercises, in which schools as a whole come to broadly held conclusions about the purposes they seek to put profiling to.

Having established our 'terms of reference', so to speak, what then are the next steps to be taken, and once again what can be adapted from the counselling approach which might be valuable? Counsellors often speak of three core conditions in interview situations which assist in the development of an atmosphere which is likely to be beneficial. Truax and

Carkhuff (1967) identified the qualities of empathy, warmth, and congruence, and all three of these have something to offer in terms of profiling interviews.

The empathetic response may be explained, basically, as the ability to see the world from the other person's point of view. Now it may seem at first glance that complete empathy with students being profiled, as opposed to counselled, is not absolutely necessary, and perhaps this is true. On the other hand, and particularly with personal recording systems, the need to be non-judgemental in our attitudes can be vital. The perception of youngsters about the value of personal achievements and qualities is often somewhat different from our own, and this may be especially true where they are considerably distanced from ourselves in terms of age, social background, and culture. What they see as creditable or discreditable may be governed by a variety of social and psychological factors outside our own experience. Therefore, if we are not to run the risk of inhibiting discourse, we need to suspend our own judgements in the first instance at least. With time, and on reflection, it may be that we feel compelled to intervene if the student's disclosures carry the potential to be damaging to their own best interests. At first, however, the ability to suspend critical comment may be crucial if the promotion of articulacy in the youngster is to be achieved.

The second quality or core condition is that of 'warmth', and this may have widespread implications for the management and organization of our profiling systems. When using the word 'warmth' counsellors frequently refer to the need to show mutual respect and acceptance of the other person's worth, if the atmosphere surrounding interviews is to be helpful. In schools, as in life generally, there is the possibility that previous encounters between individuals will colour the nature of future relationships. This is especially true where, as mentioned earlier, the custodial and disciplinary role of an establishment creates tension with the desire to maintain harmonious relationships. In a minority of cases personality clashes, and history, can make the possibility of mutual acceptance, and hence good interview relationships, difficult to achieve. This means that it could be very important to have some flexibility in the organization of a profiling framework, wherein individual students might have the opportunity to deal with an alternative member of staff if the need arose.

Finally, the third core condition is that of congruence, or genuineness, which has similar connotations for profiling as do empathy and warmth. The idea behind the congruent approach is that of a suitable and realistic reaction to the circumstances of the interview. If the context requires the student to take greater responsibility in the process of recording achievement, the teacher needs to acknowledge this, and relinquish her/his accustomed authoritative position in the relationship. The didactic role as provider of information is obviously inappropriate. Strategies to help the youngster develop their own powers of responsible self expression are required.

This brings us to a relatively mechanistic account of the kind of physical and verbal skills which are generally associated with active listening and productive questioning. The following techniques and organizational points have frequently been identified by counsellors as useful tools in the establishment of good interview relationships.

Questioning techniques Once the ice has been broken at the start of an interview, put the session on the right track by explaining the purpose of the meeting in simple terms. Then go on to:

Ask 'open' questions (i.e. those which cannot be answered with a mere 'yes' or 'no') and *listen* to replies.

Link questions to replies, or the last question asked (use reflected responses and paraphrasing).

Probe each reply to find out what the student is really saying, without putting her/him on the defensive; for example, 'Can you tell me more about that?'

Try to keep to a logical sequence of questions so that the student does not become confused.

Use silence in order to give the student time to think and to encourage her/him to say more. Look interested in order to encourage a free flow of ideas.

Avoid interrupting or putting words into the mouth of the student. Avoid ambiguous or jargon-riddled questions which only confuse youngsters.

Try to avoid criticizing the student about replies. This will only put her/him on to the defensive. Tone of voice and tentativeness of expression may be vital in order to give the other person the encouragement to reply.

Allow for negative expressions of feeling. It is important to be prepared to deal with critical comments.

Atmosphere/environment Students should feel that they have the full attention of the teacher. Therefore profiling interviews where large-scale distractions might occur should be avoided. Also, physical barriers between teacher and student, such as a desk, may be unhelpful. Telephones and access to the room by others can cause problems.

Length of interview Avoid 'clock-watching' or giving the impression that you cannot wait to get it over with. On the other hand, interviews should not go on for too long.

Self-assessment It is important for a counsellor/tutor to be able to monitor her/his own performance by developing a second level of consciousness. Active listening is important, but control over the interview must be maintained. Reflection on each session and attempts to improve upon previous performances are obviously essential.

RECORDS OF ACHIEVEMENT AND RECRUITMENT

The potential of records of achievement as useful documents in many kinds of selection processes is an issue of considerable interest to both educationists and employers. Admissions to further and higher education, youth training schemes and employment could all be influenced by records of achievement, but it is also possible to identify a potential tension or conflict between the needs of employers and the motivation of other groups mentioned.

Admissions tutors to further education or YTS managing agents may mainly be concerned with the importance of placing students on the most appropriate course or scheme. The wishes and capabilities of the individual are taken into account, and then hopefully a decision which will be in their best interest is taken.

However, when we talk about the use of records of achievement in interviews for job vacancies, we are referring to selection/rejection procedures. When companies are presented with large numbers of candidates for a limited number of posts, reasons have to be found for overlooking many individuals. If records of achievement afford the opportunity for crude comparisons to be made between school leavers, in the way that such comparisons may have been made on the basis of examination results, much of the good work accomplished during a formative process could be lost. Therefore the call to make records of achievement better suited to the needs of employers sets off alarm bells in the minds of many educationists. The interests of an employer in finding criteria upon which to disqualify candidates for recruitment may have a destructive rather than formative effect upon the motivation and self-esteem of young people. In other words, summative and formative intentions are sometimes contradictory, especially if the former is emphasized at the expense of the latter.

The Department of Education and Science has been very aware of the dangerous abuses which might be made of records of achievement. The need to guard against the problems of subjectivity and bias, for example, or the potential for readers to misinterpret statements, have loomed large in their policy documents on records of achievement.

> Records of achievement ... should take the form of sentences written for each pupil, not ticks in boxes or number or letter gradings. Such sentences are likely to be fairer to pupils, more useful to users and less open to misinterpretation.
>
> (Department of Education and Science 1984)

The requirement for personal qualities to be reported in the context in which they have been displayed, and the emphasis upon positive statements, are further evidence of a desire to protect the interests of the individual from those who might seek to use these reports in order to discriminate unfairly between school leavers.

Having said all this, what do employers think about records of achievement? It is very difficult to make generalizations about this matter. Employers are by no means an entirely homogeneous group. Different individuals hold conflicting opinions, and in any case the life of records of achievement has as yet been so short, and so few employers have actually encountered them, so it would be unwise to draw any firm conclusions. We do have a lot of evidence about what information employers are thought to need during the process of recruiting school-leavers. In many cases this has been offered without reference to records of achievement, and maybe on occasion without reference to any employers. Peterson probably hit the nail on the head with his comment,

> Employers will always make use of whatever assessment system the schools provide ... What employers need from a 16-year-old school leaver is a character reference and an assurance that he or she is literate and numerate.
>
> (Peterson 1982)

More recently, a joint research project conducted by Sandwell Local Education Authority, the West Midland Examinations Board, and the Midland Electricity Board, looking at records of achievement in particular, came up with the following conclusions:

> When a limited number of applications were being considered it seemed possible for the record of achievement to be received at the time of the initial application. The recruiter would use this additional information as an aid for selecting for interview.
>
> Where a large volume of applications were received the view was expressed that the record of achievement in addition to the letter of application would render the initial selection process too cumbersome ...
>
> Employers expressed a view that the record of achievement would be utilised in these circumstances during the interview. They considered that it would be sufficient for the candidate to submit the ... final document at the interview and that this could then be used to generate discussion and provide additional information.
>
> Where a formal recruitment procedure was in existence, candidates were often required to complete application forms which ask for detailed information on a person's interests, hobbies and positions of responsibility etc. Where no such procedure exists the ... Record of Achievement provides information otherwise not known to the recruiter.
>
> (Sandwell Local Education Authority, the Midland Electricity Board, and The West Midland Examinations Board 1987)

Subsequent conversations with employers, and the report quoted above, have uncovered evidence of strong approval for the formative processes of profiling which lead to the final document. One large bank went so far as to say that as the result of the initiation of self-assessment procedures in schools, they would now have to introduce the same techniques to their staff appraisal scheme. It was clear that different sections of a record of achievement might be of greater or lesser interest to certain employers, depending upon the nature of the vacancy to be filled. Generally the reaction of the vast majority of employers to records of achievement is very positive. The one major cause of concern relates to the time at which summative documents are made available. The summer term of the final school year is too late in most cases, with most large public and private sector recruiters conducting interviews much earlier than this. Some form of interim document available from Christmas or even September of the fifth year in secondary school may be the answer, but even then it would not be possible to guarantee that all records of achievement would be utilized in selection processes. While summative documents are considered to be the property of individual school leavers, and while many employers base their recruitment processes upon application forms and documents designed 'in-house' so to speak, the main value of the recording process may continue to lie in its formative aspects.

Indeed the whole issue of how records of achievement are explained to young people is fraught with difficulty, because of the uncertain position which they occupy in the recruitment process at the moment. Overemphasis upon the potential vocational usage of records of achievement, i.e. as documents which will supplement other paper qualifications, and hopefully be of value in securing employment, may be dangerous. Interpretations placed upon the quality of a school-leaver's achievements, and the number of appropriate job vacancies within the economy, will still be more important factors in securing employment than whether or not a detailed record of experiences and attainments is actually available. Therefore, teachers should be careful about how they describe the whole business of profiling and profiles to their students. A balanced note should be struck, emphasizing both the benefits of a formative process in terms of improved assessment practices, and the *potential* of summative documents. However, the word 'potential' is stressed since insufficient evidence is available at the moment about how they are actually being received outside the education system.

THE FUTURE?

The records of achievement movement has gained widespread approval amongst many teachers for a variety of reasons. In particular, the emphasis upon positive forms of reporting, and greater student involvement in the assessment process, have been most welcome. Now, however, many educationists are uneasy about what will become of these features with the advent of the 1988 Education Act. The model of assessment which may develop within the National Curriculum appears to have much more in common with traditional forms of testing and examining than any student-centred, formative assessment procedures. How does the attempt within profiling to identify positive achievements for all students compare with National Curriculum assessments which will not even be accessible to many youngsters with special educational needs? Where is the notion of significant student involvement in a proposed system of externally designed and nationally administered tests? The report of the National Curriculum Task Group on Assessment and Testing (Department of Education and Science 1988) comments upon these issues in more detail, and contains a request from the Records of Achievement National Steering Committee for a continued dialogue between all interested parties. The suggestion that we live in interesting times may be an understatement in the world of education at the moment. There will certainly be great interest, and concern, amongst those who have been closely involved with the records of achievement movement in the way that these tensions are resolved. Positive, student-centred assessment, and target-related, nationally prescribed tests may not be entirely incompatible, but it will take great skill and sensitivity to ensure that the maintenance of the former is not compromised by the emergence of the latter.

REFERENCES AND BIBLIOGRAPHY

Balogh, J. (1982) *Profile Reports for School Leavers*, York: Longman for Schools Council.

Buber, M. (1958) *I and Thou*, New York: Charles Scribner.

Cheesman, P.L., and Watts, P.E. (1985) *Positive Behaviour Management*, London: Croom Helm.

City & Guilds (1985) *General Abilities Profiling User's Guide*, London: City & Guilds of London Institute.

Coleman, J.S. *et al.* (1966) *Equality of Educational Opportunity: report from office of education*, Washington D.C.: U.S. Government Printing Office.

Dearden, R. (1968) *The Philosophy of Primary Education*, London: Routledge & Kegan Paul.

Department of Education and Science (1983) *Records of Achievement at 16: some examples of current practice*, London: HMSO.

Department of Education and Science (1984) *Records of Achivement: a statement of policy*, London: HMSO.

Department of Education and Science (1987) *Records of Achievement: an interim report from the National Steering Committee*, London: HMSO.

Department of Education and Science/Welsh Office (1988) *A Report from the National Curriculum Task Group on Assessment and Testing*, London: HMSO.

Goacher, B. (1983) *Records of Achievement at 16+*, York: Longman for Schools Council.

Hitchcock, G. (1986) *Profiles and Profiling*, Harlow, Essex: Longman.

Krumboltz, J.D. (ed.) (1966) *Revolution in Counseling*, Boston:

Houghton Mifflin.
Law, W. (1984) *Uses and Abuses of Profiling*, London: Harper & Row.
Lewis, E.C. (1970) *The Psychology of Counseling*, New York: Holt, Rinehart & Winston.
Peterson, A.D.C. (1982) *A Bitter Taste of the Polish Diet, Times Educational Supplement*, 21 May.
Rogers, C.R. (1942) *Counseling and Psychotherapy*, Boston: Houghton Mifflin.
Rotter, J.B. (1966) 'Generalised expectancies for internal versus external control of reinforcement', *Psychological Monographs*, **80**:1 (entire issue).
Schmuck, R.A. and Schmuck, P.A. (1974) *A Humanistic Psychology of Education*, Palo Alto, California: National Press Books.
Seligman, M.E. (1975) *Helplessness*, Reading: W.H. Freeman.
Truax, C.B. and Carkhuff, R.R. (1967) *Towards Effective Counseling and Psychotherapy: training and practice*, Chicago: Aldine.
West Midlands Examinations Board, The (1987) *The Midland Record of Achievement: an occasional paper* (Joint Project, TWMEB, Sandwell Local Education Authority, Midland Electricity Board), Birmingham: The West Midlands Examinations Board.
West Midlands Examinations Board, The (1988) *Guide to the Midland Record of Achievement*, Birmingham: The West Midlands Examinations Board.
Wheldall, K. and Merrett, F. (1984) *Positive Teaching: the behaviourial approach*, London: George Allen & Unwin.

Chapter Five

ASSESSMENT AND THE CURRICULUM

Brian Roby

HISTORICAL PERSPECTIVE

Examinations for the GCE and the CSE largely served to place pupils in rank order of ability, and there has not been any clear expression of each individual's achievement in absolute terms. Examinations have tested mainly the recall of facts and have tended to minimize the ability to reason, to solve problems, and to demonstrate successfully both practical and oral skills.

Examinations are theoretically designed to test what has been learned. The view has frequently been expressed that there was a time when public examinations dictated the content of upper school syllabuses, teaching methods and the mode of assessment. The commonly-held belief that the examination boards, particularly those associated with the General Certificate of Education, were ivory towers surrounded protectively by university thinking prevailed until the introduction of the GCSE. The lobby of those associated with Technical and Vocational Education Initiative (TVEI) curriculum development has done much to bring about rapid changes in assessment and certification.

The Mode 3 facility, promoted strongly by the former CSE boards, has always emphasized active teacher participation in the design, implementation, assessment, and moderation of new courses suited to the needs of particular groups of pupils. This examination option is again being promoted vigorously within the GCSE, and has included significant developments in new curriculum areas, such as information technology and the introduction of modular schemes.

All courses within the GCSE include significant coursework components assessed by the teachers themselves according to prescribed criteria. This continuous assessment element of the GCSE has helped somewhat to correct the overemphasis upon terminal examinations, but at the same time it has created a continuous burden for both pupils and teachers. Assessment has been brought into sharp focus by the change in emphasis from a content-dominated curriculum to one which gives importance to the acquisition of skills, the understanding of concepts and the inculcation of attitudes.

In a similar way post-16 educational provision has been changing in response to nationally-perceived economic and social requirements. The important issues of unemployment, continuity and progression between the ages of 14 and 18, education-industry liaison, the practical application and relevance of educational programmes, the requirements for flexibility to meet student needs, the economic use of resources, the rapid development of new technologies, and the value of recording student achievement in a meaningful way, have all added impetus to the development of modular programmes, the management of learning and new forms of accreditation.

This chapter will focus upon the effect of examinations on the content and management of the curriculum and upon the administration of coursework and its assessment. The curriculum will be considered in terms of the structure of meaningful learning, the identification of appropriate performance criteria, and the assessment process.

The Education Act 1988

Examinations and testing

The Government's aims for examinations as expressed in *Better Schools* (Department of Education and Science 1985a) are essentially:

> to raise standards across the whole ability range;
> to support curriculum change and teaching strategies;
> to provide clear teaching aims beneficial to pupils, teachers and employers;
> to record successful achievement;
> to measure what pupils know, understand and can do.

According to the Task Group on Assessment and Testing (TGAT) the new assessment system within the National Curriculum should meet four criteria:

1 an individual's performance should be in relation to specified measurable objectives, i.e. criterion referenced;
2 the performance criteria should express the concept of an individual's progression through the education process;
3 any grading of achievement should be capable of being moderated to enable valid comparison across groups;
4 the assessment process is essentially a formative one, the results of which are the basis of discussion between teacher and pupil to identify an individuals's needs and future education-training route way.

Records of achievement

The Government places considerable value upon a record of achievement for each secondary school pupil. The process of recording has important consequences for a pupil's curriculum. Teachers need to establish more clearly than previously each individual pupil's requirements and then to provide the opportunities for the pupil to demonstrate those qualities on which the record is intended to throw light. It is advisable that personal achievements should not be subjective but should be based upon specific examples of what a pupil has achieved and experienced, from which personal qualities and skills can be inferred. The methods of assessment need therefore to be linked closely to what is taught and to the methods of teaching and learning.

The National Curriculum

It is the government's intention to secure for all pupils aged 5 to 16 a curriculum which equips them with the knowledge, skills and understanding that they will need for adult life and employment. In the opinion of the government a National Curriculum should be backed by clear assessment through a broad, balanced range of subjects studied; by clear objectives that will challenge pupils of all abilities to achieve their potential, and by equal opportunities for all pupils by means of programmes which include the key content, skills and processes needed, for adult and working life.

Each pupil will be expected to attempt to achieve the attainment targets of the three core subjects: maths, English and science, and the appropriate targets of the other foundation subjects. For subjects such as art, music or physical education pupils and teachers adhere to guidelines rather than aim for specific targets.

The National Curriculum is a framework which uses a subject nomenclature to identify what pupils should know, understand and be able to do; but it is not the intention that the core-foundation-option subjects should necessarily be the basis of timetabling or how the curriculum should be delivered. It is difficult to envisage many schools deviating from the traditional format understood by pupils, teachers and the public at large. The availability of modular schemes does, however, offer greater flexibility in curriculum organization and the implementation of the National Curriculum.

As they evolve, the National Curriculum subject programmes of study will continue to reflect the prescribed attainment targets by setting out the overall content, knowledge, skills, and processes considered necessary for today's needs and which pupils should be taught to achieve. The prescribed minimum common content of each subject is supplemented by those areas of associated learning and themes considered relevant, but found within other subjects.

The curriculum has a broad definition which covers the content, learning strategies, assessment processes, counselling, and guidance arrangements, and the recording of pupil achievement.

Curriculum organization

Schools have been given a degree of freedom to organize the curriculum in ways most suited to the needs of their pupils according to age, abilities and circumstances (see Figure 5.1). Teachers have a measure of flexibility to select and to manage the learning experiences and to develop and implement new approaches, but it must not be forgotten that the national attainment targets are the standards against which a pupil's performances and progress are assessed. Teachers are encouraged to continue to develop those personal qualities in their pupils which cannot be written into a programme of study measured by attainment targets.

Curriculum review

In response to the perceived needs of their pupils, in relation to society, many teachers are regularly reappraising what they teach, and their learning methodologies.

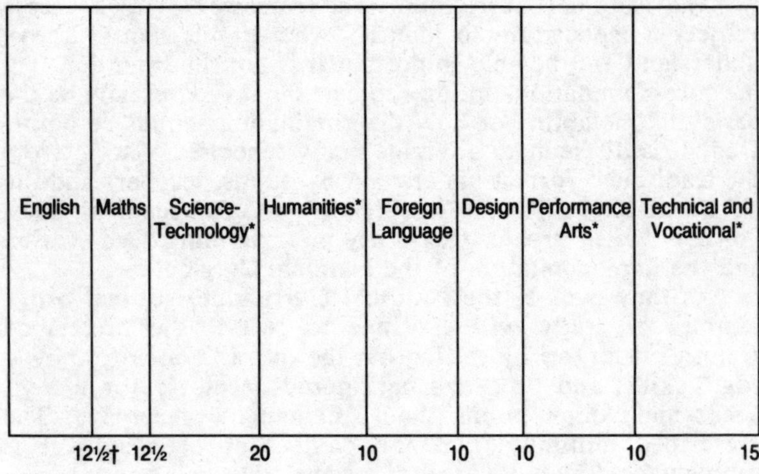

* Modular schemes permitting traditional subject titles (physics, geography, music); newer subject introductions (business studies, media studies); integrated programmes (humanities); personal development programmes (careers, work experience, physical education); thematic studies (social, economic and environmental topics).

Numbers represent percentage of time.

Figure 5.1 Curriculum model — pupils aged 14 to 16

During the next decade at least, there will be continual evaluation of curricular aims and objectives in response to National Curriculum targets and guidelines as well as to the findings of government-sponsored curriculum projects in such diverse fields as science, TVEI, information technology, and equal opportunities.

Teacher assessment of pupil performance is the basis of a school's evaluation of its own performance in achieving its aims and objectives. It requires the effective monitoring and assessment of each pupil's progress. Teachers, preferably working in teams, need to identify each pupil's strengths and weaknesses and then to provide the opportunities pupils require to develop particular personal qualities to increase their educational progress. The weakness of many schools in the past has been that they lacked detailed assessment policies which were an integral part of the curriculum.

PURPOSES OF LEARNING AT SCHOOL

The identification of each pupil's curriculum needs can only be made by relating an individual's achievement to what is generally accepted as the purposes of education. In broad terms, education may be described as a dynamic process of changing pupils' behaviours by developing within them increased knowledge, understanding and skills. In more specific terms, the aims expressed in *Better Schools* (Department of Education and Science 1985a) are generally regarded as worthwhile. They are to help pupils:

> to develop lively, enquiring minds, the ability to question and to argue rationally;
> to acquire knowledge, understanding and skills relevant to adult life and employment in a fast-changing world;
> to develop personal moral values;
> to understand the world in which they live;
> to appreciate human achievements and aspirations;
> to use language and number effectively ... and to apply themselves to tasks and physical skills.

The elements of learning

There is a general consensus beginning with HMI in 1983, reaffirmed by the Department of Education and Science in 1987 and confirmed by TGAT in 1988, that the learning and assessment processes of the secondary phase should focus upon knowledge, understanding, concepts and skills.

Knowledge and understanding

Subjects provide the framework of knowledge, but the selection of information to become the content of the curriculum needs to be related to a school's aims and objectives. Aspects of knowledge should be chosen to develop particular skills, concepts and attitudes. It is important also that the decisions about appropriate knowledge should be a collective staff exercise to avoid duplication and wastage of resources. The selected knowledge should be capable of application to demonstrate clear understanding by the pupil and not be just a collection of unrelated facts.

The fundamental principles of the curriculum are that it

should have a breadth as a whole and in its parts it should introduce the pupil to a wide range of experiences, knowledge and skill. A balance should be achieved in each area of the curriculum by allocating it sufficient time to make its specific contribution. Through a practical dimension to learning, the content of subjects can be made relevant to a pupil's own experience and the application of knowledge, understanding, concepts, and skills can be shown to be of continuing value in adult life. The principle of relevance requires teachers to skilfully utilize pupils' experiences. A practical approach to learning is being encouraged by the Department of Education and Science (1985a) and the GCSE across the curriculum. No longer confined to physical skills in drama and physical education, nor manipulative skills in home economics and CDT, practical activity is regarded as a foundation of learning in maths, science, humanities and foreign languages.

Concepts

These are essentially key ideas, which enable a pupil to clarify, to organize, or to understand knowledge and experience. Such a concept might be: 'Technological innovation has been a necessary condition for industrialization.' Here the educational focus is on discovering the prerequisites for industrialization with perhaps particular reference to one industry. It is important to identify something as an example of a particular concept so that its treatment may be more clearly understood.

The GCSE criteria promote the concept of 'values education', the acquisition of a sensitivity to different values people place on issues, and the ability to empathize so that pupils will learn to appreciate the significance of the attitudes and values of people in particular situations of the past and the present. At the same time it provides opportunities for pupils to develop their own values, self-concepts, and decision-making skills.

Multicultural understanding is extremely relevant to all pupils' curricula. The Department of Education and Science, in *Better Schools* (1985a), advises that pupils should be educationally prepared for an ethnically mixed society and the GCSE criteria draw attention to the value for all pupils of incorporating material which reflects ethnic diversity.

The National Criteria stipulate that each syllabus should be designed to help pupils to understand the subject's relationship to other areas of study and its relevance to a pupil's own life through an awareness of economic, political, social, and environmental factors.

In response to the importance given by the GCSE to socio-economic concepts, a number of cross-curricular 'subjects' have been developed under titles such as 'world studies'. The approach is usually thematic, dealing with topical issues: peace and conflict; wealth and poverty; human rights; nuclear power. Alternatively, the structure may be modular with, for example, history, geography, religious education, and social studies contributing units that may be combined in different ways under the title 'integrated humanities'.

Skills

Schools are being encouraged to develop in their pupils a wide range of abilities that will be of lasting value. There is a belief that teachers could help themselves to be more effective if they saw the pursuit of certain types and levels of skills as an important aspect of their curriculum planning, especially in a whole-school context. Departmental co-operation is a valuable step towards securing a coherent school curriculum.

TVEI has been instrumental in encouraging new thinking about the 14 to 18 curricula, including the promotion of the abilities to:

solve problems and make decisions;
find and organize information;
think critically and creatively;
analyse, synthesize and evaluate;
communicate effectively and clearly;
co-operate with others to achieve common aims;
cope with changing and unfamiliar situations.

A skills-related approach to learning can enhance a more traditional academic approach. A certificate is more meaningful if the examination grade can be described in terms of the skills and competences that underpin the award. For the student, skills-statements may represent clear definitions of positive achievement, whereas grades alone can portray degrees of failure.

Most schools will probably wish to encourage the development of a wide range of skills from those of a semi-automatic type, acquired usually as a result of repeated practice, to competences dependent upon complex thought processes such as problem-solving. Those 'basic skills' essential to everyday life are quite likely to find a place in learning programmes for all ages. Some skills have a more generic nature, being applicable to a range of activities in different contexts. The ability to transfer such skills successfully to new situations is in itself regarded as a valuable asset, but it will only be achieved if there is a deliberate curriculum policy to provide suitable learning opportunities and pupil motivation.

Skills cannot be taught like knowledge and understanding. They can be demonstrated or described by the teacher, but can only be acquired by practice and experience. Learning methods for skills are more limited than for acquiring knowledge which enables the teacher to choose from various strategies: note-taking, resource-based learning, discovery methods. For a pupil to learn a skill the teacher must become a resource and not the source of knowledge.

All experiential learning must have a reflective stage, otherwise it will be less effective. Pupils should be debriefed to ascertain if the learning objective has been achieved and the learning method successful. The reflective process can make pupils aware of skills that they own and the potential for the transfer of these abilities to new contexts.

Schools have clearly demonstrated that there is a place for skills-based learning within various educational contexts. It may be an integral part of subject courses, modular programmes, personal development courses, tutorial-pastoral arrangements, or specific skills programmes designed to achieve cross-curricular objectives such as communication skills.

Integrated courses

The National Criteria for 'integrated courses' apply to those schemes where there is a clear demonstration of the integrated nature of knowledge, skills and attitudes. Knowledge is defined as that which enables the pupil to understand social, economic, political, environmental, technological, cultural, and aesthetic factors. The development of a core of skills relevant to an individual's future needs in work, further education, and leisure is given prominence.

The integrated course criteria also required examination boards to ensure that all pupils taking such courses followed a curriculum programme which was broad, balanced, relevant and differentiated in terms of the government's White Paper *Better Schools* (Department of Education and Science 1985a), and a pupil's curriculum must include English, maths, science, humanities and technology. This requirement has been confirmed by legislation in the Education Reform Act (1988).

It is envisaged that an active student-centred style of learning will be adopted, encouraging: pupil self-analysis; independent learning; group activities; discussion and reflection; and, set within the context of work, residential and community experiences. The terms 'integrated', 'foundation' and 'pre-vocational' are interchangeable. The whole of a pupil's 14 to 16 curriculum is essentially pre-vocational in that it is the preparatory base for all post-16 activities.

In 1985 Business and Technician Education Council (BTEC) and City and Guilds of London Institute (CGLI) combined as the Joint Unit to rationalize their 14 to 16 pre-vocational provision. The original courses offered by BTEC and CGLI for 14 to 16-year-olds had primarily been directed toward pupils for whom the more traditional academic approach was not considered suitable. The new provision, known as Foundation Programmes, evolved as a curriculum framework for all pupils. It is an example of the new trend whereby examination and validation boards are involved in curriculum development, rather than just in the provision of an examinable syllabus.

Foundation Programmes offer a school flexibility in designing the learning experiences within a framework of the five 'skill areas': information; social and interpersonal; making, creating and controlling; decision-making; application. The approach is thematic: people; technology; arts and design; money. All are delivered within the four possible contexts: self and environment; business adminstration and distribution; services to people; production and technical services.

The modular structure of Foundation Programmes is based upon modules which integrate a theme and a context. Four examples are shown in Figure 5.2, from the BTEC-City and Guilds document, 'The Framework Description'. The learning experiences are mainly case studies which can either be internally differentiated or designed at different levels of achievement.

This pre-vocational framework illustrates the importance being attached to the integration of assessment and the learning process within 14 to 18 educational courses and modular programmes. Achievement is recorded by continuous assessment according to performance criteria statements, and pupils are directly involved through a process of negotiation and reflection with their teachers.

Within a school's scheme the modules offered must be such

as to cover more than one theme. At least two of the themes offered must be developed in relation to more than one context. All skill areas must be included.

A possible scheme model would be:

- skill areas developed through the modules:

  technology in the context of business administration and distribution;
  technology in the context of production and technical services;
  money in the context of business, administration and distribution;
  money in the context of production and technical services;

and conformity with scheme criteria.

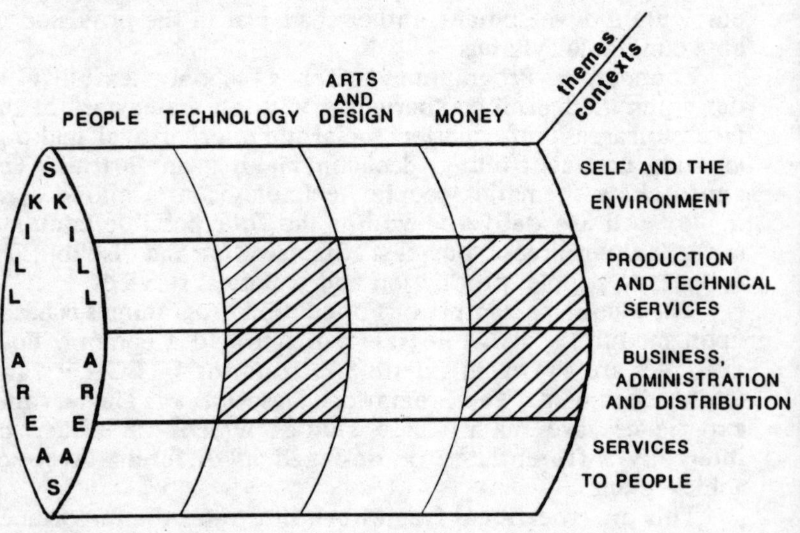

Figure 5.2 BTEC-City and Guilds foundation programme
Source: Pre-vocational Programmes for Pupils aged 14-16, Business and Technician Education Council-City and Guilds of London Institute 1987

The Northamptonshire TVEI Modular GCSE Scheme, initiated in 1985, aims to provide an effective bridge from school to work by ensuring relevance to the needs of the wider community. The content, context and styles of learning are those advocated for integrated courses. The structure is one of Foundation Modules and Option Modules within the fields of community, media, design, IT, business, and modern language. Four foundation modules may be combined under the title 'Industry, Technology and Society'. Examples of other possible combinations are shown in Figure 5.3. The GCSE subject-specific National Criteria may impose restrictions on module combinations.

Curriculum area	Foundation modules	Option modules
Community studies	CS1	2, 3, 6
Media studies	MS1	2, 5, 7, 8
Design technology	DT1	9, 15
Information technology	IT1	3, 6
Business studies	BS1	
Business language	BL1	

Programme	GCSE title	Selected modules
Foundation programme	'Industry, technology and society'	
Subject specific	'Community studies	
	'Media studies'	
Multidisciplinary	'Information/Design Technology'	

Figure 5.3 Northamptonshire TVEI modular scheme

The advantages of student motivation, flexibility of organization, and economical use of resources afforded by modular curricula, were recognized by Coventry LEA in a report published in 1982. The TVEI pilot project in 1984 initiated a pre-vocational modular framework which has stimulated long-term development across the whole curriculum. The TVEI modular framework is structured on a core-plus-options arrangement under specific GCSE titles. For example: the 'leisure studies' programme is made up of the two core modules 'leisure and recreation' and 'lifestyles'; plus any three option modules from: 'photography'; 'marketing'; 'product development' or 'sport and media'.

The Leicestershire Modular Framework (LMF), a major GCSE curriculum development, was created in 1983 and comprises free-standing units that could be clustered under family titles within curriculum areas. This scheme has now been modified to a core-plus-options arrangement to give more coherent programmes in line with GCSE National Criteria. It illustrates the rapid evolutionary nature of some modular schemes.

The organization of learning

Pupil involvement

An important aim of any learning programme should be to raise a pupil's confidence by building upon his or her personal knowledge and experience through the creation of new situations in which, initially at least, the risk of failure is minimized. As pupils see themselves improving, they learn that making mistakes is part of life, and that the ability to identify personal weaknesses enables progress to be made more quickly. This implies that forms of experiential learning and self-study integrated with active pupil self-assessment, counselling and guidance is an arrangement that will have many benefits for pupil and teacher alike.

A great deal has been written about the mismatch between what schools offer and what pupils actually see themselves receiving in learning experiences. Boredom is common among older pupils, as is a fear of getting things wrong. Pupils appear to value their education more when they are involved in the assessment process as a joint venture with their teachers. The development of pupil profiling, with pupils participating in the completion of their personal document, is a valuable way of assessing and recording the progress pupils make in the curriculum. This requires arrangements to be made for continuous formative assessment; the process can be extremely time-consuming for all concerned. Pupil self-assessment has been found to be a means of making the system more manageable, but it requires careful training of the pupils if the recorded outcomes are to be valid and reliable.

Prerequisite knowledge, understanding, and skills

When a pupil can relate new knowledge to concepts already acquired, then learning ceases to be rote and long-term memory is strengthened. New learning often makes more sense to a pupil when it is presented as part of a carefully thought-out sequence of experiences, each of which builds, at least in part, upon what has already been acquired. For subjects built on a modular structure with sequential units building only to a limited extent on previous units, mastery of core competencies in one module does not necessarily prepare pupils for the core of knowledge and understanding in subsequent units.

If the first module of a programme contains the essential core knowledge, concepts, and skills, a pupil may then be able to extend his or her learning through other selected units that permit the application of the core at a higher level of understanding.

Instruction

The learning style of a pupil is related to the way in which the individual represents information in memory. This may polarize towards either a verbal or an imagery form, and it focuses attention upon the relationship between learning style and the form in which material is presented, i.e. whether it is written or pictorial.

Research at the University of Birmingham has found that students whose memories highly rely on imagery perform well on tasks that can be visualized, but perform less well on those presented verbally. For those pupils whose memories polarize towards a verbal form, the reverse is true. It would also appear that, generally, introverts use the imagery mode while extroverts use the verbal mode.

The verbal mode is fairly flexible and can be applied satisfactorily to most learning situations. This encourages high performance amongst those pupils who favour this style. In contrast, pupils who prefer imagery do not perform as well as might have been expected because the imagery mode is not always the most appropriate form in which to present information.

Memory codes information as verbal, mathematical, or pictorial, and the mode of representation in memory has important implications for the organization of learning experiences. For the best results, the learning method and material should be chosen to be compatible with the learning style of the pupil, if the individual's potential is to be fully realized.

Rate of presentation

There are two aspects to the learning process: 'assimilation', which is the reception and analysis of new information; and 'accommodation', when the new material is related to existing knowledge within an individual's memory. A critical stage in the memory process is that of analysing the information received by sensory means into the short-term primary memory before it can be committed to longer term storage and retrieval in secondary memory. Analysis takes place relatively quickly but each pupil's ability to learn is related to the individual's speed of analysis.

Pupils following instructions must analyse each sentence before it is displaced by the next. Verbal instructions at too fast a rate will result in some students only partially storing the information in long-term memory. This will usually result in their future inability to complete tasks successfully, causing demotivation. A reduction in the rate of presentation improves learning performance. Repetition of some activities is likely to have a similarly beneficial effect.

When the assessment system is not based upon terminal course examinations there are potentially better opportunities for a pupil to demonstrate their capabilities fully. Course planners and module programme designers should provide sufficiently demanding tasks for all levels of ability, and also on as many occasions as time allows. Examination boards will probably wish to extend their acceptance, found in GCSE musical performance, of the one-off examination as an obsolete concept in today's educational system. The principle of allowing a pupil to present the best performance, even after repeating a task a number of times, is a perfectly valid means of determining what each individual knows, understands and can do.

Learning sensitivity

Pupils differ in important ways in their ability to handle new information and experiences. Some pupils perform better if the task is structured, while others can extract relevant information from a complex context, and successfully organize the material to achieve desired outcomes.

Structured questions, for example, can act both as a guide to pupils and as a stimulus for imaginative responses. The questions may be presented in sets, to achieve in their collective short answers a coherent whole response to a theme or topic. Questions may be designed to be open-ended in nature, catering for pupils of varying abilities. The levels of response will depend to some extent upon the degree of complexity of the learning experience. Whatever the situation, the questions and source material should interact, and the mark scheme should be integral to the whole experience.

Learning strategies

If pupils are to realize their full potential and enjoy their education, then it is essential that what is taught and how it is learned is matched to the varied abilities and aptitudes of individual pupils.

In designing learning tasks, the concepts necessary to make the learning meaningful should be identified, and steps taken to ensure that they are known and understood by the pupils. The language by which ideas are communicated may itself be a barrier to understanding. This problem is not confined only to pupils whose first language is not English. All verbal and written forms of communication are worthy of careful scrutiny. A most effective form of differentiation to help individual learning is in the teacher's use of different kinds and levels of language with different pupils, in varying the pace of introducing new materials and ideas, and in carefully organized practice and revision of knowledge and skills.

Groups of widely varied ability make heavy demands upon a teacher's expertise to select and design suitable tasks and then to implement them successfully. Classes are frequently organized in sets or bands of similar abilities in an attempt to facilitate the learning process. This does not always help each individual pupil, whose needs may on occasion be considerably different from the rest of the group.

Bands or streams can colour a teacher's perception of levels of teaching and learning ability. With mixed ability groups the need for accurate assessment is very important. The teacher is responsible for identifying individual pupil strengths and weaknesses and matching up appropriate learning assignments. Since pupils in mixed groups do not work at the same speed then individual programmes cannot be collectively assessed at the same time. Mixed ability groups highlight a number of difficulties due largely to the organizational pressure upon the teacher. Such problems include: a tendency to subjective assessment; the need for considerable time associated with preparation and implementation; and the relatively complex and detailed recording of achievement.

The GCSE General Criteria require that all examinations are designed to ensure proper discrimination, so that candidates across the ability range are given opportunities to demonstrate their knowledge, abilities and achievements. Where timed written papers are not used, or where they form only a small proportion of the total marks, then it is expected that teachers will use other techniques such as structured questions, orals, or projects.

Group size is important on two counts. Firstly from the point of view of what is to be achieved, be it individual special needs, team investigation, small group practical, or large group dissemination of information. Such arrangements may all involve a team of teachers working closely together on task-planning and assessment. The importance of this organizational strategy is now being emphasized in respect of the pupils themselves and is the second reason why group learning tasks are to the fore. Such activities are beneficial in developing a range of skills, including those of problem-solving, decision-making and of an inter-personal nature.

A major shift in the new examinations is away from the traditional didactic teaching approach towards a more pupil-centred experiential learning methodology advocated as an integral part of all programmes of study across the curriculum. The concept of 'enterprise education' is an example of the new approach that aims not only to develop in pupils business acumen, but more the competences of problem-solving and decision making, and the personal qualities of initiative and perseverance.

Assessment

Frameworks

It is very important to draw up clear guidelines indicating how and when assessments are to be made, what tasks are to be assessed, and the performance criteria by which levels of achievement will be measured. For the purposes of moderation it is advantageous to have at least some tasks common to all groups.

There are two frequently used approaches to assessment.

The first may be described as a practical approach whose process is essentially: to assess the learning activities; to analyse the results in order to discriminate amongst the pupils; to adapt the assessment criteria to accommodate all outcomes; and finally to award grades for achievement.

The second approach is: to determine in advance the assessment objectives that will achieve the aims; to identify performance criteria at different levels; to design and pre-test learning tasks and assessment techniques in order to establish suitability according to content, perceived outcomes, and the pupil's age-ability range. The minimum levels of competency are the grade thresholds, and as such are fixed. The problem for most teachers is that the pre-testing stage is initially omitted because of lack of time. Learning assignments are frequently designed on the basis of teacher experience of what is perceived as good practice. Human error is not unknown, and it may be necessary to refine the criteria and consequently the grade thresholds.

The learning outcomes should be expressed in behaviour terms as precise, unambiguous statements in a form such as, 'The student can/is able/has ...' Sometimes regarded as restrictive or mechanistic, such assessment objectives have been found to be essential to achieving aims and they provide clear, measurable targets for pupils, as well as informative statements for parents and employers. Objectives should be written with concrete action verbs such as 'write', 'list', 'describe', and not with verbs such as 'know', 'appreciate', 'understand'. The statements should also indicate such content and contextual information essential to a full appreciation of the performance criteria. These may be factors of time, speed, accuracy, location, equipment, or sequence. For example: 'The student can type instructional text of approximately 100 words [content] on an electric typewriter [context] at a minimum speed of 25 words per minute, with an accuracy of at least 95 per cent [criteria].'

Bloom's (1956) taxonomy of cognitive objectives: knowledge, comprehension, application, analysis, synthesis, evaluation, is a hierarchical assessment framework frequently used by curriculum designers. An adaptation of this taxonomy is used by the Coventry TVEI Modular Framework, stated as four major assessment objectives: knowledge; comprehension/enquiry; application; evaluation. It is interpreted more specifically by each module through sub-objectives.

Any assessment system should focus upon particular key questions. Will the assessment benefit the pupils? Will the information on attainment be useful? Do the performance criteria identify positive achievement? Are there important aspects of the course not covered by the assessment? Are the assessment techniques appropriate or valid for the learning experiences? Is the mark scheme reliable?

Validity and reliability

People need to have confidence in the results of any assessment process. If the results are expected to be similar, irrespective of when the task was completed, then the assessment may be said to be reliable. The results of a test can be affected by a pupil's understanding, and also by how and when the task was tackled. A pupil's performance may vary and a single response may be an unreliable measure of true ability. Targets may be achieved by different pupils in different sequences. Aggregations of target achievements can be reported with greater reliability, but the repetition of assessments can become a burden upon teachers and pupils to the extent of detracting from the value of the learning. It is important to minimize the amount of information to be collected about a pupil's abilities, but to maximize confidence in the stated achievements.

Assessment will be a more accurate reflection of attainment if the process concentrates upon a small number of assessment objectives or profile components. To have increased value, the interpretation of achievement must be related to national standards. Level of attainment descriptors are often tied to a points-rating scale to assist teachers in recording overall achievement in a course. The process is more reliable when short scales are used with a small number of profile-objectives components.

The Leicestershire Modular Framework for GCSE identifies five assessment objectives: recognition of a problem; location of information; application; communication; and evaluation. For each one there are four levels of achievement, the descriptions for which can be written in module-specific terms. Each stated criterion of performance spans two points on an eight point assessment scale (Figure 5.4).

To be valid, assessments must use the technique most fitted to the learning experience and the objectives to be achieved. Practical skills, for example, cannot be tested by written responses. On the other hand, communication skills may be assessed by oral, written, graphical, or dramatic techniques.

Figure 5.4 Leicestershire Modular Framework: visual communications module

Assessment objectives	*Attainment descriptors*			
Mark range	1 2	3 4	5 6	7 8
A Recognition	Can explain what is meant by visual communication in relation to specific design brief.	Can define visual communication and propose limited ideas to demonstrate its usefulness, in relation to a chosen brief.	Can plan a varied range of solutions to demonstrate understanding of visual communication in response to a chosen brief.	Can analyse the advantages and disadvantages of a variety of proposed solutions to a chosen brief.
B Location	Can collect or identity a limited selection of resources relevant to a design brief.	Can collect or identify a variety of resources relevant to brief and make some comments about their usefulness.	Can gather a varied selection of resources relevant to brief and compare the suitability of the content and methods of presentation.	Can gather a wide range of relevant resources and critically analyse their strengths and weaknesses in relation to a chosen brief.
C Application	Can use basic methods of visual communication and answer simple questions about their work.	Can use some visual communication techniques and show simple development of ideas.	Can use appropriate visual communication techniques and provide evidence of the development of a chosen idea or solution. The chosen solution will be based on a comparison of at least two techniques.	Can use appropriate visual communication techniques and provide clear and coherent evidence of the development of a chosen idea or solution. The relative merits of these techniques will have been compared to lead to a reasoned choice.
D Communication	Can produce a limited folio of information relevant to the brief with supporting practical outcome if appropriate.	Can produce a folio showing a range of ways of communicating information relevant to the brief, with modifications noted in a rudimentary manner, and practical outcome when appropriate.	Can demonstrate a variety of ways of recording, developing, and presenting a folio and practical outcome. Can keep an accurate record of modifications.	Can demonstrate sensitive use of appropriate materials and techniques when communicating ideas. All modifications will have been recorded in a detailed and systematic manner.
E Evaluation	Can produce basic statements describing outcome of brief and how it was done.	Can identify some problems encountered and describe briefly and simply how they were overcome.	Can identify strengths and weaknesses of the outcome of the brief giving reasoned arguments for modifications.	Can present a coherent comparison between their aims and the actual outcome of the brief, including references to limiting factors and constraints. Can show awareness of the work of others and everyday applications.

Source: Leicestershire Modular Framework, Leicestershire Education Authority, 1988.

Validity is probably the most important quality of any assessment and may be regarded as the extent to which an examination measures those aspects of achievement that it was designed to measure, as outcomes of a specific course. What is to be achieved must be clearly defined. Examination boards formerly published only brief outlines of content and assessment and left the teacher to speculate upon the purposes of teaching the material. The gradual shift towards statements of aims has resulted in GCSE courses that explicitly identify aims, objectives, methodologies, and performance criteria. There is, however, a danger in implicitly believing in assessment instruments and it is necessary to be mindful of human error associated with results, despite careful test design.

The creation of valid and reliable assessment schemes is difficult and time-consuming. Observational schemes of assessment change the teacher's role to that of tutor, counsellor, facilitator of learning rather than the didactic purveyor of knowledge, and such a role is not welcomed by everyone.

In constructing valid and reliable tests, a number of factors need to be carefully considered:

- the length of the assessment, which if it is too short will be inadequate;
- the choice of test technique, be it essay or short answer, structured or unstructured;
- the language of instruction to avoid creating communication barriers;
- the importance of sound administration and clearly presented examination materials;
- the questions should reflect the content and learning strategies and address the objectives;
- the need for objective marking linked to realistic performance criteria.

Coursework

The assessment of coursework as part of an examination system is not a new idea, but what is new is its inclusion in every GCSE subject. It focuses attention upon the ability of every teacher independently to assess their own pupils in a reliable manner. There may be a conflict between the analytical objective marking required by examination boards to establish reliability and the teacher's marking, which may be designed to act as a spur to low-achieving pupils.

Continuous assessment of coursework tasks usually takes

place periodically throughout a course as and when an exercise is completed or a test administered. Marks are totalled to give an end of term unit order or grade. Normally classwork, homework and periodic test marks are aggregated but they will probably have been awarded on different criteria and should not be combined without some adjustment which may be difficult to achieve.

Without moderation, marks awarded on the basis of a pupil's response may be regarded as a record of progress rather than attainment. Such progress marks or grades may be sufficient to enable a teacher to recognize and record individual differences and achievements. Teachers may feel that assessment is a means of determining present achievement as a guide to future potential and as a means of developing pupil–teacher relationships. In contrast, the public view of assessment leading to certification is essentially comparative and competitive.

Assessment of coursework must be as carefully planned as would be a series of external tests, and this is very demanding upon teachers. It is not unusual to find teachers marking to different standards even when different classes have taken the same examination. The differences are greater when classes have worked with different teachers using different approaches and emphases, even though they have been following broadly the same course. To be objective about attainment there must be uniform standards of marking by all the teachers concerned with a group of pupils. For any certificated course or module assessed by 100 per cent coursework, sound moderation within and across centres is vital.

The claimed advantages for coursework assessment include:

- improved validity as all the syllabus can be assessed;
- tasks completed under normal learning conditions without stress;
- a wider range of skills/abilities can be measured;
- immediate feedback on progress to pupil and teacher;
- a single poor uncharacteristic performance may not affect overall achievement;
- innovation and experimentation in learning methods are possible.

Any learning experience requires three elements: knowledge to understand the context and the expected outcomes; skills to demonstrate achievement; and positive attitudes to act. In designing assessable coursework tasks, the teacher should consider what the pupil must be able to do on completion; the contextual learning conditions; and how it will be recognized that the pupil is performing at the required level of competence. The following assignment is taken from a 'Land Based Industries' modular programme designed by Holme Lacy College of Agriculture, Hereford.

> *Machinery limitation survey*: Before starting any job, whether large or small, it will require some degree of planning. You are going to plan and research what type of machines will be required to extract timber from a forest plantation.
> *Practical activities involved*: locate position on map; measure inclines using clinometer; interpret machine limitations graph; carry out survey; measure distances with survey tapes;
> *Location of learning*: forest plantation.
> At the end you should be able to produce a worksheet of instructions for the extraction of timber, stating loading point, direction of extraction, and equipment required. You should also be able to use map, compass and clinometer.
> *Assessable skills*: communications: map reading; following instructions. Social: working as a team; accepting responsibilities. Decision making: assembling information on worksheet.

Formative processes

The examination system is moving in a direction away from the labelling and grading of pupils to well-planned diagnostic assessment, i.e. from normative to criterion referencing. The old system compared the performances of pupils and produced rank orders of ability to fit anticipated normal curves of distribution. As a result, teachers expected all 'good' examinations to produce normal curves of distribution. However, diagnostic assessment does not emphasise such general attainment. Instead it records specific attainments which, for a group having followed a course of learning, do not conform to a normal distribution.

It should at least in theory be possible for the whole of a group of pupils to achieve the highest level of attainment described by a set of acceptable performance criteria. There is frequently a conflict in the minds of teachers over the high levels of performance achieved by pupils and the teachers' perceptions of pupils' abilities. Examination boards have traditionally produced rank orders and the comparative grading of pupils. Criterion referenced attainment is not meant to serve such a purpose, because it could produce a mismatch between absolute achievement and grading for certification.

It is not unknown for pupils to achieve 100 per cent mastery of predetermined outcomes without actually having followed a specific learning programme. Such results are often regarded with suspicion, and claims made that the assessment must be at fault. This arises out of a long-held view that testing is for reporting and comparative purposes.

Musical performance examinations have always been designed on the principle of levels of achievement recorded as numerical grades. The attainment to be demonstrated by the pupil is specified at particular levels of ability, the criterion. The attraction of such an arrangement to pupils is that they can take the tests when they feel competent. In the wider context, public examinations have been age-dominated despite the claims that GCE, CSE, and now GCSE, can be taken by anyone. From a school's point of view it is organizationally more convenient and practical to have an upper school core plus options arrangement, linked to external accreditation rather than to have all-age classes determined by similar ability levels. Accordingly age groups of pupils are 'prepared' for external examinations set in the same year.

Teachers need to think differently about the role of assessment such that the diagnostic model can be used in a more formative context. Well-planned diagnostic assessment focuses attention upon the needs of individual pupils and it is particularly valuable for pupil-centred learning. Pupils can become more aware of their own strengths and weaknesses when they understand that the assessment is an integral and valuable part of the learning process. There are advantages in promoting diagnostic assessment as an end in itself rather than as part of a grading system.

Continuous coursework assessment is a formative process enabling teachers to know pupils better, and providing immediate feedback on the value of the learning tasks. Syllabuses need to be planned in detail before criterion assessment can be devised. One approach to curriculum design that has been found satisfactory is first to define a series of concepts and skills to be understood and mastered during the course. It is then necessary to select performance criteria appropriate to the age of the pupil; in the case of the GCSE these would be applicable to a 16-year-old about to complete compulsory schooling. Using the identified attributes exemplar learning experiences can be selected to illustrate the concepts and skills.

The learning strategies associated with diagnostic assessment require a marked shift from teacher-directed courses to pupil-negotiated programmes. This is particularly the case with modular schemes. Teacher exposition and questioning have been minimized in favour of individual pupils working on assignments, then finding out, organizing, creating, and evaluating outcomes, with teacher guidance only when requested.

Evidence of achievement

Profiling and graded certification both record a pupil's achievement, but the supporting evidence of attainment is frequently omitted from profiling. Before a GCSE grade may be awarded it must be clearly shown how a pupil demonstrated a particular level of attainment. A curriculum designer who subscribes to the principle that the assessment process is integral to the learning experience should have no difficulty in identifying predictable outcomes. However, the emphasis now prevalent in assessment upon process skills, group tasks, the more extensive use of oral techniques, and observational recording using competence check-lists, has focused attention upon a number of issues with regard to evidence of individual pupil attainment; not least within modular schemes.

Student-centred learning uses an assignment or task methodology focusing upon an individual's ability to research, organize, understand, communicate, and evaluate knowledge, concepts and skills that are within the individual's experiences and relevant to a pupil's immediate future lifestyle.

Products resulting from the learning can be assessed with minimal difficulty by measuring the quality of the outcome. If the product is of an ephemeral nature then its long-term retention for external assessment is impractical. The problem may be overcome by using photographic evidence.

Artefacts can give an experienced assessor a fair indication of the level of skills employed by a pupil in handling materials, tools, and equipment, and can indicate the degree of productivity within a time constraint. Using end products as a means of measuring process abilities cannot cover all skills satisfactorily, for example the ability to read an instrument accurately; equally, it may be argued that assessment by observation is not always reliable. Product and process are related and integral parts of any assessment scheme.

Process skills required to achieve an end product are now regarded as more important than simply the quality of the artefact itself, and this has presented teachers and assessors alike with a problem of verifying the teacher's records of pupil performances. A degree of professional trust needs to be established between the teacher-examiner and the external assessor. The assessor, as the examination board's appointed agent, is the upholder of national standards, and as such will need to be convinced, at least in the first instance, that the recorded performances are a true reflection of each candidate's ability. For this reason it is essential to show a clear relationship between the assessment objectives and the performance criteria as demonstrated by the content and contexts of the learning experiences. All of this needs to be clearly and concisely documented and supported by the teacher's assessment records.

Problem-solving within modular schemes is frequently the main approach to learning. This is exemplified by the Shropshire GCSE modular scheme 'Technology for All' which promotes the concept of 'technological capability' across the curriculum. A pupil completes a core module plus four other personally selected modules. Within each module a pupil has the opportunity to develop a range of competences and apply them to designing solutions to the type of problem they may encounter in their daily lives. The pupil's performance is matched against the appropriate level of attainment descriptor for each of the assessment objectives in a module.

The team approach to problem-solving in real-life situations has been translated significantly into the new style education, promoted by TVEI and encouraged by the DES. The process of working together co-operatively is relatively easy to record, but difficult to measure. The individual's contribution may, on the other hand, be clearly seen but still difficult to measure objectively. For this reason it is important to decide what is to be assessed for certification and what may be more valuable as a descriptive statement for a record of achievement. Selectivity is essential if the evidence is to be valid and reliable.

Tasks should each be carefully analysed in respect of presentation, operation, and response. Attention needs to be paid to the mode of communication used at each of the three stages. If a variety of modes are used in coursework assignments then pupils will feel more at ease with externally provided examinations. The mode of communication also determines the form of the evidence. For example, an open-ended assignment may use a written/visual mode of presentation, a practical/oral mode for the operation stage, and expect an oral/written assessment mode in the response.

Coursework that develops skills and understanding requires more structuring than that which traditionally emphasized the acquisition of knowledge. A series of small-scale assignments frequently replaces a single large project. This is clearly demonstrated in many modular schemes. The single coursework project sometimes found in modules highlights the importance of knowing exactly what is to be assessed and how the various elements are to be valued or weighted. Mistakes in presentation and operation will more seriously jeopardize responses than may be the case with a series of shorter assignments, whose outcomes are aggregated to achieve an overall set of module performance descriptors for each pupil. It is valuable to sub-divide each process task into parts, each with criteria checklists written as 'can do' statements. The danger to be avoided is an emphasis upon very low order skills or a mechanistic approach.

Modular approaches to the curriculum can be of equal standing to the more traditional courses, but to be so they must make in-depth demands upon pupils. By means of differentiation the tasks within each module must provide opportunities for pupils of all abilities to demonstrate their highest possible achievement. Structurally there are a variety of means by which different levels of response may be achieved. Whatever the means chosen, the form the evidence will take should be identified by the teacher and clearly communicated to the pupil before the task is tackled.

The language of communication used to convey instruction must be simple enough to be understood by all pupils with minimal teacher input; otherwise, the value of active student learning is reduced and obstacles are placed in the way of pupils demonstrating what they can really do. The GCSE is a single examination for an ability range greater than either of its predecessors, and it highlights the importance of language in the structuring of coursework assignments and examinations.

Equal opportunities for all pupils to demonstrate what they know, understand, and can do irrespective of gender, race, culture, or ability is a part of GCSE philosophy. Despite very careful curriculum design, assessment results are likely to show differences between and within groups. Attention is focused upon the effects that content, context, and question format can have upon individual achievement. Where choices can be made about the content of the curriculum, account should be taken of the diversity of pupils' cultural experiences. The curriculum should aim to create an understanding of the different environments, systems, societies, and cultures throughout the world, as well as in the various communities which make up the local and national scene.

Practical assignments are frequently used within modular programmes to achieve TVEI-style aims and objectives, which include equal opportunities for all pupils. As a form of learning they are both difficult to organize and time consuming. As in other experiences, that which is to be measured must be precisely identified. For example, in geographical landscape model-making is geographical understanding to be tested and/or model-making skill? The validity of a practical test can be improved if broken down into a series of sub-tests. At the same time any aspect that can be validly tested by other means should be eliminated from the practical assessment and measurement should be confined to performance using a short marking scale.

Manipulative activity is central to the assessment of practical skills and can itself be broken down into a series of actions: dexterity, movement, sequencing within a time constraint. Such activity can only be assessed satisfactorily at a particular performance level as it takes place, and cannot be measured through a write-up of what happened. On the other hand, the processes of planning, selection, safety, communication, and evaluation, which are abilities enhancing practical skills within any truly educational experience, can be assessed by written outcomes. What cannot be assessed using this mode is whether knowledge and understanding are actually applied in the manipulative activity.

Having exercised selectivity on what is to be assessed, the form of the evidence supporting recorded achievement can be identified and should be in manageable quantities. Courses and modular programmes should not be over-assessed. Quality of assessment is more important than quantity. The number of learning objectives will often exceed the number of attainments to be measured.

Project work is a valuable learning experience but, as with other tasks, it requires careful thought on the part of the teacher, and clear understanding on the part of the pupil, as to the nature of what will be acceptable as an assessable outcome. The assessment should mirror the skills and abilities developed by the project activity. Where pupils can negotiate their own project then common assessment criteria need to be devised to cover credit for presentation, research, content, and conclusions, each being appropriately weighted. Alternatively, more specific abilities may be identified such as knowledge, enquiry, comprehension, application, and evaluation, with these major objectives expanded into sub-objectives to facilitate effective assessment.

Inexperienced pupils undertaking project tasks will initially need structured guidance. If pupils are to be provided with opportunities to demonstrate high levels of achievement then the guidance must to an extent be open-ended so that each pupil's attainment may be determined by the level of the individual outcome. There will be a higher standard of work when the teacher and the pupil are both clear about the performance criteria. The problem to be tackled, rather than simply a topic title, should be manageable, relevant to the pupil's experience, and should be clearly stated. Data collected at first hand is more valuable than copious copying from books. The real measure of high ability will be the extent to which the pupil can demonstrate the higher order abilities of analysis, synthesis, and evaluation.

Teachers assessing projects should avoid the 'halo' effect of judging the quality of the achievement solely according to effort and standard of presentation. While these are important attributes they may demonstrate only neatness and thoroughness, without providing evidence to support the real abilities being assessed and certainly not those of a higher order. Shorter projects have the merit of encouraging selectivity of material, concentration on the main issues and the exclusion of irrelevances by pupils.

The content of a project may be regarded as less important than what the pupil acquired in experience, skills, and understanding. The question of authenticity is raised whenever a pupil completes substantial pieces of work outside the normal classroom environment where the teacher does not exercise a watching brief upon an individual's skills and attitudes. Individual contribution within group project tasks is not always easily recognizable. Oral assessment may quickly reveal the true extent of individuality and the amount of assistance provided by others.

Oral assessment techniques as traditionally applied towards the end of a two-year langauge course generate nervous strain in many pupils, and may result in inaccurate evidence of a pupil's true communication ability. Oral testing requires very sensitive teacher management, and even then it is doubtful whether many pupils can maintain a natural free-flowing conversation. In modern language, the new examination courses place greater emphasis upon verbal ability than upon other language skills. The demands upon teacher time and energy to prepare, implement, and moderate orals are very great and it is questionable whether the one-to-one formal oral is either worthwhile or cost-effective.

Partly for these reasons, and more importantly to develop social communication in a more realistic and relevant context, teachers are increasingly using group discussions as a means by which individuals can express their thoughts. These interpersonal skills are not confined to traditional language subjects but are finding a place in other curriculum areas, such as technology, science, and creative arts.

If the assessment of communication skills for an individual pupil in a one-to-one situation is difficult to conduct, then the assessment of a pupil within a group situation poses more difficult problems. Such difficulties may be reduced by adopting one or more strategies. An oral with an individual pupil may be audio-recorded and the assessment completed later. Group work requires video taping and it is very time-consuming to assess each individual, as the tape will need to be played a number of times. There is the added difficulty of ensuring a video of adequate clarity.

Group orals need to be with small groups of four to five pupils, and the teacher must exercise care to ensure that each pupil has a fair chance to contribute and that the assessment is based upon a reliable amount of evidence. A pupil's participation is not measured by quantity, but by the quality of the contribution.

To judge quality it is recommended that a small mark scale is used, each point on the scale being identified by a brief but clear descriptor of the level of achievement. It is doubtful if many teachers can carry a large assessment scale in their head and conduct the oral without risking confrontation with at least one pupil. A strategy used in some modular schemes is to conduct the oral with an independent teacher-examiner present who can concentrate upon applying the assessment criteria to each individual in the group.

The composition and arrangement of a group may influence the contribution of individuals within it. Groups may be self-selective or teacher-organized. The latter may achieve a more balanced composition of pupils. A way of increasing reliability and reducing the impact of oral tests is to spread them throughout a course. Within a module of 30 to 40 hours this is still feasible, but is still difficult to manage, and problems such as occasional pupil absences may cause insurmountable difficulties.

The spreading of oral tests may result in a less pressurized, more manageable arrangement, allowing for greater variety of oral work under more natural learning conditions. The varied maturity of pupils focuses attention upon the timing of the oral tests. This problem may be mitigated by introducing a series of very short orals. However, single, short test situations can be fragmented and cast doubts upon the validity of the assessments. Within a course the short oral may not adequately cover the syllabus, but within the shorter contextual situation of a single module, orals may be more realistic. Whatever strategy is adopted it should not be forgotten that many pupils take time to settle down before demonstrating their true attainment level.

In curriculum areas other than languages the oral technique may be found to be advantageous as a method of examining, since increased flexibility enables pupils to discuss their work more freely, and more able pupils can respond in depth. The teacher can adjust the level of questioning to suit pupils of all abilities. Orals are less reliable than written tests, but many pupils achieve a higher standard of work through orals.

MODULAR CURRICULUM ISSUES

The overloading of the options systems, as more and more subjects were added in a mistaken belief that this increased the breadth of pupil choice, frequently resulted in a fragmented, imbalanced curriculum for many individuals. From this situation arose the 'core' concept as a safeguard for all pupils age 14 to 16, with a particular emphasis upon English, maths, and science. There has evolved the concept of a 'common curriculum', with elements of human knowledge and experience to which all pupils should be entitled and expressed intentions as to pupils' personal and social development. In an attempt to provide a broad and balanced curriculum for upper secondary pupils, schools and LEAs have turned to modular curriculum frameworks.

The time span of 20 to 40 hours over a period of 10 to 15 weeks is frequently used to deliver pre-16 modules. The programme may either be made up of a prescribed group of modules, or contain some degree of pupil choice — be it core modules plus options or entirely free-standing units. Modular programmes bring more sharply into focus a number of issues associated with the assessment and moderation process which have already been referred to.

The actual teacher-pupil contact time within the majority of GCSE modules is of the order of 25 to 35 hours, with some a little less or a little more. Programmes for certification are usually made up of four or five units. There are no examination board regulations that require a minimum time commitment, but various board guidelines indicate what is considered to be reasonable in terms of achieving the GCSE full range of grades. There is a notional view that at least the same amount of time should be available for a certificated programme as was regarded essential for GCE and the newer GCSE courses. The origins of this principle are lost in the mists of time but are quite possibly derived from the grammar school curriculum concept of a core of subjects, later embellished by the options systems. This resulted in some 2 to 3 hours per subject each week which over a two-year course provided 150 to 200 hours of timetabled lessons for a subject.

The content of a module is perceived as that which must be covered within the timescale. The new style of learning, with greater emphasis upon skills, does not fit this idea. Nevertheless, the notion of minimum time still prevails. Modules, because they are relatively so much shorter than a full course, pose questions about what can be learned in a unit, and more importantly as to what standard various abilities can be demonstrated.

There has developed within modular schemes the concept of a content-free programme. The emphasis is upon competences, the ability to demonstrate an understanding and application of various processes which may not always result in a measurable product.

The process and product outcomes of the learning experiences may be affected by a number of factors. Performance criteria for GCSE are related to what it is expected that a pupil at 16, about to leave compulsory schooling, should be capable of demonstrating. Although all such pupils will officially be in their final year at school, there could be nearly 12 months age difference in any group. The level of maturity, the degree of individual motivation, and the wide ability range of such an age group will all affect the results.

Most of the learning will be pupil-centred activities, and will not be confined to timetabled sessions. The socio-economic circumstances of the pupils will affect the opportunities each individual may have to realize his or her potential. This is not an unusual feature of learning situations, where the availability of materials and equipment are important considerations. The small time-scale of a module also requires learning to take place outside of the classroom.

The degree of help received by a pupil is often difficult to determine. A pupil's high achievement while studying or working in the context of the local community may result from high motivation and the opportunity presented to realize and demonstrate specific abilities. Such a pupil should not be viewed with suspicion because the teacher's perception of the pupil's ability in other circumstances within the school indicates a capacity for lower achievement.

The use of community, residential, and work experiences commonly found in modular schemes sometimes requires adults other than teachers to judge the level of achievement of a pupil. There is nothing wrong in anyone measuring and recording performance on behalf of a teacher provided that they are fully conversant with the assessment framework, including the criteria by which levels of ability are to be measured.

The pace of delivering modular programmes can be frenetic. This is particularly true where the change-over to new modules takes place every 10 weeks or so. Within the relatively short time-span of the module there must be completed: the implementation of experiences; monitoring, counselling and guidance; the assessment and recording of achievement; and the negotiation of new modules. Added to this, shortly after the module ends, will be a layer of internal moderation where more than one teacher is involved.

It is not surprising if pupils and teachers resort to short-cuts in order to achieve the desired end results. Teachers may revert to didactic teaching to ensure that all the module content is covered. Learning may be targeted specifically towards end of module test papers. This focuses attention upon the security of examination materials. Unlike two-year courses with terminal examinations that are set once and kept secure until the day of the test, modules may run a number of times with different groups over a one- or two-year cycle. Is it valid and reliable to use a test more than once? One solution is to have a bank of test material from which particular examinations may be produced according to an agreed format.

The frequency of assessment in modular programmes generates a feeling of over-assessment among pupils and teachers. Such an impression may also be true of some courses. The danger is the traditional one that the examination system begins to control, rather than respond to the needs of, the curriculum. Limited assessment objectives and careful selection of the learning outcomes to be measured go some way towards improving the quality of the assessment.

Throughout a two-year course a pupil has the opportunity to acquire and to progressively develop a range of abilities which may be assessed periodically, as part of a formative process, with a final summative statement of the highest levels achieved. A well-constructed modular scheme takes account of the need for continuity and progression by designing an assessment framework applicable to a whole programme, irrespective of the modules of which it is composed. When the modules of a programme are hierarchical they provide opportunities for pupil development as might a two-year course. When modules are free-standing there is no guarantee of progression.

Progression, continuity, and coherence are important aspects of any educational programme. A course broken down into units merely to facilitate delivery could be said to be still coherent as a subject. The opposing view holds that some Mode 1 GCSE courses built up of units do not demonstrate coherence because there is no explicit integration of each part to create a wholeness. Modular schemes which permit any combination of units under a title such as 'Interdisciplinary Studies', must clearly demonstrate that, whatever the choice, the units are not fragmentary unrelated pieces. A pupil must have the opportunity to progressively develop abilities across the selected modules and not merely to repeat skills in different contexts but all at a relatively low level.

Differentiation within each module may help or hinder a pupil's development and realization of individual potential. Differentiation within the earliest modules may make demands which are too great for a pupil, and there is a risk of demotivation. This may happen when all modules in a scheme are regarded as equal in value or weighting. Each module attempts to provide opportunities to achieve the highest levels of performance irrespective of the preparedness of the pupil. Added to this is the possibility that some skills are specific to a module and can be assessed only a few at a time, and some skills common to all modules within a programme can be assessed more frequently over many months.

It may be possible to weight the modules or to assess them at different levels using graded criteria. In a sequential arrangement such a solution is feasible. The Midland Record of Achievement has a facility permitting the design of units at ten levels, the top seven of which may be related to GCSE grades (Figure 5.5). An alternative model is to assess, for example, four modules by means of coursework techniques, completing the programme with a fifth integrating module which utilizes and applies previously acquired knowledge, concepts, skills, and understanding to an unfamiliar context. The Redbridge GCSE Modular scheme makes provision for pupils to select either a 'practical project' module or an 'enquiry' module to complete particular programmes. Some schemes have supplemented module coursework assessment, with an overall terminal examination which negates some of the claimed motivational advantages of modular programmes.

GCSE: 'Applied Vocational Skills' – a personal development programme					
	10	*Assessment objectives:*		*A*	*GCSE programme grade:*
	9		expressed as Outcome	B	(A-G) derived by
Unit	8	Knowledge	Statements (criteria)	C	matching the three
Levels	7	Skills	in the context of	D	module grades (a–g)
	6	Experiences	each learning	E	to a profile
	5	Concepts	experience	F	arrangement system;
	4			G	e.g. aba = A.
	3				*Foundation stages*: Uncertificated but also part of Record of Achievement.
		Module programme:	3 × 60 hrs from:		
		Computing Today	Electronics		
		Visual Communication	Consumer Services		
		Design Technology	Design Production		
		Land Based Industries	Performing Arts		
		Business Office Services	Business Technology		
		Food Hospitality Industry	Community Care		

Figure 5.5 Hereford/Worcester TVEI pilot-modular GCSE 1988

Achievement

Results

The results of assessments should be in terms of varying degrees of positive achievement rather than of a pass-fail nature. Assessment information about pupils may serve different purposes:

formative: positive achievement recognized and used for the planning of further individual programmes;
diagnostic: learning difficulties identified and solutions devised;
summative: systematic recording of overall achievement.

All three aspects of assessment are part of modular schemes arising from the shift in the balance of assessment objectives to emphasize competencies. This requires more assessment time, more skill in the examiners, and a reduction in the usual pupil-teacher ratios if the assessment process is to be successful. The GCSE has probably created more problems for teachers in carrying out their new role in assessment rather than in accommodating new syllabuses or shifts in emphasis.

To record a pupil's achievement accurately, the performance must be standardized against agreed performance criteria. This will require moderation between teachers and across schools. The process will be less onerous and more effective if performance criteria can be agreed prior to the implementation of the learning programme. This will still permit some adjustment at the moderation stage to accommodate the unusual or unexpected, but valid, outcomes.

It is very important to be able to show a clear relationship between the assessment objectives, the content and context of the learning experiences, the performance criteria, and any marking scheme used to confirm the recorded achievement. It is also essential that the achievement is supported by clear evidence. Model exemplar assignments, highlighting the relationships described, can serve both as in-service instruments for teachers and as acceptable standards against which the actual outcomes can be evaluated.

The results may be expressed as profile statements; as distinction, pass, fail categories; or as grades, as in GCSE. A profile of criteria statements is regarded by many people as a far more useful expression of a pupil's achievement than an overall grade, but there is evidence that some employers still prefer nationally validated grades. The seven-point scale, A to G, of the GCSE is considered by some to be too detailed and certainly difficult to achieve if it were to be based upon seven criteria. The pass-fail classification of pupils will be rejected by most people because it is alien to the philosophy of positive achievement. The linking of the former GCE grades with the newer GCSE grades, although made no doubt to reassure people of the maintenance of standards, unfortunately perpetuated the old feelings that anything less than grade C is a failure.

Within modular schemes the modules themselves may be assessed against the seven-point GCSE scale on the principle that each is an assessment component, in the same way that assessment techniques are used in more traditional courses. The results of each component or unit are aggregated to determine the overall modular programme or course achievement for a pupil. Coventry TVEI Modular Scheme (Figure 5.6) uses this system.

Assessment Objectives	C F	E D	C B	B
Knowledge/ understanding	Identify knowledge of information relating to syllabus content (using description and elementary level of understanding).	Identify and explain knowledge of information relating to syllabus content.	Shows knowledge of syllabus content using description/ explanation/ operations in order to pursue a process or single line of argument.	Pursues a process or line of argument showing clear evidence of breadth and depth of information by using appropriate knowledge of syllabus content.
Comprehension/enquiry	Can select/extract single items of data from a limited number of sources. Can, with help, convey ideas and information in an elementary form.	Can extract multi-items of data and begin to show the relevance of information to the specified topic by basic classification and selection. Conveys ideas/ information in an elementary form with some resemblance of structure, using appropriate methods.	Can clearly select/ extract relevant information appropriate to the topic and can then infer/predict a possible outcome in a basic form. Conveys ideas/ information with clarity in a structured and appropriate manner.	Can make an analytical or critical assessment of the relevance of a range of information to the particular problems or topic with clear evidence of the ability to infer/predict possible outcomes. Conveys a sequence of ideas in a fluent manner by the most appropriate means.
Application	Can apply basic information skills and processes and/or concepts to reach an outcome at an elementary level.	Can apply information skills, processes or concepts to reach an outcome.	Can select and apply in a co-ordinated way a range of concepts, skills, processes and information with a demonstration of basic implications.	Can synthesize a range of concepts, skills, processes, and information to reach an outcome and demonstrates a clear understanding of the implications
Evaluation	Can describe what occured and is able to make judgements in a structured situation.	Can draw conclusions from the learning experience and make independent judgements.	Can draw conclusions and make a basic justification of their own interpretations using support material.	Can draw conclusions and make a reasoned and balanced justification of their own interpretations using a variety of evidence.

Note: Differentiation Grade descriptions are provided to give a general indication of the standards of achievement likely to have been shown by candidates awarded particular grades. The grade awarded will depend in practice upon the extent to which the candidate has met the assessment objectives overall and it might conceal weakness in one aspect of the examination which is balanced by above average performance in some other.

Source: Coventry TVEI Modular Scheme, City of Coventry 1987.

Figure 5.6 Performance indicators: for judging final GCSE grade boundaries within a module the above criteria are intended to provide a general indication of the abilities to be assessed within each of the assessment objective categories.

Certificate grading

How can marks or grades from different sources be combined in a meaningful way to give valid overall achievement? Modular GCSE schemes have tried out different methods of arriving at the overall reading of a programme of modules. It is doubtful if anyone can authoritatively claim that a particular method is more appropriate or more accurately reflects absolute pupil achievement. But seeking new forms of accreditation in response to TVEI criteria certainly encouraged the development of modularity and, because of the perceived value of GCE and now GCSE, a means had to be found to grade each pupil's achievement.

Employers and institutions of further and higher education expected the GCE to predict future performance and have grown accustomed to graded pupils and students even though it can be demonstrated that a seven-point grading system is not a very practical instrument and that the allocation of pupils to grades is often subjective. Traditionally there has developed a cut-off point below which pupils were regarded as failures. The move to criterion performance requires 'can do' statements which are more explicit and useful than overall grades. This is probably very true of complex modular schemes. Public pressure has, however, very much against the wishes of teachers, led to the conversion of statements to numerical or alphabetical grading systems.

The more usual practice is to grade the performance of a pupil within each module and then to aggregate the results to achieve the overall programme grade. The assessment process, for example, may show module achievement by a percentage score; the seven grades a to g, or in levels such as 1 to 4, where 1 is the highest. Each module performance is then aggregated and the result of an overall GCSE grade recorded. This is achieved in a number of ways. The percentage scores may be standardized before aggregation.The grades a to g may be converted to a points score, when for example a = 7; b = 6; c = 5, etc., and following aggregation the total score is matched to a predetermined score pattern relating to GCSE grades. Alternatively, grades a to g and levels 1 to 4 may be expressed as an arrangement or profile such as a, a, c, b, e; or 1, 1, 2, 4. The order of achievement is not important in arriving at the final grade, which is determined by matching the pattern of achievement to GCSE grade criteria patterns. For example, in a four-module programme a candidate achieving a, b, a, a may be regarded as equivalent to GCSE grade a overall.

The profile is more explicit than the arguably arbitrary points system, because it indicates the different levels of achievement within the modules of a programme. If accompanied by criteria-related statements specifying outcomes the results are found to be a valuable record of pupil achievement.

Teachers have commonly used a five-part lettered scale A to E for internal assessment purposes. Not all teachers, however, use a scale in the same way. Some feel that 'A' signifies perfection and seldom award it. Some teachers never use 'E' because it is felt to be discouraging to pupils. Whatever grade scale is used it must be applied uniformly across all subjects by all the staff, otherwise pupils, parents and employers will mistakenly equate a 'C' in English with a 'C' in history. The use of grade-related criteria, if applied properly, can produce more useful results. The introduction of the GCSE brought with it some problems for teachers who had to grade pupils, in some subjects, many months in advance of the final examination in order to decide which papers or for which levels of examining a pupil should be entered. This is extremely unfair on pupils, because it discourages the continuous development of abilities and last-minute determined efforts to raise personal standards.

The central aim of the Leicestershire GCSE Modular Framework (LMF) is to develop a range of skills that are applicable to any modular programme irrespective of the combination of modules. The skills are expressed as assessment objectives and attainment descriptors (Figure 5.7).

The LMF consists of five assessment objectives, each expressed by statements of achievement at four levels of response. The framework criteria are interpreted in the context of the module. The four levels lie along an eight-point scale which is used to refine the position of each pupil's achievement. At the end of the five-module programme, marks representing the profile of attainment in each objective across all five modules are aggregated. This is matched to a predetermined points pattern related to the GCSE grades. By this method, due account is taken of a pupil's increasing and progressive development. The end result is not affected by a slow start in initial modules nor by an uncharacteristic later module achievement. The framework applies to all modules and the criteria are, as far as is humanly possible, interpreted to the same standard throughout.

Assessment Objectives	Attainment descriptors			
Mark range	1 2	3 4	5 6	7 8
A Recognition	Can decide on a way to proceed.	Can identify a number of alternative ways of proceeding.	Can chose and develop an overall plan.	Can develop an effective plan, working through a range of alternatives and anticipating outcomes.
B Location	Can identify appropriate information.	Can select appropriate information, concepts, processes and skills.	Can select with reasons different concepts, processes and skills.	Can gather and synthesize a selection of concepts, processes and skills.
C Application	Can apply straight-forward information.	Can apply appropriate information concepts, processes and skills.	Can apply in a co-ordinated way a range of concepts, processes and skills.	Can synthesize a range of concepts, processes and skills with purpose and precision.
D Communication	Can communicate a recognizable outcome.	Can communicate purpose in the outcome.	Can communicate the outcome of learning.	Can communicate the structure, purpose and outcome of learning.
E Evaluation	Can describe the task and the way it was done.	Can describe the task and the way it was done; and can draw conclusions from content.	Can identify the strengths and weaknesses of the methods used in the task and draw conclusions from content.	Can evaluate alternative methodologies applicable to the task and inferences from content.

Figure 5.7 Leicestershire Modular Framework assessment framework

Brian Roby

Post-16 developments

A level courses

Proposals for the replacement of the Advanced Level of GCE by other schemes during the past twenty years have not met with government approval. The widespread feeling in higher education that it would be of great benefit to establish what was common ground amongst their new entrants led to the identification of common cores for the major subjects. The examination boards have produced the A level syllabuses which the schools and colleges are required to teach, but choice of syllabus is maintained by the use of optional elements in many subjects.

The codification of A level cores was a useful exercise but did not address the needs of future students in the 1990s. The importance of continuity from compulsory schooling to the courses and qualifications offered post-16 should not be underestimated. Some A level syllabuses are in tune with the spirit of the GCSE by stressing the importance of investigative problem-solving approaches and the practical applications of knowledge, concepts, and skills.

The debate over the issues of breadth and depth has been pursued for many years and is likely to continue in the foreseeable future. The recommendations of the Higginson Committee in 1988 to broaden A level curricula to five subjects for all students did not meet with government approval, on the grounds that it would sacrifice the rigour of the existing system. This view was not shared by many eminent people in higher education.

Despite reservations, important changes are taking place within A level subjects, particularly with regard to active learning strategies and supported self-study, rather than the mere passive absorption of considerable factual material and the regurgitation of other peoples' views and ideas. There is a move towards the more systematic and rigorous development of study skills at A level. Reservations have been expressed that the shift in emphasis in most GCSE subjects from the academic skills of analysis and evaluation will leave more students ill-prepared for A levels. Structured questions in GCSE, that only require short answers, do not encourage the development of abilities to interpret information, to plan and to structure extended essays. Assignments in the GCSE have been criticized because they often contain trivial tasks and have forced pupils to work at levels below their potential.

A further criticism of the GCSE syllabuses is that the course content is likely to be less than the old O levels, and as a result the factual basis to build on at A level is reduced. The problem is compounded by the variations of GCSE syllabuses between the examining boards. The backgrounds of students in a sixth form college may be so varied as to require an initial consolidation phase before A level work can be started in some subjects. A move to reduce A level content would have a similar effect upon higher education establishments.

In contrast, the continual assessment of coursework increases students' motivation to compete with themselves, developing intellectual and study skills, and more confidently tackling problem situations. Provided there are opportunities to practise critical information retrieval and analysis the new GCSE approach can be a sound basis for A level work.

Modular A levels

Initiatives in schools and colleges have increasingly pointed to modular schemes as a means of achieving many educational goals. The advocates of modular A levels draw attention to the advantages of flexibility of course design; enhanced, broader A level syllabuses; the emphasis on practical, applied, problem-solving learning strategies; continual coursework assessment; and results that reflect more accurately the abilities of the students.

The A level module bank developed at Cambridge was initially an attempt to meet the perceived needs of TVEI projects. The performance grades achieved by a candidate in each of six modules are aggregated to determine the overall A level grade for a subject specific programme.

AS levels

The principal objective of introducing AS examinations was to broaden the A level curriculum without diluting academic standards. A distinction has been drawn between broadening within an A level subject and broadening which results from studying within, say, sciences and humanities at the same time. Students may take A level subjects in which they wish to specialize, and at the same time broaden their curriculum with contrasting AS levels. Alternatively, some students may study a range of AS subjects or, as in the Cambridge scheme, accumulate credit for three modules equivalent to an AS level award.

Certificate of Pre-Vocational Education

The Certificate of Pre-Vocational Education (CPVE) was introduced in 1985 by the Joint Board (BTEC and CGLI) at the request of the Secretary of State for Education. It provides young people at 16 in schools and colleges with the opportunity to develop their general education and vocational skills. The scheme provides a formal link between education and the world of work. Students can negotiate their own course content within a given framework of a core, vocational studies and additional studies, and it provides opportunities for progression to the main national qualifications.

Because there are no formal entry requirements and because of the negotiated structure, the CPVE appeals to students with a wide range of abilities. The flexibility of CPVE makes it equally suitable both for those who find traditional academic courses inappropriate, and for students taking A and AS levels who wish to explore new areas of study, develop personal interests, and have the opportunity of work experience. This is possible with a CPVE programme spread over two years.

The CPVE framework is a cohesive whole made up of interrelating modules and projects. It is an important part of CPVE that a student understands how different activities relate to each other and enable progression to be built into a programme.

The Core concentrates on providing relevant basic skills within the eight areas:

Communication	Science and Technology
Numeracy	Information Technology
Problem Solving	Social Skills
Practical Skills	Industrial, Social, Economic Studies

'Personal and Careers Development' and 'Creative Development' are no longer part of the core aims and objectives for assessment. They are, however, still a vital part of any CPVE programme. There will be further changes in the light of pilot developments.

The similarities between such core elements, the advice of NCVQ; *Better Schools* (Department of Education and Science 1985a); TVEI criteria; GCSE National Criteria;

integrated course criteria; requirements within BTEC and CGLI main stream courses is very apparent, and it highlights the importance attached by curriculum designers to the issues of educational continuity, progression and relevance.

In CPVE the common core competences are developed through the focus of the vocational studies which also encourage students to explore their talents and interests. The modules are defined in the three stages: introductory, exploratory, preparatory; each with a more specific vocational focus. For some students, 'additional studies' are included as a contribution to fully rounded programmes of work.

The CPVE is an effective framework for delivering TVEI post-16. Students can complete their own selection of modules that are accredited by the Joint Board in a Record of Pre-Vocational Experience. Developments in National Vocational Qualifications (NVQ) have accelerated the move towards credit accumulation and the linking of CPVE preparatory modules to the mainstream courses of BTEC and CGLI.

The CPVE is unlike other qualifications in that it does not grade its students. Academic examination certificates are not particularly reliable predictors of performance in employment situations. The CPVE formative profiling strategy reflect, record, review, revise; records each student's achievements as 'can do' statements relevant to further education and employment. The CPVE philosophy encapsulates the new thinking in the post-16 education world.

SUMMARY

The government of the 1980s has emphasized the need for a high quality, cost-effective education and assessment system. The introduction of a National Curriculum is an attempt to remove curriculum clutter and to raise standards by means of nationally validated criteria at all levels and for all students aged from 5 to 16. There is an acknowledged need for the assessment process to be dynamic, responsive both to the needs of students and those of society.

Staff within schools and colleges are developing a greater understanding of the advantages and disadvantages of assessment processes and they are now more aware of the possibilities of examinations dictating sterile learning styles. There has been a noticeable shift from examination boards to teachers of the processes of planning, design, implementation and assessment so that what is measured more accurately reflects current curriculum practice. The pursuit of accountability throughout the educational system has encouraged a more open attitude from examination board officers and teachers. The changes have highlighted the need for highly professional teachers in schools and colleges; motivated, able to diagnose individual student needs, and capable of evaluating programmes and results. Staff are being encouraged constantly to question the validity of existing arrangements.

Learning styles are changing with a marked shift, in both secondary and further education, from didactic teaching to active learning methods and the use of new technologies. There is a new emphasis upon creativity, imagination, practical application, and co-operative ventures using meaningful materials and tasks. Relevance is coupled with breadth and balance both within subjects and across an individual's curriculum. At the same time there is a tendency to shift away from specific subjects to cross-curricular themes and the introduction of new educational elements and experiences. Modular structures are being used to increase the flexibility of delivery and to stimulate students to realize their true potential. Society is focusing attention upon a number of important social, economic, and technological issues that are all being given educational priority.

Assessment is now accepted as an integral part of the learning process. A much wider ability range is receiving national recognition through different forms of recording achievement. There is wider use of assessment techniques and a noticeable shift from the written mode to the recognition of other abilities and aptitudes. The process of learning is at least as important as the product. The 'big bang' terminal examination has given way to more user-friendly continuous coursework assessment. The knowledge explosion and new technologies have reduced the importance of recall, but have stressed the value of a much wider range of skills or competences.

The recording of achievement is now clearly focused upon the individual whose performance in any given context is measured, not against other individuals as in a normative system, but against criterion referenced performance levels. Assessment is diagnostic, with the young person negotiating with the teacher personal targets, as part of the student's formative process of development. There is marked tension between diagnostic assessment and assessment for certification where the latter is shown by grades.

The new emphasis upon rewarding positive achievement, success not failure, is accompanied by a move to replace marks and percentages with concise, unambiguous criterion statements that identify clearly what a student knows, understands and can do. The time-scale for certification is also being extended so that credit for achievements may be accumulated over the period of time most suited to the individual.

The major and rapid changes in the assessment and testing of young people aged from 5 to 19 has drawn attention to the advisability of a coherent whole-school or college policy with regard to all forms of external assessment, national curriculum, records of achievement, and the dissemination of information. The accuracy of records is very important, and the tendency for teachers to over-assess needs to be replaced by a policy of assessing less often but placing greater reliance upon the results. School and college assessment arrangements should provide economically accurate information about pupils' attainments when it is needed and in a form most appropriate for whoever requires it.

REFERENCES AND BIBLIOGRAPHY

Bloom, B.S. (ed.) (1956) *Taxonomy of Educational Objectives Handbook 1: cognitive domain*, New York: McKay.

Business and Technician Education Council (1987) *The Certificate of Pre-Vocational Education*, London: BTEC.

Business and Technician Education Council-City and Guilds of London Institute (1987) *Pre-Vocational Programmes for Pupils aged 14-16*, London: BTEC.

Cambridgeshire Technical and Vocational Education Initiative (1987) *Modular A levels - Guidelines*, Cambridge: Cambridgeshire LEA.

City of Coventry (1987) *Coventry TVEI Modular Scheme*, Coventry: Coventry LEA.

Department of Education and Science (1985a) *Better Schools*, London: HMSO.

Department of Education and Science (1985b) *GCSE: The National Criteria*, London: HMSO.

Department of Education and Science (1987) *A Report from the National Curriculum Task Group on Assessment and Testing*, London: HMSO.

Frith, D.S. and Macintosh, H.G. (1984) *A Teacher's Guide to Assessment*, Cheltenham: Stanley Thorne.

Higginson Report (1988) *A Level Review*, London: DES.

Leicestershire Education Authority (1988) *Leicestershire Modular Framework*.

Midland Examining Group (1988) *Modular Schemes-*

Regulations for GCSE.
Northamptonshire Education Authority (1988) *Northamptonshire TVEI Modular Scheme*
University of Cambridge Local Examinations Syndicate (1988) *GCSE Advanced Level Module Bank*
Warwick, D. (1987) *The Modular Curriculum*, Oxford: Basil Blackwell.
Watkins, P.R. (1982) *Modular Approaches to the Secondary Curriculum*, London: Schools Curriculum Development Committee.

Chapter Six

ASSESSMENT AND RECRUITMENT OF SCHOOL LEAVERS FOR TRAINING AND EMPLOYMENT

Mary Jones

This is an analysis of assessment and recruitment procedures for training and employment based on evidence taken from employers and managing agents for Youth Training Schemes (YTS), using a Midlands careers service, and research into recruitment to YTS based on nine Midland careers services.

ASSESSMENT AND RECRUITMENT FOR TRAINING

To see how the recruitment process for YTS operates let us look first at:

1 how information about schemes becomes available to pupils;
2 the extent to which the careers service affects the recruitment process;
3 the selection methods employed by managing agents.

Research based on nine Midland careers services, including the one used in this survey, showed that each produced a directory of local YTS provision which was made available to all interested young people. Each service organized a YTS convention or a convention incorporating YTS as one of the post 16 year options, and each held details of vacancies in YTS and referred young people for submission. All except two of the services processed application forms, i.e. acted as a clearing house, collating details of application and passing completed application forms to chosen schemes. The information given about the schemes in the directories varied in content and form. Here is an analysis of entries in six directories.

Directory (1)

The name of each YTS is under an occupational heading, e.g. retail and distribution — 'Midland Link is part of National Link Training Scheme. They offer retail and warehousing in most parts of [the region]. Many different types of shops offer on-the-job training and experience. Off-the-job training is at local colleges and at Link's own Training Centre.'

Directory (2)

All the schemes are listed under occupational headings. A description of each scheme is given in terms of location, number of places, scheme content described in brief terms, qualifications obtainable and qualifications required.

Directory (3)

All the schemes are listed under occupational headings. No other details are available in the directory but entries may be supplemented by YTS information sheets on which hours of work, qualifications needed, what you will learn, is included.

Directory (4)

All the schemes are listed under occupational headings, e.g. 'Hotel and Catering Training Board — A country-wide scheme with approximately 30 places available in this area covering many of the job skills required in the hotel and catering industry. Off-the-job training takes place at the Hotel Catering Training Board Centre and can lead to Caterbase and City and Guild qualifications. Work experience is arranged locally in hotels, restaurants and cafés, and with individual and commercial caterers. To apply, complete a YTS application form, available from your Careers Officers or Careers Teacher.'

Directory (5)

This gives details of work experience, off-the-job training, qualifications obtainable and entry requirements, e.g. 'NIH Training Services —

Work experience: placements at local retail outlets include product knowledge, customer relations, security, lay-out, pricing and shelf-filling, payment procedures, stock control.

Off-the-job-training: based on correspondence course leading to City and Guilds, also residential course, driving lessons and projects.

Entry requirements: basic maths, physically fit, strong, pleasant manner and appearance.'

Here are some examples of entry requirements for schemes listed:

Engineering: entry requirements — No specific requirements but preferably with good standard of GCSE in maths, English and craft subject, in order to cope with the studies and work requirements.

Agriculture: entry requirements — No formal qualifications are required. All people with a genuine interest in the industry and a will to succeed are welcome to apply.

Hotel: Entry requirements — We ask for no set qualifications but are looking for young people with aptitude and the right appearance and approach for high-class hotels.

Research and leisure: Entry requirements — no specific requirements but a genuine desire to work in the leisure industry.

Travel Agency: Entry requirements — (a) Have a sound secondary education, (b) be well motivated towards a career in the tourism and leisure industry, (c) be suited for a career within the industry, (d) because of the nature of the industry the young person should like working with and being involved with people.

Directory (6)

This directory has brief descriptions of schemes available, e.g. 'Halifax Building Society — The largest national building society has training places at a number of local branches in [the region]. Recruitment is usually by individual branch managers.'

It can be seen that schemes' criteria for selection are not always available to the applicant. In some cases schemes state that an aptitude test will be given, but what the tests are designed to establish is not stated. Formal qualifications may be required, or a scheme may say no formal qualifications are required, only an interest in the industry. General terms are often used, e.g. 'a good standard in GCSE maths, English and science'; 'have a sound secondary education'; 'be suited for a career in the industry'; all of which beg the questions, what is 'good'? what is sound? what is it to be 'suited to the industry'? what is taken as evidence of 'interest'?

The survey showed that very few schemes detail the content of their programme. There is little said about the duties likely to be specified. There are clearly implications for the preparation of young people for YTS choice. This leads to a consideration of the extent to which the careers service affects the recruitment process. It can be seen that, as things stand, the careers officer has a significant role in trying to match what they know of occupations, training, and the provision of local schemes to their clients. The careers officer is often seen by managing agents, parents, and young people as an influential intermediary, although careers officers are sensitive to this fact, given that they see their role, in most cases, as essentially non-directive. They will therefore try to identify objective criteria for the clients to judge for themselves — type of training, whether the scheme offers premium or basic places, qualifications obtainable, location, knowledge of placements, likelihood of permanent employment. They will try to help the client understand the relationship between the scheme's duties and the client's self-assessment. It can be seen, however, that whilst acknowledging the non-directive approach, the careers service does become an important element in the assessment of young people for YTS. The greater the willingness of managing agents to work in conjunction with the careers service to establish their criteria for selection for all to see, in a way which is clear and specific, directly related to establishing suitability for future training and to providing fuller information to all parties concerned, the less subjective and inefficient the process becomes.

The recruitment process has so far been analysed up to the point at which young people go to an interview with managing agents. To establish what happens at this stage, five managing agents were approached within one Midlands Local Authority and asked to complete the following questionnaire. Scheme (1) is the only scheme surveyed which recruits premium and basic trainees. All the others offer basic places. Scheme (1) offers off-the-job training at its own workshop and looks to employers within the community for its work experience. Scheme (1) has 165 places. Schemes (2), (3), and (4) are with large (i.e. over 50 employees) companies who provide the work experience element of their scheme at their own workplace. Scheme (2) has 20 places, Scheme (3) has 11 places and Scheme (4) has 37 places. Scheme (5) arranges work experience both at its own establishment and with other employers in the community. All training is provided 'in-house'. Scheme (5) has 60 places.

Questionnaire

1 Do you recruit young people (i.e. under 18 years of age) directly into employment, and if so into which occupational area?

Scheme (1)	No
Scheme (2)	Yes. Engineering, clerical.
Scheme (3)	Yes. Clerical, warehousing, but usually referred to YTS.
Scheme (4)	No.
Scheme (5)	Not normally

2 Do you recruit young people into YTS and if so into which occupational area:

Scheme (1)	Yes. Motor vehicle, general building, engineering.
Scheme (2)	Yes. Engineering, clerical.
Scheme (3)	Yes. Retailing.
Scheme (4)	Yes. Retailing, catering, clerical.
Scheme (5)	Yes. Warehousing.

3 Approximately how many of your YTS trainees go directly into employment related to their chosen occupational area?

Scheme (1)	Approximately 85 per cent in each area.
Scheme (2)	99 per cent.
Scheme (3)	99 per cent.
Scheme (4)	Majority in all categories.
Scheme (5)	75 to 80 per cent.

4 **What recruitment and selection procedures do you use?**

Recruitment	*Selection*
Scheme (1)	
Entry in YTS directory. Some direct applications by letter. Application through careers service.	Completion of application form giving qualifications, hobbies, interests. Interview.
Scheme (2)	
Entry in YTS directory. Letter to each school with details of schemes. Some direct applications by letter. Notification of available places at careers centre.	Application form. Preliminary test, i.e. a maths test is given for engineering places which establishes competence in fractions and decimals; the ability to continue a sequence of numbers; knowledge of elementary trigonometry. For clerical places a test is given in arithmetic and spelling, and a short essay is required.
Scheme (3)	
Entry in YTS directory. Direct applicants are referred for submission via the careers service. The intention for 1988/89 is to advertise through each school and ethnic minority papers. Notification of available places at careers centre.	Performance at interview to demonstrate communication skills. Oral communication skill is the main criterion. A test is available to the recruiter which involves arithmetic (addition, subtraction, long division and multiplication), problem solving (e.g. working out staff discount involving percentages), and writing a paragraph on a given subject.

Scheme (4)

Entry in YTS directory. Details of scheme sent to all schools. Attendance at YTS and school careers convention. Notification of availability at careers centre.	Everyone is given a test. The average result is the pass mark. The test consists of basic numeracy (i.e. the 4 rules), a communication exercise, and a problem-solving exercise. Interview.

Scheme (5)

Entry in YTS directory. Notification of available places at the careers centre.	A test of basic numeracy. Interview which looks for interest in storekeeping and sales; motivation and readiness to participate.

5 What requirements do you specify?

Scheme (1)	None	
Scheme (2)	For engineering (craft):	
	GCSE:	Maths grade E
		English grade E
		Physics/Science grade E
		Practical subject grade E
	(technician):	
	GCSE:	Maths grades A-C
		English grades A-C
		Physics grades A-C
		Technical drawing grades A-C
	For clerical:	
Scheme (3)	None.	
Scheme (4)	Keenness, enthusiasm, willingness to learn. Ability to pass the selection test. It is helpful if the applicants can express themselves well.	
Scheme (5)	Reasonable maths and literacy.	

6 What factors are relevant to your choice?

Scheme (1)	Interest shown.
Scheme (2)	Interest and intention to make a career in the occupational area chosen.
Scheme (3)	Good communication, basic literacy and

numeracy, i.e. can read, write, work with the four rules of number, clean appearance.

Scheme (4) Genuine desire to go into this particular occupational area, enthusiasm/ability to communicate. Not necessarily smart appearance but personal hygiene needs to be good.

Scheme (5) Simple maths test, commitment to examinations, attendance at school.

7 What factors are the best predictors of success?

Scheme (1) Interest, effort.
Scheme (2) Enthusiasm, showing interest.
Scheme (3) Communication, i.e. able to answer questions in more than one syllable.
Scheme (4) Leadership qualities, e.g. applicants who have been prefects, guides/scouts, outgoing personalities.
Scheme (5) Interest, enthusiasm, team work, commitment to work, acceptance of authority.

8 How well do you feel examination results correlate to your job requirements?

Scheme (1) Qualifications are not a real indicator.
Scheme (2) We have to have specified qualifications because some training boards have stipulated them. Applicants are recruited on the strength of mock exams. If they are not met exactly by craft recruits there is some flexibility, but technicians not reaching the specified standard would have to re-sit.
Scheme (3) Not at all. As a matter of technique, the interview of applicants is done without recourse to estimated results initially.
Scheme (4) Personality is the most important.
Scheme (5) They are relevant, especially maths and English.

9 Have you ever been presented with a record of achievement by an applicant? If yes, how relevant has it been to your selection procedure?

Scheme (1) No, but it would be helpful.
Scheme (2) No, but it would be useful, if accurate.

Scheme (3)	Yes, on 2 occasions. They were useful. Comments are useful if they include weaknesses. It is important not to rely on academic qualifications.
Scheme (4)	No.
Scheme (5)	No.

In the schemes surveyed, three out of the five always used tests as part of the selection. Why? Scheme (4) is very popular, hence the test could be seen as having a sieving effect, or it could be assumed that there is a level of competency which the test establishes, below which applicants are likely to have difficulty in reaching set standards. Only one of the schemes, (2), specified academic qualifications. Two of the others said no requirements were specified: (1) and (3). Two schemes, (4) and (5), specified the need for evidence of numeracy and literacy. When pushed to specify factors which would be relevant to their choice, Scheme (3) did refer to basic literacy and numeracy, i.e. ability to read, write and do the four rules of number, although communication skills were seen as paramount.

Before drawing conclusions from this analysis, I intend to look at assessment and recruitment for employment.

ASSESSMENT AND RECRUITMENT FOR EMPLOYMENT

Employers will recruit through a variety of avenues. They may not need to advertise vacancies in the press or at careers or job centres because they are well known enough to attract speculative enquiries. Some recruit through personal contacts or through word-of-mouth amongst the existing workforce, and some employers will now recruit young people into employment through taking their YTS trainees on to their workforce. The careers service operating in the area covered by this analysis contacts the larger, traditional recruiters of young people in January/February of each year to establish whether they are likely to be recruiting school leavers, and any such vacancies will be circulated to all schools/colleges in the education authority. The following is a catalogue of vacancies notified to the authority's Careers Service during two weeks of the summer of 1988 and may well serve to illustrate some of the issues relating to assessment and recruitment for employment.

Job Title	*Requirements Specified*	*Duties*	*Age*	*Observations*
Trainee sheet metal worker	Previous experience helpful but not essential	To be trained in all aspects of sheet metal work.	16 years preferred.	What kind of experience could be helpful?
Clerical trainee (employed under YTS)	GCSE in maths and English useful but not essential. Will take clerical aptitude test.	To work on all duties.	16 years preferred.	What does the aptitude test examine? GCSE in maths and English — what does it mean? Is it simply sufficient to have taken the exam?
Engineering technician (employed under YTS)	GCSE grade C in maths, physics, English, craft, design and technology (CDT). Will take an aptitude test. Must be interested in engineering.	To follow a company training scheme.	16 years preferred	What does the aptitude test examine?
Craft apprenticeship (employed under YTS)	GCSE in maths, physics, English. Grades not important. Candidates take aptitude test.	To be trained in the workshop.		What does the aptitude test examine? Are grades unrelated to standards required for vocational courses?

Job Title	*Requirements Specified*	*Duties*	*Age*	*Observations*
Trainee moulder (employed under YTS)	Must be capable of taking a college course (City and Guilds and E.I.T.B. Certificate). Will sit aptitude test.	YTS eligible.		What does the aptitude test examine? How does an industry with a poor local local image make itself attractive and likely to be incorporated in a careers education programme?
Trainee bricklayer	Some experience in brick-work, stonework is required. Prefers ex-YTS young person.		17–18 years.	The demand for experience dictates the need for an ex-YTS trainee, but at 17 years the most likely recruit would be in the middle of YTS and, in leaving the scheme, s/he would jeopardise prospects of obtaining a vocational qualification.
Trainee printer	GCSE grade C in maths, English, and science. Mechanically minded to maintain machinery.		16–17 years only.	Why are the grades required? The group who hold such qualifications are more likely to be considering further and higher education.

				Printing may not figure as an occupational area much discussed in careers education, because of providing few openings and an image of de-skilling.
Production control clerk (employed under YTS)	Reasonable GCSEs especially in maths. Some clerical experience is an advantage.		16–17 years.	What is a 'reasonable' GCSE in maths? What arithmetic ability is required? What would constitute 'clerical experience'? Business studies at school?
Apprentice toolsetter (employed under YTS)	Must be keen and have an interest in engineering. Should have taken related subjects.	Setting up machines, putting plastic moulds into machines.	16 years.	The choice of subjects taken at school is seen as more important than grades. Why? Is the *choice* an indication of interest? Does having taken a related course assure sufficient potential for training if the 'interest' is there?

Job Title	*Requirements Specified*	*Duties*	*Age*	*Observations*
Apprentice toolmaker (employed under YTS)	GCSE grades A–C in metalwork, maths, and technical drawing.	To train to make plastic injection moulds.	16 years.	The requirements are almost those of technicians within the industry. Would the vacancy as it stands attract that calibre of young person? The typical candidate considering engineering at craft level would be unlikely to reach that level.
Dental surgery assistant	Preferably GCSE English and maths.	To learn all aspects of dental reception and nursing.	16 years.	GCSE maths and English the only stated criteria. Will it be sufficient just to have sat the exam and obtained the basic grade? How does this requirement relate to the job?
Assistant to electrician	Must be good with hands. Aptitude more important than qualifications.	Drilling, fitting screws. Support work for the electrician.	School leaver.	

General assistant	GCSE English, maths, grades D/E. Must be able to count (dealing with stock, 3,000 items).	General warehouse duties, counting stock, putting up orders. (There is the possibility of taking a correspondence course).	16–17 years.	
Sewing machine operator	Some experience preferred.	General sewing work plus overlocking.	16+ years.	It is highly unlikely that someone who had not done relevant YTS would be competent enough to apply.
Trainee contracts clerk	GCSE English and maths, grade C and above. Ability to type. Typing test at interview.	Sales ledger work, dealing with credit notes: checking and filing invoices and contracts.		What numerical and communication skills are required?
Maintenance trainee and toolroom technician apprentice	At least two GCSEs grade A–C in maths and science, and preferably in English too.		16 years.	No description of duties. Note the discrepancy between technician apprenticeship requirements and apprentice toolmaker (craft level) requirements earlier recorded.

Job Title	Requirements Specified	Duties	Age	Observations
Trainee telephone sales	Must be good at figures and be capable of calculating lengths and weights. Good communication by phone and letter.	To be trained in all aspects of sales work, enquiries, quotations, orders.	16–18 years.	
Trainee machine manager (employed under YTS)	GCSE in maths and English, grade C/D. Must have eye for detail, not colour blind.	To do general and machine printing.	16 years.	What mathematical and language skills are actually required? What are the duties to which the requirements relate?
Office junior	Must be keen, able to type; have a flexible approach to employers.	Typing, telephone and reception work.	16 years.	How is keenness to be evaluated? — choice of relevant subjects? Effectiveness at interview? Commitment to school work. What level of typing ability is actually required?

Trainee maintenance fitter	Must be keen and willing to learn; reliable, numerate, literate	To repair and maintain industrial machinery, also cranes, tractors, excavators, and diesel engine repair.	16–18 years.	Keenness, willingness to learn, reliability could be difficult to establish at time of submission. A school report may have been for the use of the careers office at the time of the vocational guidance interview but this information is given in confidence and may, in any case, have little or nothing to say about keenness or willingness to learn in the context of employment.

What factors for consideration have emerged?

Imprecise or unspecified selection criteria

As in the case of recruitment to YTS, vague terms, open to wide interpretation, are being used. What are 'reasonable GCSEs'? The extent to which the terms can be made precise depends upon the willingness of the employer to describe the duties and relate them to minimum competencies, thus specifying their assessment criteria. This procedure does not come easily to most employers, and obviously there are implications for the training of vacancy-taking staff and for those writing recruitment literature.

Inadequacy of information base

Analysis of skills and aptitudes is an important factor in the recruitment procedure, but employers can specify characteristics such as 'hard-working', 'reliable', as the sole assessment criteria. How one person interprets 'hard-working' or 'reliable' may not be the same as how someone else interprets it. In some cases the report from school may indicate this,but it may not. Should I, as the careers officer, not submit, therefore, or should I deduce the information from other comments; and how valid would this be? Conversely, the requirement for academic qualifications is often substituted by employers for personal characteristics, i.e. 'have three GCSEs at grade C' may be equated with being a reliable, hard-working person. Factors considered as important by both employers and managing agents, such as interest and commitment, may well be established, it is felt, by interview; but how effective an instrument of selection is the interview? An interview presents an immediate impression at a moment in time. The interviewee is seen out of context, out of the environment in which s/he usually functions, which may present a distortion of the truth. The interview is a dialogue and will be bound by the limits the interviewer imposes. The difficulties presented by the interview as a technique of selection can to some extent be mitigated by supporting evidence, but who provides this information? Is it valid? Can it be used effectively?

School reports produced for the use of careers officers for vocational guidance are confidential and not for the benefit of employers. Reports produced for parents may equally be inadequate in providing the kind of information employers require. Different ways of recording information to take account of competencies related to employment and characteristics sought by employers and managing agents are needed. The foregoing has implications for the development of records of achievement as a way of dealing with these problems. The government aims to set in place by 1990 national arrangements for the introduction of records of achievement. As a result, school leavers will be required to have a completed record of their achievement. A profile is a document which can record others' assessments of pupils across a wide range of abilities, including skills (subject, specific, and cross-curricular), attitudes, personal qualities and interests, achievements, experiences, and subjects attainments. The development of the profile ought to involve the pupil at all stages, and is generally known as the formative process, or profiling. The summative document, sometimes known as the record of achievement, draws together the various strands of the profiling process. One of the obvious uses of such a document could be in presenting a more rounded picture of candidates for jobs or courses than can be provided by a list of examination results or an interview, thus helping potential users to decide how candidates could be employed, and for which jobs, training schemes, or courses they are likely to be suitable.

Lack of established competencies

As well as using examination passes as a personality indicator, employers seem to be asking for certain examination results as a quick and easy way of assuring themselves of an adequate level of competency in reading, writing, and comprehension. Employers will not know what having GCSE in English at grade C means. Careers officers will know, however, that the pool of young people with grade C passes in English and maths who will want to apply for a specific vacancy is much smaller than that pool of young people with average competency in oral, written and number work. The GCE/CSE results in Table 6.1 reinforce the point.

The onus is on the educational establishment to explain the level of competency which the receiver of a grade D, E, or F has acquired. There is something unsatisfactory about an educational system which leaves employers and trainers still specifying the need to establish levels of literacy and numeracy by using their own tests.

Table 6.1 DES 10 per cent leavers survey 1979

GCE/CSE results in:	*English (% per grade)*	*Maths (% per grade)*
Grade		
A }		
B }	34.5	25.6
C/1 }		
D/2	13.1	8.2
E/3	14.1	11.6
E/4	11.6	13.9
E/5	4.7	9.1
U or fail	3.9	8.8
Not entered	18.6	22.8

Source: Department of Education and Science.

Lack of awareness of youth labour market

From the survey of vacancies it could be seen that some employers have not caught up with the trends relating to youth employment. This is particularly important given the dramatic reduction in the youth labour market that will shortly begin to take effect.

Technician recruitment has long been difficult because employers are looking for a calibre of applicant which very often sees its future in further or higher education. A young person with four GCSE passes will more likely to be encouraged into the pursuit of a professional rather than a technician-level career. This may have implications for devising new ways of training technician apprentices, starting at a different base and extending the training period.

Employers who are not aware of the system of recruiting to YTS may well miss out on suitable applicants if their timing is wrong. The YTS recruitment procedure has become centralized through the careers service. There is early knowledge, in the main, of where places are going to be offered. It has the facility of offering places early and without any great effort or need for 'hunting' on the part of the young person. Young people in the system, with the offer of a place, are loathe to start looking outside it for alternatives. Employers need more than ever, therefore, to notify vacancies early so that they are considered when decisions are being made.

Similarly, young people with an offer of YTS may prefer to gain the training offered rather than accept a job without training, so more employers may be forced to offer training themselves. Likewise, young people who have spent some time on YTS may not wish to actively seek work midway through, and as a consequence lose out on obtaining qualifications.

Lack of adequate job descriptions

Very few of the sources of recruitment information surveyed gave anything but the briefest of job descriptions. There is the assumption that everyone knows what is entailed in the job simply by reference to the job title. This has significant implications for the preparation of young people through careers education programmes.

A survey of six careers education programmes spread throughout five local authorities illustrates that the recruitment issue is dealt with in terms of job seeking skills, application form filling, interview techniques, letters of application, and curriculum vitae preparation. Two specifically looked at selection tests. In terms of providing occupational information, it is interesting to note how the programmes tended to approach the subject. Occupational information in the schools surveyed is approached through occupational groupings. Three out of the six careers education programmes uses Jobs, Ideas and Information Generator Computer Assisted Learning (JIIGCAL). Pupils are required to indicate interest areas which are linked to jobs. The interest groupings are practical, natural, economic, artistic, social services, literacy. Other schools tended to use groupings based on CRAC's 'Signpost' headings — scientific, social service, general service, persuasive, literacy, artistic, computational, practical, nature, outdoor/active. The programmes tend to encourage an individual or group investigation of an occupational group or an individual job study based on pupils' interests. I relate this to a finding I noted when looking at vacancies notified to the careers service, i.e. that in some cases employers may be offering jobs in occupational areas that are not readily identifiable in the occupational groupings, or which are not easily assimilated into a group, or which are not likely to be evidenced within the careers education programme because they represent jobs or industries which are not well known or fashionable and are unlikely to be chosen for research by pupils initiating their own job research. The validity of using such categories as 'persuasive', 'artistic', 'literacy', may be questionable. At the level where the heading 'literacy', for example, is going to be significant and characteristic, the majority of pupils will be excluded by lack of qualifications. Occupational groups may be a useful device to organize information but it would be more helpful if the groupings were derived from local/regional opportunities at a level at which school leavers are likely to enter. The need for more localized information on the labour market, and the job types commonly entered, exists, and such information needs to be fed into careers education programmes. One accepts the need for a balance between the parochial and limited view of opportunities and the school of thought which maintains that 'anything is possible', but what is being argued for here is the need for a realistic approach using local information, making careers education programmes relevant to pupils' likely experience rather than starting with interests, strongly linked to subjects, which force job 'connections' which are often competitive, untypical, scarce, or regional.

Chapter Seven

ASSESSMENT METHODS AND EQUAL OPPORTUNITIES

Merlin Rangel

The purpose of this chapter is to examine current assessment practices, their strengths and weaknesses, and to suggest ways in which such methods may be used to enhance equal opportunities in relation to gender, race, and social class.

The Sex Discrimination Acts, 1975, 1986, makes it unlawful to discriminate directly, or indirectly, on grounds of sex or marital status, or to apply requirements or conditions which have a disproportionately disadvantageous effect on people of a particular sex or marital status where these cannot be justified. The Race Relations Act, 1976 makes it unlawful to discriminate directly, or indirectly, on grounds of colour, race, nationality, ethnic or national origin, and to apply requirements or conditions which have a disproportionately disadvantageous effect on people of a particular racial group, and which cannot be justified on non-racial grounds. Each act makes it unlawful to use discriminatory employment advertising and to apply pressure to discriminate or to aid discrimination by another person.

The 1960s and early 1970s witnessed increasing resistance to assessment in educational guidance and the counselling professions. Such views are still held quite strongly in some circles, especially as assessment of personal and social attributes are complex and often highly subjective.

Changes in the labour market and the emphasis on skills training have led to a renewed interest in assessment techniques for recruitment and selection by employers and training agents. The most recent developments in the National Curriculum and the associated requirements for assessment and testing at regular intervals leave us in no doubt that assessment is here to stay for the foreseeable future. How, then, do practitioners deal with the conflicting demands of assessment methods and the needs of those subjected to them? Clearly the issue is a complex one and no simple solutions are offered here. Rather, current studies are reviewed which indicate the merits and limitations of different methods of assessment for a variety of purposes.

The need for assessment *per se* is not questioned, since its value as an indicator of progress or as a facilitator of change is generally recognized as a positive thing. However, the requirements of the Sex Discrimination Act and the Race Relations Act raise questions about the fairness of methods used, and consequently the justification of some commonly held assumptions which until recently have been taken for granted; for instance,the view that boys are better than girls at science or that ethnic minorities unrealistically over-aspire. Some of these assumptions and practices are examined in relation to educational choice, educational attainment, vocational aspirations, and the recruitment, selection, and training of potential employees.

EDUCATIONAL CHOICE AND ATTAINMENT

It is well known that subjects studied by girls vary widely from those studied by boys beyond the third year of secondary education. Other than core curriculum subjects, a larger percentage of girls take biological science, languages and vocational subjects. Boys, by contrast, more frequently study sciences and technical subjects. These differences are later reflected in differences in occupations entered into by women and men.

The impact of the Sex Discrimination Act on subject choices was investigated in 1980, five years after its implementation. The findings are well documented in a report undertaken on behalf of the Equal Opportunities Commission by NFER-NELSON (Pratt, Bloomfield, and Seale, 1984), and is highly recommended reading. Some of its findings are briefly examined here. The survey found that although the pattern of educational provision in schools had changed to some extent, the pattern of subject choices had not altered as much. The majority of schools (75 per cent) tended to abide passively by the act in so far as they did not deliberately discriminate in the options offered to their pupils. A minority (10 per cent) had been pro-active in establishing strong equal opportunities policies and practices to promote non-traditional subject selection, while a similar minority (15 per cent) displayed poor practices. They found some evidence of discrimination in a few schools where some subjects were still being offered to one sex only!

Factors influencing subject choices were broadly related to gender, administrative constraints, and stereotyped attitudes of teachers and pupils alike. (Unfortunately, parental attitudes were not included, but would have been a valuable source of information since parents continue to be the strongest single influence on the educational and occupational choices of young people.) The most statistically important factor determining subject choice was the sex of the pupil. The majority of pupils continued to opt for traditional subjects. However, where non-traditional subjects were chosen in the third year, there was a tendency to maintain this pattern in relation to further and higher education courses and vocational training.

Choices were also limited by timetables and the structure of option groups rather than by pupils' desire to study particular subjects. In some cases, such as science and technology, links with other subjects were a limiting prerequisite.

Attitudes of teachers frequently influenced the advice given about the suitability of subjects. Teachers who were least inclined to encourage non-traditional choices were those who taught physical sciences, craft, and technical subjects. They believed that lack of ability and irrelevance to girls' careers were justification for excluding them from their subjects. A more indirect approach was taken by other teachers, who took the view that providing neutral information enabled pupils to make independent choices. Of even greater relevance to the issue of subject selection were the stereotyped views held by the pupils themselves. They were even less inclined to believe that both sexes were equally *capable* of studying all subjects. Their perceptions of occupations and domestic roles displayed similar stereotyping.

Assuming that the above-mentioned factors influencing subject choice are based on pupils' achievement and experiences up to and including their third year at school, it would not be unreasonable to conclude that some teachers' and pupils' perceptions of differential aptitude and attainment are that abilities are gender-related. Their views would appear to be based largely on subjective assessments.

These views are challenged on the basis of more objective evidence, which shows that measured abilities are age-, rather than sex-related, and that pupils' cognitive skills are more similar than they are different up to and including the third year of secondary education.

The figures in Table 7.1 show average scores of third year pupils from a representative sample of Birmingham schools for six mental abilities.

Table 7.1 Average socres of third year girls and boys on six tests

Mental ability	*N*	*Girls* *x*	*S.D.*	*N*	*Boys* *x*	*S.D.*
Non-verbal	1,102	49.58	16.20	707	47.87	16.58
Spatial	1,466	28.12	12.53	1,005	29.14	13.60
Clerical	164	209.72	55.22	240	186.32	55.64
Speed						
Clerical	164	5.39%	4.46%	240	6.40%	5.57%
Accuracy		errors	errors		errors	errors
Numerical	105	10.72	5.58	161	10.59	5.49
Verbal	105	10.75	5.58	161	11.62	6.57

Note: N = number in sample; x = mean; S.D. = standard deviation.

The tests were used as an aid to subject choices in some secondary schools in the Birmingham Local Education Authority. The differences in sample sizes are due to the fact that most schools used tests to measure those abilities they were less likely to have information on, and a few used additional tests.

The average scores on five mental abilities are nearly the same for girls and boys. The only test which shows an apparently greater difference in performance between the sexes is clerical speed. The girls' average scores are slightly, but not significantly, better than the boys for non-verbal reasoning, clerical speed, clerical accuracy, and numerical reasoning. The boys' average scores are slightly, but not significantly, higher for spatial ability and verbal reasoning.

A brief description of each test and the way it relates to subsequent educational attainment demonstrates that differences in measured abilities between girls and boys seem to be more closely associated with learning rather than with inherent sex differences. The test of non-verbal reasoning (sometimes known as general reasoning) measures the ability to solve problems using diagrams and sequential thinking. It correlates strongly with attainment in the sciences and humanities and gives a good indication of level of ability. The test of spatial perception measures ability to visualize two and three dimensional figures and to understand abstract ideas. It correlates well with scientific, technical and practical subjects.

Clerical speed gives a measure of the rate at which information is checked, while clerical accuracy indicates the percentage of errors made on the degree of accuracy acquired in checking information. These two mental skills are weak predictors of educational attainment, but more efficient measures of training in clerical skills. The numerical and verbal reasoning tests measure attainment and reasoning skills with words and numerical concepts. The tests correlate strongly with mathematical and verbal subjects, and in particular with maths and English.

Each of the tests have been correlated with CSE and O level examinations in twenty-eight subjects (Rangel and Pendlebury 1980) using a sample of 2,169 pupils' scores. Correlation coefficient range from 0.04 to 0.80. The total profile of six mental abilities is a strong predictor of examination and educational attainment. (The correlation coefficient is in the order of 0.76.) The three best predictors of general learning ability are verbal, numerical, and non-verbal reasoning.

The data in Table 7.1 show that the abilities of boys and girls in the third year are similar rather than different, and that pupils can and should be encouraged to consider a wide range of subjects. The data also supports the view that access to non-traditional subjects and occupations is not limited by gender. It is unwise at this early stage to restrict subject choices to narrow vocational avenues. The emphasis should be a broader educational and personal development which enables the individual to be flexible about occupational decisions and benefit from new opportunities as they emerge.

One further issue affecting the nature and development of measured mental abilities needs mentioning, as it has far-reaching implications for fair assessment. Spearman's (1927) theory of universal positive correlation claims, on the basis of empirical evidence, that any two measured skills are positively related and that each consists of a 'g', or general factor, and an 's', or specific factor. The implications for educational and occupational choices suggest pupils who demonstrate ability in one area are likely to demonstrate ability in other areas and that differences in test scores tend to reflect differences in experience rather than a lack of ability.

VOCATIONAL ASPIRATIONS

Debate about the process of occupational choice remains inconclusive, with some social scientists emphasizing the constraining influences of personal, social, and economic pressures, while others argue for a rational, informed, developmental approach to decision-making. Research to date strongly suggests that occupational choices of school-leavers are largely accidental and are based on inadequate knowledge (Clarke 1980). Some of the factors influencing occupational choice are reviewed in order to gain some insight into the relative meaning of the concept of choice. These are social class, sex, ability, and interests.

Clarke (1980) found that level of aspiration was closely related to parental education and occupation, regardless of the child's own ability. School-leavers frequently choose the same careers as their parents. Pupils whose parents worked in unskilled and semi-skilled jobs tended to leave education early, while those from more affluent homes had higher rates of entry into further education. Likewise, pupils from grammar school were more likely to enter university and professional occupations, while those from secondary modern schools were less likely to continue their education, and had less ambitious aspirations. Gupta (1977), in studying the effects of race on educational and vocational choice, found an upward trend in occupational mobility between pupils and their parents. He also found that Asian pupils were more ambitious than their English counterparts, and explained the differences in terms of greater motivation and parental expectations. Changes in occupational level are increasingly accompanied by higher levels of educational attainment, though they are not always reflected in careers advice received or jobs obtained.

It has already been stated that males and females do not differ in their potential ability. However, patterns of occupational choices show marked differences between the sexes, and three observations are associated with these differences. First, that the national ratio of girls to boys opting for science and maths is 1:6; second, girls are less ambitious (or less confident) than boys in their choice of higher education courses and institutions; third, that women are inclined to be motivated by occupations of 'social benefit' while men are motivated by 'self-benefit' (Clarke 1980).

The effects of ability and attainment are possibly the strongest influences on occupational aspirations. More able pupils are motivated by positive self-images and aspirations. Less able pupils, on the other hand, tend to base their choices on negative reasons, often because they are unable to fulfil their original ambitions or because they have limited alternatives (this is as true of subject choices as it is of occupational choices). It is important to distinguish here between perceived and actual ability. Perceived ability is known to have a strong influence on attainment, in terms of self-fulfilling prophecies which may lead to under-achievement with some and unrealistic over-aspiration with others.

The effect of interests on occupational choice is less obvious than the effect of abilities. Practical interests seem to be linked directly with practical occupations, but other areas of work are less clearly related to interests. Interest in some academic subjects also appears to have connections with job preferences; for instance scientific, technical, and some social careers have related subject-entry requirements. The influence of interests on occupational choice and occupational success is often confused by teachers and counsellors who are unable to distinguish between the relative effects of interests and abilities on occupational choice and occupational success. Knowing what interests an individual can assist him/her to make appropriate choices and maintain the motivation to succeed. However, the strength of interest alone does not indicate the likelihood of occupational success, since success is primarily dependent upon competence which in turn may be enhanced by interests. For these reasons measures of interest are just as important in the decision-making process of an individual of low or average ability, who may have a smaller range of choices available to him/her, as they are to the more able individual who has a potentially wider range of occupational choice.

The complexities of factors affecting both educational and vocational choice only serve to highlight the need for individuals to be well-informed about themselves and about the opportunity structure. Only then can a realistic compromise between the two types of information result in personal satisfaction and optimum use of human resources. The process of self-evaluation is best achieved by a combination of assessment methods. Some positive approaches associated with educational and vocational choices are:

- look for indications of positive achievements;
- supplement information which is lacking or absent by some other method of assessment;
- examine the reliability of information on which recommendations are made;
- encourage non-traditional choices, particularly where they enhance personal development or increase opportunities;
- encourage active participation by the individual in the assessment and decision-making processes.

ASSESSMENT FOR RECRUITMENT AND SELECTION

Assessment for recruitment and selection was, until relatively recently, based largely on information obtained from application forms, references, and interviews. Common to each of these methods is the highly subjective nature of the assessment. The need to reduce bias and improve objectivity led to an increase in the use of psychometric tests, and in particular to tests of ability and interest; personality assessment was less common but is now gaining ground. Objective assessment, however, is not necessarily synonymous with fair or valid assessment. Poorly designed, improperly administered, and incorrectly interpreted tests are almost certain to result in poorer selection decisions than those based on some well tried and tested subjective methods. It is ultimately the responsibility of the test user to ensure that his/her choice of tests meets the minimum requirements. These are given below in relation to test construction, administration, and interpretation.

Item content

Test items or questions must be, and must be seen to be, related to the skills required on the job. They should not be biased in favour of one gender or ethnic group. Mechanical test items, for example, appear to be more obviously associated with performing mechanical tasks than the diagrams in a test of non-verbal reasoning which claim to measure non-verbal or general ability. Items with ambiguous meanings are misleading and should be eliminated. On the other hand, those items which appear to have some connection with the job or learning task can enhance motivation. By comparison, a familiar criticism of questions asked at interviews is that some have doubtful meaning or no relevance to job performance and can be difficult to justify.

Sampling

A test is designed for use with a particular group or population and should be standardized or put on trial on such a group. It should not, therefore, be used for individuals who differ widely from the original sample, as this will lead to errors in the meaning of scores. Tests that have been standardized on an all white population, for example, should not be used with individuals from ethnic minority groups as their respective experiences are likely to be quite different. Likewise, tests standardized on an all-male population should not be used to select females. It does not follow that the standards required of one group are necessarily the same for others.

Norms

Norms are closely associated with sampling. A test score is of little value unless it is compared with other scores from which it gets its relative meaning. It is necessary that comparisons of scores be made with appropriate norm-groups. For instance, norms based on 14 to 16-year-old school pupils would not be relevant for the selection of computer programmers. Although one may be a sub-group of the other, the two represent quite different samples. Similarly, norms based on male engineering apprentices cannot be used for the selection of female apprentices, as the experiences and therefore measured abilities of girls may be quite different. Girls may be just as successful in occupational training with lower selection scores. Pearn (1977) found this to be true of Asian apprentices for whom the average score of successful trainees was similar to the average score of unsuccessful white trainees.

Some employers argue that separate norms amount to setting double standards or the lowering of standards in favour of one group. This is not so. What they fail to understand is that tests are not equally fair assessment tools for different gender and ethnic groups, since they measure achievement as well as aptitude or ability. If separate norms are used they should be validated and should demonstrate that the (lower) scores are equally efficient predictors of subsequent performance. The Civil Service has successfully used separate norms in order to improve its representation of potential female employees in its selection procedure (Pearn, Kandola and Mottram 1987).

Reliability

The reliability of a test is a measure of the extent to which test scores remain consistent from one occasion to another, or the extent to which a test is internally consistent. The reliability of a test indicates the amount of trust that can be placed on a score as a measure of the presence of some human attribute. Two types of reliability are generally given in test manuals — test re-test reliability, which is a measure of the extent to which test scores remain consistent from one occasion to another, and split half reliability which is the extent to which a test is internally consistent. Reliability is expressed as a correlation coefficient, which is the degree of agreement or relationship between pairs of test scores. Although there is no agreed minimum reliability coefficient, it is unwise to use a test with reliability lower than 0.80. In other words, the lower the reliability, the more likely the score is to vary significantly if the test is taken again. By comparison, the average reliability of subjective assessments such as reports, performance ratings and, in particular, interviews, ranges from 0.20 to 0.40. This is not surprising since subjective judgements are influenced by a wide range of factors, only some of which are relevant to the attributes being assessed.

Validity

The validity of a test is a measure of the extent to which a test actually measures what it claims to measure. Validity is also expressed as a correlation coefficient. Three types of validity are of interest to test users. The first is construct validity, which is the extent to which test items measure a particular construct or human attribute such as word fluency, interest, or anxiety. The second, concurrent validity, is the extent to which a test correlates with a parallel or other test of proven validity. It is most useful as a means of checking the consistency of a behaviour or skill where other information is lacking. The third type, criterion validity, indicates the accuracy with which subsequent performance can be predicted or estimated from a test score; for example, success in examinations or occupational training.

Validity coefficients range from -1.0 through 0.0 to +1.0. A -1.0 (minus one) indicates a perfect negative relationship between two variables; for example, altitude and density of air. A 0.0 (zero) correlation indicates no relationship between two variables, for example ability and size of head. A +1.0 (plus one) correlation shows a perfect positive relationship between two variables. Because human characteristics are complex and difficult to control, perfect correlations are unobtainable. However, the higher or closer a correlation coefficient is to +1.0 the stronger the relationship between the two variables. Correlation coefficients of +0.40 and above show that there is a definite relationship between the test score and the predictor variable, and that the score should be taken into consideration, though other information should not be ignored.

Data on test validity is seriously lacking in a large number of tests currently in use. A survey undertaken on behalf of the Institute of Personnel Management (Incomes Data Services Ltd 1985) found that over 50 per cent of the test users they surveyed had not undertaken any validation of their tests and of the remainder, the studies were considered to be inadequate. Unless a test is validated there is no way of knowing what it is measuring, let alone whether it is an efficient indicator of some subsequent behaviour.

Standardized administration of tests

Rigorous standardization of test administration increases the probability that all individuals undergo the same procedure. This process in turn improves the reliability of the test score and reduces the number of error factors that might influence the score. The standardization process also permits comparisons to be made between different individuals at different times and in different places. Similar comparisons are difficult to obtain with subjective assessments such as teachers' or trainees' ratings, and are even less likely with self-assessment.

In order to meet the requirements of standardized administration, test users need to be trained to varying levels of competence, depending upon the degree of sophistication of the tests. Potential test users sometimes criticize the training requirements as being overly stringent, but unless standards are closely adhered to the strengths of the objective psychometric assessments are likely to be undermined, with the consequence that the value of the information is reduced.

Interpretation of scores

As with administration, so too interpretation of test scores is a complex issue which justifies the training demands made by test publishers. Interpretation of test scores can be divided into presentation of factual information and analytical interpretation. The further test users stray from the recommended rules and guidelines, the more likely they are to introduce subjective bias and inaccuracies.

A test score does not indicate the amount of knowledge or psychological attribute an individual possesses in absolute terms. It is an indication of how well s/he has performed in relation to others. It is a more accurate measure than subjective ratings so far as a test score indicates the relative position of an individual in relation to others as well as the percentage who have more or less of a given characteristic. In these respects, test scores are similar to examination scores, but superior to rating scales which only indicate relative position.

Test scores do not provide cause-effect explanations and therefore interpretations needs to be made with caution, and in conjunction with other biographical data. Thus while the score itself is important, of equal or greater importance is the meaning or interpretation given to the score. A score interpreted as aptitude can have a more limiting effect than if it is interpreted as attainment. Aptitude is sometimes understood to mean potential or inherent ability. Consequently, an applicant may be rejected because s/he is thought to lack the necessary skill. Attainment, on the other hand, is interpreted as skill level reached at a particular point in time. This interpretation of a score is more flexible, as it recognizes the role of training or learning in raising levels of competence. The distinction sometimes made between aptitude and ability is misleading, since a score which represents measured ability is the result of a complex interaction between aptitude and attainment which has not yet been satisfactorily understood or explained.

Interpretation of assessment which results in disproportionate representation of one gender or ethnic group is illegal. Anyone considering using tests may wish to take into account the following points (Rangel, 1987):

1 Establish a policy and code of practice, i.e. consider:
   - why tests are used;
   - when tests are used;
   - training for test users;
   - how results are fed back to successful and unsuccessful applicants;
   - how long results are kept 'live'.

2 Identify skills/attributes to be tested:
   - undertake job analysis;
   - identify any other relevant features.

3 Choose appropriate tests and refer to manual for:
   - 'design' sample;
   - reliability data;
   - norms;
   - validity data.

4 Norms should:
   - be representative of an organization's needs;
   - not discriminate on grounds of sex;
   - not discriminate on grounds of race.

5 Generate 'in house' norms:
   - collect raw scores within the organization;
   - feed back scores to publisher;
   - keep separate norms for sub-groups;
   - review and update norms at regular intervals.

6 Establish a selection procedure:
   - inform applicants of sequence of events;
   - send applicants information or example questions in advance.

7 Test administration:
   - allow adequate time, with a break if necessary;

- follow standardized administration;
- keep groups small (manageable) to permit close supervision;
- explain the purpose of the tests;
- use tests with practice examples;
- explain feedback process before applicants leave.

8 Interpretation of results:
- avoid cut-off points or scores;
- use 'bands' of tolerance;
- use other biographical data as well;
- look for alternative evidence where low scores occur.

9 Feedback of results:
- successful applicant should be informed at interview or as appropriate;
- unsuccessful applicants should be informed as soon as possible in some meaningful way;
- consider whether unsuccessful applicants can reapply at a later stage.

10 Validate tests:
- follow up progress of trainees;
- monitor training progress of sub-group;
- modify selection criteria if necessary.

11 Monitor selection procedure:
- keep records of applicants; percentage male, female, ethnic group;
- check percentage success/failure rates;
- modify policy and practice to ensure equal opportunities for all applicants;
- monitor training progress of sub-group;
- modify selection criteria if necessary.

ASSESSMENT AND ETHNIC ORIGIN

The Swann Committee, in its investigations into the educational achievements of ethnic minority groups compared with the majority white population, reported that a School-Leavers' Survey taken in six Local Educational Authorities with large ethnic minority populations showed that West Indian children in every measure did much less well in examinations than their white peers. Asian children, on the other hand, achieved very much on a level with their white counterparts with the single exception of examinations in English (Swann 1985). An earlier Government Select Committee (Select Committee on Race Relations 1977) and the Rampton Committee (Rampton 1981) repeatedly found that black children, especially West Indians, achieved less well in the British education system than white pupils. Achievements are examined under three broad headings, namely teachers estimates or reports, public examinations, and psychometric tests.

Studies of teachers' estimates or reports are scarce, but Haynes's research (1971) provides some valuable insights into the inherent inequalities of the process of assessment as well as their consequences. Haynes examined the value of learning tests (in preference to intelligence tests) as predictors of the learning ability of 125 Asian pupils with poor knowledge of English and 40 English pupils in the first year of junior school. The results of the tests were compared with teachers' assessments of pupils' performance at the end of their second year and with 28 personal and social variables. Although the samples are small and the results cannot be generalized, they shed light on some important relationships between achievements and cognitive abilities, as well as on social and personal factors.

From her results, Haynes concluded that learning tests were more efficient predictors of learning ability for English pupils than they were for Asian pupils. The scores of English pupils were significantly different from those of the Asian pupils on both learning and intelligence tests. Verbal learning tests in particular were the best predictors of subsequent learning but were superior predictors for English pupils. Non-verbal intelligence tests were better indicators of subsequent achievement for Asian pupils. Similarly, teachers' estimates of pupils' achievements were less reliable for Asian than for English pupils. Of greater interest was the relationship between pupils' performances on tests and teachers' attitudes and expectations. There was some indication that schools with higher percentages of immigrant pupils, and positive attitudes and expectations of teachers, were associated with better scores on all tests obtained by Indian pupils. Examining the issue of educational progress, Scarr's study (Scarr *et al.* 1983) of over 1,000 pupils in a Warwickshire town showed that West Indian pupils lagged behind white and Asian children from pre-school age to the end of their school careers. The gap in achievement widened with years spent in school, and average scores declined for the West Indian children between the ages of 8 and 12 years by 4.6 IQ points, and increased for the Asian children by 4.4 points. While these differences in scores are in themselves cause for concern, the interpretation placed on them is likely to have even more damaging results. Scarr reported that only 2 per cent of West Indians gained places in 'grammar streams' of local secondary schools, compared with

75 per cent of white middle-class pupils.

The need for valid assessment methods cannot be overstressed when made in relation to critical decisions. Haynes (1971) drew attention to an article in *The Times* December 1969, which mentioned evidence of an increase in the number of immigrant pupils being transferred to special schools for the educationally subnormal based on restricted measures of mental ability. The long-term consequences of such inappropriate judgements carry moral as well as educational and vocational implications.

Public examinations

It is recognized that assessment is often necessary to facilitate change or indicate progress. As a source of information it can act in at least two ways. Positive assessment is a measure of the presence of ability. Negative or low assessment, however, is not necessarily evidence of lack of ability; it may be lack of evidence of ability. It is necessary, therefore, that scores are not interpreted at face value only. Where assessment methods are likely to be less valid for a particular group, underlying causes may be an equally important part of the interpretation. Examination results of ethnic minorities fall into this category (but the implications may also be applicable in relation to social class and the indigenous population).

Rutter's research (1982), carried out over several years on the achievements of black (West Indian) pupils only who stayed on in education beyond the fifth year, challenges some stereotyped assumptions and research evidence associated with low achievement of black pupils which is said to reflect the social and educational deprivation of West Indian homes and parents. His study was based on 2,700 pupils from twelve inner London comprehensive schools, of which 800 pupils were in the fifth and sixth forms; 650 white and 150 black. His findings are examined here in further detail.

Rutter found that a larger percentage (47 per cent) of West Indians stayed on in the sixth form and made 'dramatic' gains both in their exam results and in their job prospects. By comparison, the 24 per cent white pupils who stayed on also benefited, but to a lesser extent. Eleven per cent of West Indian pupils left school at Easter without any qualifications, compared with 28 per cent of white pupils. Apart from the top 7 per cent white pupils who had five or more O levels, compared with 1 per cent West Indians, the latter group obtained better examination qualifications overall.

Rutter noted that of all pupils who stayed on in the sixth form for an extra year, a quarter gained five O levels and after two years nearly two-thirds gained at least one A level. Even those who did not improve their grades improved their prospects of getting better jobs. Only 20 per cent of sixth form pupils went into unskilled work, compared with 40 per cent from the fifth form. Similar comments have more recently been made about pupils on Certificate of Pre-Vocational Education (PVE) courses, implying that the extra year in education enhances their social and personal development.

Commenting on IQ scores, Rutter points out that the average score for all pupils staying on for one extra year was 103, and for two years it was 108. However, in both instances more than one in ten had IQ scores below 90. West Indian pupils' measured IQ and reading scores were lower than those of the white pupils, but higher than those of West Indian born and educated, or partially educated, overseas. The gap narrowed by the age of 14 years, except for reading where those born in Britain did better.

With regard to family background, it was found that although West Indian pupils came from more deprived homes, their parents were more likely to take an active interest in their school work than white parents. Although their educational qualifications were as good as the white parents, West Indian parents were twice as likely to be in unskilled jobs. He concludes that the lower achievements of West Indians in the fifth year confirms that they are no better than white pupils at passing exams. However, beyond the fifth year, evidence of greater commitment (i.e. higher attendance rates, especially with girls), and aspirations, result in sharper differences in achievement in favour of West Indians.

Similar results were found in a later study undertaken by the Postgraduate School of Studies in Research in Education, University of Bradford, in relation to the achievements of Asian and English pupils (Gajendrak 1984). Researchers concluded that Asian teenagers from poorer backgrounds than white pupils, in spite of being placed in lower streams at school, had higher aspirations and achieved as well as, if not better that, white pupils. Their findings contradict the claims made by some teachers and careers officers that Asian pupils unrealistically over-aspire. They criticized the negative attitudes of teachers and careers officers whose assessment and guidance reflected stereotyped assumptions, and actually discouraged achievement. These two studies provide positive evidence of the achievements of West Indian and Asian pupils, and point to the urgent need for teachers, careers officers, and employers to be more discerning in their judgements based on methods of assessment that are not equally fair or valid for members of ethnic minority groups.

Two observations are brought to the reader's attention. Positive attitudes and dedication can, and do, improve pupils' achievements to differing degrees. Factors affecting educational development and progress are not the same for all pupils; in the case of ethnic minorities, differences in basic verbal competence as a fundamental learning skill are still grossly underestimated and misunderstood. Those who have taught or learned a different language will appreciate that it is easier to learn to converse than to write in a foreign language. It is a fallacy to assume that because individuals from ethnic minority groups are born and educated in this country, their lower initial achievements are a reflection of lower potential ability rather than differences in experience. Bilingualism and cultural experiences account for some of the differences in rates of learning which are reflected in achievements measured by culturally biased assessment methods. Flexible attitudes which encourage and promote achievement directly, and more often indirectly, coupled with a variety of assessment methods and appropriate guidance can result in moderate gains for many, but significant vocational benefits for some.

Psychometric tests

The growth and widespread use of psychometric tests in the United States of America has not kept pace in Britain. Similarly, research into the validity and limitations of tests as diagnostic or measuring instruments with members of ethnic minorities groups in this country remains relatively unexplored. Although the search for culture-free tests has long been abandoned, the expectation that culture-fair tests exist and might be the solution to complying with Race Relations legislation reflects a misunderstanding of the term 'culture-fair'. Tests, by their very need to be relevant and meaningful, are developed within a cultural environment. Consequently, the greater the difference between the indigenous culture and that of members of ethnic minority groups with whom the tests are used, the more likely is their performance to be adversely affected by 'error' factors with the result that scores are less reliable than they are for members of the indigenous population. Research in this area, though sparse, repeatedly shows that average scores of ethnic minority groups on mental abilities are lower than those of the majority population, though individuals may do as well as, or better than, some individuals in the majority culture.

The outcome of a comparative study undertaken in eight Birmingham schools (Rangel 1986) of 623 pupils' scores on six measures of ability is summarized below. The tests are non-verbal reasoning, spatial perception, verbal reasoning, numerical reasoning, clerical speed, and clerical accuracy. The sample was representative of the comprehensive but not of the grammar school. Three ethnic groups were compared: white English, Asian, and West Indian. Differences in sample sizes were indicative of proportions in the chosen schools, but not of the city. These were 306 English, 229 Asians, and 44 West Indians.

The results showed that the two ethnic minority groups obtained lower average scores than the English group on all the tests. On each test the English pupils obtained the highest average scores. In five out of six tests, the Asians got the second highest average scores and the West Indians did better than the Asians on one test, that of verbal reasoning.

The average scores on all tests for the English sample were higher and significantly different compared to the average scores of the Asians and West Indians. The differences between the average scores of the Asians and West Indians, however, were smaller and were not significant. The largest difference between the English and the other two groups was, not surprisingly, on the test of verbal reasoning. There appears to be a smaller and consistent difference of half a standard deviation between the average scores of the English sample and the two minority groups on each of four tests, namely non-verbal reasoning, spatial perception, numerical reasoning, and clerical accuracy. The difference on clerical speed is smaller and equivalent to about a quarter of a standard deviation. The consistent differences between average scores of English, Asian, and West Indian pupils seems to suggest that some consistent influence or factor is contributing to the uniformly lower scores. These findings support the need for separate norms to be used for ethnic minority groups. The samples were too small to indicate whether norms should also be kept separate for each ethnic group.

When the distributions of scores were examined and compared with expected normal frequency distributions, some interesting differences were revealed. The English pupils' scores were the most evenly distributed above and below the mean and were the most similar to expected frequencies. The scores for clerical accuracy were symmetrically distributed above and below the mean. The scores on the non-verbal and spatial tests were over-represented above the mean by 6 per cent and 7 per cent respectively. The scores for clerical accuracy were 24 per cent over-represented above the mean. However, the scores on the verbal and numerical reasoning tests were under-represented above the mean by 6 per cent and 7 per cent respectively.

The distributions for the Asian pupils scores showed that they were equally distributed above and below the mean on clerical speed only. They were over-represented above the mean by 7 per cent for clerical accuracy. On the other four tests they were under-represented above the mean and therefore over-represented below the mean. The corresponding percentages were: 9 per cent on non-verbal reasoning, 11 per cent on spatial perception, 20 per cent on numerical reasoning, and 30 per cent on verbal reasoning. These scores indicate that Asian pupils do less well than English pupils on six measures of mental ability,but that they are least disadvantaged on the test of clerical checking, which requires them to check lists of names and numbers for similarities and differences. They are relatively more disadvantaged on tests of non-verbal or diagrammatic reasoning and on spatial perception. They are even more strongly disadvantaged on the test of numerical reasoning and most disadvantaged on the test of verbal reasoning.

The distributions of scores for the West Indian pupils were similar to the Asians, with the exception of clerical speed where they were under-represented above the mean. The scores were as follows: on the test of clerical accuracy they were over-represented by 10 per cent above the mean. They were under-represented on the other five tests. The corresponding percentages were: 9 per cent on clerical speed, non-verbal and spatial perception, 25 per cent on numerical reasoning, and 27 per cent on verbal reasoning. These scores indicate that West Indian pupils are least disadvantaged on the test of clerical accuracy compared with English pupils. They are more disadvantaged on the tests of non-verbal reasoning, spatial perception and clerical speed. They are most strongly disadvantaged on tests of numerical reasoning and verbal reasoning respectively. Compared with Asian pupils they are less disadvantaged on the test of clerical accuracy and spatial perception. They are more disadvantaged on clerical speed and numerical reasoning. The distribution of scores on non-verbal reasoning are almost the same for both groups but the West

Indian pupils do better at verbal reasoning.

The implications of the differences in average scores between the three ethnic groups need further consideration. Although pupils from ethnic minority backgrounds did less well on all the tests, they did considerably worse on verbal reasoning and numerical reasoning than on spatial perception, non-verbal reasoning, clerical speed and accuracy. It does not automatically follow that the last four are less culturally biased, although their effects on selection and vocational advice may be less disadvantageous. If the tests were used for selection purposes using the same norms for all applicants, the lower scores and unequal distributions would result in disproportionately larger numbers from the two ethnic minority groups being rejected. Second, as batteries of tests almost always include measures of verbal and numerical attainment, the chances of being selected are considerably lower for Asians and West Indians. Thirdly, where specialized skills for scientific and technical careers or training are sought through tests of spatial perception, the chances of being selected are reduced for minority applicants whose scores on tests of spatial and numerical ability are lower. Consequently they are less likely to benefit from the occupational growth areas, such as engineering and technology. If, on the other hand, separate norms were used for each ethnic group, the probability of members of each group being equally selected would still be unlikely, but ought to be improved.

The lower performance of Asian and West Indian pupils on tests of mental abilities will inevitably raise doubts about the validity and fairness of using psychometric tests as measures of achievement for ethnic minorities. In order to understand their relative value as assessment tools, it is helpful to consider some of the reasons why members of minority groups do less well. The reasons have been grouped into 'intrinsic' and 'extrinsic' factors (Pearn, 1977).

Intrinsic factors refer to the psychological attributes an individual possesses as a result of personal, educational and cultural experiences. Lower scores on tests may therefore reflect a lack of experience rather than a lack of potential ability. Extrinsic factors refer to conditions external to the candidate and associated directly with test administration. These include the following:

- Unfamiliarity with the testing procedure can increase anxiety or result in confusion caused by reluctance to ask questions. The rigorous standardization procedure alters the teacher-pupil role and may discourage 'normal' rapport.

- Language-oral and/or written instructions may be unclear and may result in ambiguity of meaning with the result that candidates are unable to follow the principles required to solve problems. Crawley (1975) found that West Indian pupils made more mistakes on practice questions than white pupils.
- Anxiety caused by confusion or fear of failure is demotivating and can result in candidates switching off or pretending to cope.
- Motivation is important for all candidates; it has been suggested that individuals from third world countries do not have the same sense of rivalry as western society promotes, and it is not uncommon to find pupils in school 'helping' each other and being less affected by time constraints.
- Test content or cultural bias is unquestionably a major reason for poorer performance by ethnic minorities. Verbal tests seem to be the most culturally biased measure of ability. The evidence that non-verbal tests are relatively less biased is, as yet, conflicting.

Two courses of action are open to those considering using psychometric tests for assessing individuals from ethnic minority backgrounds (Rangel 1985):

- avoid psychometric tests;

  or

- include tests but make allowances for the disadvantages by supplementing tests scores with biographical data.

If the decision is taken to avoid psychometric tests, it should be made in the knowledge that other conventional assessment methods such as teachers' estimates, school reports, supervisors' ratings and examinations are also likely to underestimate the individual. They, too, are less reliable and less valid measures for ethnic minorities than they are of the indigenous population. On the other hand, because average scores conceal individual differences it should be remembered that some individuals (albeit a small number) from minority groups do as well, or better, than some members of the majority population. If tests were omitted, some positive information would be missed. The solution depends to some extent on what other relatively more reliable and valid information is available or can be obtained.

If the decision taken is to include psychometric tests then the quality of test scores can be improved or optimized by careful adminstration and sensible interpretation. Some practical suggestions are offered:

- Group size — keep group sizes small to *ensure* that individual attention and close supervision is possible.
- Group composition — keep groups as *homogeneous* as possible; individuals with specific difficulties may have to be tested separately.
- Language — the level of language or instructions should be appropriate to ensure that the principles of problem-solving are understood and that candidates are well motivated.
- Oral instructions must be clear and easily understood; unfamiliar accents can cause confusion and adversely affect understanding of the task.
- Written instructions for candidates to follow should be the same as oral instructions or appropriately abbreviated to avoid confusion; written instructions are helpful for those who may be unclear about the task and need to check the information at their own pace.
- Objective — explain the objective of the exercise and its relevance to subsequent performance, as this can improve co-operation and motivation.
- Use tests with practice items and allow adequate time for them to be completed. Assist as appropriate those who get practice questions wrong; positive feedback enhances performance.
- Coaching or practice is sometimes helpful, but usually for the less able; beyond a certain level practice results in diminishing returns.
- Allow adequate time for entire test administration; if administration is rushed it leads to unstandardized practice, and candidates may become anxious and under-perform.
- Test scores should be interpreted in relation to other biographical data, never in isolation; 'over-interpretation' (Pearn 1975) must be avoided; tests measure specific areas of behaviour, and interpretation must be made in relation to appropriate behaviours only.
- Test scores should be interpreted with discretion; advice on predictions should be short term, and should be updated at regular intervals to take account of personal development.

CONCLUSION

We are constantly reminded that the impact of technological advancement on the employment structure will paradoxically reduce and expand opportunities. Although it is difficult to predict with certainty the degree and nature of these changes, a recent memorandum by the National Economic Development Council to the Secretary of State for Employment, and the Chairman of the Manpower Services Commission (April 1988) outlined some of the implications. Technology will reduce the need for unskilled and semi-skilled labour and increase the need for skilled personnel of technician level and above. New jobs will require new skills which in turn will need to be regularly updated. More complex economies will require professional management. Finally, it warns that the longer people remain unemployed the more difficult it will be for them to re-enter the job market.

Set against this background of relative uncertainty it is imperative that trainers, counsellors, and individuals themselves understand the need for vocational planning to be based on sound information about the individual's own strengths and weaknesses, preferences and dislikes. The process of educational and vocational choices should seek to encourage the development of a wide range of skills that will enable the individual to benefit from new opportunities rather than be hampered by diminishing traditional occupations. The increased participation of women in the economy should be reflected in all types and levels of work. Personal and social skills should encourage more confident and reliable members of society who are capable of co-operating and communicating within and beyond the working environment.

Central to the identification and enhancement of these personal and social skills is the role of assessment. It is noteworthy that the most recent developments in assessment methods emphasize the need for positive attitudes as well as positive methods. The former position of the 'expert' assessing the 'client' is replaced by a more negotiated approach between the assessor and the assessed. Recognition of achievements is seen as relevant to all levels of ability, not just the academically more able. Assessment should provide a comprehensive record of positive achievements which include educational attainment, work experience, extra-curricular activities, and personal and social achievements. Perhaps the most radical indication of positive assessment is the encouragement of active participation by the individual in planning and controlling the development of personally relevant achievements. The relative merits of each assessment method from the tutorial, through the interview, supervisors ratings, teachers' report, examinations, and psychometric tests point to the need for assessment to include a combination of the most appropriate techniques in preference to single isolated methods. The real test of equality of opportunity will be seen, not so much in well-documented policies and codes of practice, as in the reflection of a truer representation of members of society in relation to race and gender.

REFERENCES AND BIBLIOGRAPHY

Birmingham Careers Service (1982) *Norms for Pupils ages 12 to 15 months*, unpublished survey.

Clarke, L. (1980) *Occupational Choice: A critical review of Research in the United Kingdom*, London: HMSO.

Crawley, R. (1975) *A Preliminary Study of the Effects of Cultural Experience on Aptitude Test Performance as a Background to Careers Advisory Work*, Birmingham Careers Service, Unpublished BA dissertation, University of Aston, Birmingham.

Department of Education and Science (1987) *Interim Report on Records of Achievement*, London: HMSO.

Gajendrak, V. (1984) *Problems of Vocational Adaptation of South Asian Adolescents in Britain, with Special Reference to the Role of the School*, University of Bradford: Postgraduate School of Studies in Research in Education.

Gupta, Y.P. (1977) 'The educational and vocational aspirations of Asian immigrant and English school leavers: a comparative study', *British Journal of Sociology* 28.

Haynes, J.M. (1971) *Educational Assessment of Immigrant Pupils*, Windsor: NFER.

Incomes Data Services Ltd. (July 1985) *Psychological Assessment* Study 134; Surrey: Unwin.

Institute of Personnel Management (1984) *Schools and the World of Work: what do employers look for in school leavers?* London: IPM.

National Economic Development Council (1988) *Skills for the Future: memorandum by the Secretary of State for Employment and the Chairman of the Manpower Services Commission*, London: NEDC.

Pratt, J., Bloomfield, J., and Seale, C. (1984) *Option Choice: A Question of Equal Opportunity*, Windsor: NFER-NELSON.

Pearn, M.A. (1977) *Selecting and Training Coloured Workers*,

London: HMSO.

Pearn, M.A., Kandola, R.S., and Mottram, R.D. (1987) *Selection Tests and Sex Bias: the impact of selection testing on the employment opportunities of women and men*, London: HMSO.

Rampton, A. (1981) *West Indian Children in Our Schools*, London: HMSO.

Rangel, M.V. and Pendlebury, A.C. (1980) *Validation of Six Tests and Twenty-Eight O level and CSE Examination Subjects*, Birmingham Careers Service: Unpublished Report.

Rangel, M.V. (1985) *Testing Pupils from Ethnic Minority Groups for Educational and Vocational Guidance*, Birmingham Careers Service: Unpublished Report.

Rangel, M.V. (1986) *A Comparative Study of Asian, English and West Indian Pupils on Six Mental Abilities*, Birmingham Careers Service: Unpublished Report.

Rangel, M.V. (1987) *Improving Fairness in the Use of Tests for Selection* Birmingham Careers Service: Unpublished notes for YTS managing agents.

Rangel, M.V. (1988) *A Pilot Study on the Improvement of the Objectivity and Usefulness of Records of Achievement for Assessment for Employers*, London: CEGB.

Rangel, M.V. (1988) *Adult Guidance and Training*, Ashiya University, Japan: 6th International Conference on Vocational Guidance.

Rutter, M. (1982) *Fifteen Thousand Hours*, London: Open Books.

Scarr, S., Capanilo, B.K., Ferdman, B.M., Tower, R.B. and Caplan, J. (1983) 'Developmental status and school achievements of minority and non-minority children from birth to 18 years in a British Midlands town', *British Journal of Developmental Psychology* 1: 31-48.

Select Committee on Race Relations (1978) *The West Indian Community*, London: DES.

Spearman, C. (1927) *The 'Nature of Intelligence' and the Principles of Cognition*, London: Macmillan.

Swann, M.M. (1985) *Education for All: a brief guide to the main issues of the Report*, London: HMSO.

Chapter Eight

FUTURE TRENDS IN ASSESSMENT

Richard Riding

Assessment faces a future which consists of several opportunities made possible by new developments and discoveries. It also inherits from the past a range of problems to be solved. In order to emphasize a positive approach, the opportunities will be discussed first.

DEVELOPMENTS AFFECTING ASSESSMENT

Possible changes in the improvement of assessment include those related to educational initiatives, psychological research into learning and evaluation, and technological developments.

Educational Initiatives

There have long been two recurring concerns in education. The first has been that the curriculum should be relevant to the lives of those who receive it, and the second is that the quality of the education should be monitored.

A curriculum that is relevant for life

Common sense suggests that education should enable those who receive it to develop their potential to allow them to live their lives to the full. There will always be contention, of course, about the ways in which value systems affect the content of education and also about how much of a particular value system should be included. However, most are likely to agree that education should have a clearly defined benefit rather than a supposed usefulness. To achieve this outcome both the distant aims and the skills learned need to be relevant to the individual.

It may be argued that much education in the recent past has been too academically orientated and too dependent on memory. The secondary school curriculum of the 1970s and 1980s developed from the university entrance requirements as taught in grammar schools and reflected in the School Certificate and the General Certificate of Education. When the Certificate of Secondary Education was introduced in the 1960s, instead of opting for a more practically orientated vocational approach, it was modelled on the contents and emphases of the GCE. Hence, in essence GCE/CSE mathematics, for example, was a preparation for A level mathematics, which in turn was the preparation for a degree in science or mathematics. Since only a relatively small percentage of the population does, and should, follow an academically based professional career, it is not an appropriate curriculum for all to follow. In the past, much too little attention has been paid to the career and life directions of pupils and consequently many pupils have found sections of the curriculum inappropriate to their interests, aptitudes and life's work. The curriculum and its related assessment needs to move from focusing on the narrowly academic to being more broadly utilitarian based.

A further requirement is that, in terms of the skills learned, the focus should not be so exclusively on memory. Inspection of many GCE and CSE papers indicates that there has been great emphasis on the ability to learn, and then in the examination to reproduce a definition or fact in a fairly rote manner. There are several limitations to this approach: (a) it does not test understanding of the concepts learned or their application to new situations; (b) it does not reflect what often happens in everyday life, where knowing where to look for information is important; (c) it does not acknowledge the rate of change in some areas of knowledge, where in the future the ability to retrieve and find out will be increasingly important; (d) it does not encourage critical thinking and problem-solving skills; and (e) it tests only quick, short-term activity and not persistent effort over a longer period of time such as is typical of real life — the move towards coursework assessment in the GCSE is useful in this respect.

National assessment initiatives

During the 1980s two interests in the quality of education

emerged. The first was at the level of the individual and was aimed at improving motivation and involvement. There was a desire to involve pupils in recording their own levels of achievement and in setting their own goals. The second was initially a concern about, and then a move to monitor, the standard of educational attainment of pupils throughout their schooling on a national basis.

Records of achievement That pupils should be involved in being aware of their educational progress and of mapping their positive achievements is a welcome development. It has the advantage that it is possible to increase motivation because pupils feel that they have a greater say in what they are doing, that their goals are established in consultation with them, and that they monitor their progress in discussion with their teachers. This is useful for all pupils, but is particularly so for those who are likely to lack motivation because the purpose of education is not clear to them since they are thereby made more responsible for considering where they are going and what they are achieving. It is also helpful to those of more limited ability since the goals can be negotiated in units that they can accomplish in a reasonable time and with success. It is useful for both pupils and teachers since it focuses attention on the relevance of education to future work and life, and causes pupils to think about their career development, and it encourages teachers to consider the content of instruction.

There is scope for further development of records of achievement and pupil profiles as long as it is done efficiently and effectively — efficiently in terms of staff time since it would be counter-productive to spend so much time discussing attainment with each pupil that there was little time left to attain anything, effectively in that it is easy for good initiatives in the hands of enthusiasts to succeed but to degenerate into mere ineffectual formality when forced upon an unwilling staff. Clear systems and guidelines need to be worked out to allow the best features of recording achievement to be developed and incorporated into educational practice.

The quality of education The move to monitor the level of attainment of pupils has great potential for the improvement of the quality of education, since it is a long and cumulative process and beyond the span of an individual teacher who may only teach a pupil for a year or even less. Those who are involved in its beginning have little vision of its ending, and it is difficult for a teacher to have an overview of the whole.

Clearly, without monitoring it is not possible for any single teacher at a particular point to be sure that a pupil is on course for his or her ultimate educational destination. A nationally agreed content of the curriculum, together with careful attention as to how it is taught, could dramatically improve the standard of the education of many pupils who, without long-term monitoring, may for a variety of reasons fall behind.

In this respect national assessment at 7, 11, 14, and 16 years old for all pupils is to be welcomed. To be effective it must assess validly both in terms of measuring what it sets out to assess and what is educationally real. It must also do this efficiently so that assessment is kept as the servant of education and does not become its master. If it is effective then it will also aid communication between pupils and teacher, and between teacher and parent, in considering and making meaningful decisions about the pupil's progress.

Psychological research

Recent research into the relationships between achievement and the learning style and personality of the pupil have implications for the nature and validity of assessment. Pupils vary along several personality and style dimensions, which have considerable bearing on their performance and on the ways in which it will be influenced by the type of assessment used. Two aspects of the mode of assessment will be discussed, (a) set exam versus coursework assignment, and (b) form of question or assignment.

Set exam versus coursework assignment

Two common modes of assessment are in terms of a set written examination with a fairly short time-limit and an extended coursework assignment over a period of several days or weeks. The set written examination favours pupils of a more extrovert and stable personality, since they perform well in a situation which requires activity for a limited time and is relatively arousing. By contrast, more introvert and nervous pupils do not perform so well in the pressured examination situation which requires a quick response in a tense atmosphere and allows little opportunity for leisured reflection.

The coursework assignment which is undertaken over an extended period, and which probably represents a more true-to-life situation, is generally done better by the introvert pupil who is more diligent and willing to concentrate over a period of time and who is more able to think clearly in the less stressful situation where there is less immediate time constraint. The extrovert, by contrast, is inclined to become bored with a long task, is more willing to be distracted, and is more likely to give up or to submit incomplete work.

It is important to allow a variety of types of assessment in order to permit pupils to demonstrate what they can accomplish in a variety of situations and also to reflect the range of activities that are encountered in everyday life situations. In the past, much assessment has been restricted to very short-term, intense activity and has omitted longer term tasks. A balance is required if assessment is to reflect real life and be fair to individuals.

Form of question or assignment

Questions in set examinations, and assignments in many subject areas, can be presented either in verbal or visual form. For instance, knowledge about an electrical circuit can be assessed either by a verbal description of a problem or by means of a diagram and a question. A question about a geographical feature such as an escarpment can be presented either wholly in verbal form or with an illustration or diagram.

There is now a considerable body of research which indicates that some pupils are predominantly verbal in their preferred mode of representing information in memory, while others utilize mental imagery (see, for instance, Riding and Dyer 1980, and Riding and Calvey 1981). Riding and Anstey (1982) and Riding and Cowley (1986) found reading performance in children to be related to verbal imagery learning style and extroversion. Riding and Ashmore (1980) showed that imagers learned better from pictorial presentation and vebalizers from written presentation.

Since learning style really has little to do with intelligence, questions should be designed to accommodate a range of styles. If assessment is to be fair to pupils then there should be a balance between the verbal and the visual emphasis in the form of presentation of assignments.

Technological developments

The major technological development that has implications for the content and methods of assessment is the area of information technology which has been made possible through computer developments. The two most significant of these developments are the increased accessibility of information from large databases, and the potential for the computer as a controller of instruction.

Information retrieval and critical thinking

Since the late 1970s there has been a very rapid development in personal computers and in computer networks and communications. This has implications for society and work, and consequently for the curriculum and examinations. One effect of the development is a shift of emphasis from learning and remembering a body of knowledge to knowing how to access, retrieve, and handle information. Obviously there is still knowledge that is worth internalizing, but in a rapidly changing situation and one where information can be readily accessed, what is useful for work in business, industry, and the professions is different from that required a generation ago.

In this context it will be useful to consider three technological developments and the directions in which they may be leading. These are the personal computer, networking, and mass storage. The personal computer has developed since the mid-1970s from a limited toy for computer enthusiasts to a very powerful and relatively inexpensive tool that is extensively used and found in many work situations. Year by year the computer of a given price level has increased in capacity and speed of operation, and this trend shows signs of continuing in the future.

The development of the 'stand alone' personal computer has been paralleled by an increase in the facilities for connecting computers together in networks and that of linking them to larger computers via telephone lines. This has provided the possibility of communication between computers and of accessing large databases of information quickly and efficiently.

There has also been an increase in storage capacity in the personal computer, such that compact disk devices are capable of storing one million pages of A4 on a single disk. This is sufficient space to store approximately twenty ten-volume encyclopaedias, together with a retrieval system that would allow topics to be searched, cross-referenced and displayed in a few seconds. This capacity will increase over the next decade.

These three developments make possible the easy storage and quick search and retrieval of a very large amount of information. The consequence of this for education is that what is required is the learning of skills in retrieval and the manipulation of information, rather than learning vast numbers of facts. This means that not only must the curriculum reflect this change but so also must assessment. There will be a need to assess skills in retrieval of information and in critical thinking and the ability to use information to solve new problems.

The computer as an intelligent tutor

During the 1980s the computer had relatively little impact on schools and education. There have been several reasons for this: partly it was because teachers were reluctant to come to terms with technology such as computers and video; partly it was because little incentive was given to computer manufacturers to develop reasonably priced machines suitable for the education market; partly it was because, to be used effectively in education, computers need to be reasonably powerful in terms of speed, memory and storage capacity; and partly it was because little attempt was made to identify which aspects of instruction computers are best suited to, and to develop extensive software packages to exploit this in the main subject areas.

The future will see a change in all these areas. The introduction of the National Curriculum and other educational changes has produced a reconsideration of teaching methods. The move toward an industry standard in computers and their increased use in business and the home will produce the basis for an economical machine for education. Coupled with this is a considerable increase in power. This opens the opportunity to explore what the computer is capable of doing in an intelligent tutor role. In other words, acting as a teacher would, as a sort of educational expert system. The potential is not only for suitable basic skills to be taught and the learning to be monitored by the computer, but also for problem solving and critical thinking to be facilitated. In several respects it will be possible to go beyond what the teacher can do and provide.

PROBLEMS THAT NEED SOLVING

There are a number of problems that need to be tackled if assessment is to be effective and make a real contribution to education. If they are not solved, there is the danger that, far from improving the standard of education, assessment may reduce it. Measurement in any branch of science is often not simple and this is particularly so in learning where both the product (education) and the vessel that contains it (the human student) are respectively difficult to define and functionally very complex. It is therefore not surprising that evaluation in education is currently facing several tensions. This section will focus on some of these: (a) reliability versus validity; (b) formative versus summative emphasis; (c) moderation; and (d) cultural background.

Reliability versus validity

Assessment and the content of education

It is desirable, of course, that assessment is both reliable and valid. Reliability refers to consistency of measurement, validity to the need that the object of the measurement is actually assessed. The problem in education is that what are often spoken of as laudable aims (understanding, appreciation, critical awareness, creativity and the like) are difficult to define and measure, and that what can be measured reliably (rote learning, etc.) has little educational validity. Here is a dilemma — do we teach only what can be measured? If the answer to this is yes, then the effect is to limit the curriculum to fairly low-level objectives and to omit many higher order cognitive skills that are difficult to define. If the answer is no, then the result opens two possibilities: (a) that all that is taught will not be assessed (no great problem perhaps); or (b) that the curriculum becomes fanciful in that the time is spent on activities that have very doubtful educational validity, and that educational fictions arise that have more in common with the king's new clothes.

There is no simple answer to the dilemma. The most sensible solution would appear on the one hand to be to concentrate on increasing the extent to which valid educational notions can be operationalized into assessable objectives, and on the other to critically analyse current exotic educational practices.

Objectivity is important not only so that teachers can agree on the content of the curriculum and its assessment, but also so that the result of assessments can be compared — from class to class, school to school, country to country — and communicated to pupils and their parents.

The tension between formative and summative assessment

The distinctions between the two types of assessment

Formative assessment refers to evaluation made during the instructional phase to inform the teacher about progress in learning and what still needs to be learned. Summative assessment is the terminal measurement of performance at the end of the instruction. Formative evaluation differs in purpose and in nature from summative evaluation. There is, however, a real danger that, all too often, while the difference in purpose and timing may be recognized, the difference in nature may not. This leads to summative assessment tests and procedures being used during the course with the misconceived intention of formatively evaluating the learners. The problem may arise in part from the dominant effects of summative evaluation not only on assessment but also on the whole of the school curriculum. A further restriction is that summative assessment can limit the use of pupil profiles and records of achievement.

Even when the mastery learning approach is adopted, with the course broken down into manageable units, thus providing reasonably short-term objectives for the learners, the tests at the end of each unit consist of items derived using the same principles as the summative evaluation at the end of the course.

In some cases the tests consist of parallel, or even identical items. Such tests will be of limited help in providing specific guidance to the learners who have failed to achieve mastery levels on a particular test. Tests of this type, however, can be used as an alternative approach to summative evaluation by final examination. The total time available for assessment is increased and so is the coverage of the content. If the opportunity to retake the tests, without penalty, is available to candidates who do not reach mastery, the level of anxiety associated with traditional testing could be reduced for many learners.

The prime consideration of summative assessment is the

determination of the extent to which an individual has mastered the knowledge and skills associated with a course, as opposed to revealing the processes by which the learner achieved these outcomes. The latter is the purpose of formative evaluation. Ausubel (1985) describes this neatly as the difference between considering the logical aspects of a subject, its principles, procedures, and information base, and the psychological aspects where the ways in which an individual learns about that subject are also included. The essential function of formative evaluation is to inform the learner and the teacher not only about the present level of the learner's knowledge, but also about the ways in which this knowledge and understanding was acquired.

In summative evaluation, the assessment is designed to test learning outcomes against a set of objective criteria as in the new GCSE examinations. The structure of questions may reflect Bloom's (1956) taxonomy of the cognitive domain, but they are intended to measure learning outcomes in terms of an individual's performance at the particular point in time when he or she is examined. The questions are unlikely to be suitable for revealing the details of the route which the learner followed in reaching that point, details which are essential in the process of formative evaluation. In the ideal case, formative evaluation takes the form of a dialogue between the learner and the teacher with a loosely structured agenda determined by both participants.

It is argued that these issues must be addressed in the design of assessment for formative purposes, since it is necessary to provide the learner and the teacher with this kind of information if the individual is to receive specific advice on ways of dealing with topics or skills which are causing him or her difficulty. It is important to distinguish this type of formative assessment which is aimed at the vast majority of learners in school or continuing education, from the highly specialized diagnostic tests employed in the case of individuals with severe learning problems.

Formative evaluation and grading

One problem is deciding at what point the instruction ceases, particularly in the application of summative assessment on a national scale to young children at, say, 7 and 11 years old. Consider the case of two 11-year-olds who are asked to write a short story. They bring their efforts to their teacher who reads them both and assesses them, perhaps on different occasions, to be of an equal standard of, say, 55 per cent. Now suppose further that ways of improving their stories in terms of structure, vocabulary, plot, use of paragraphs, etc., is discussed with each child and each is asked to re-write its story, which when re-submitted are graded as now being worth 85 per cent and 60 per cent. Clearly one child has been able to improve its performance much more than the other. If the first assessment had been taken as the indication of performance level they would both have been equal; if the second, one child is much superior to the other. This raises the question, when is instruction of a scheme of work sufficiently complete to justify the summative assessment?

A further aspect is that stressing the summative nature of the assessment of coursework may severely limit the use of formative evaluation and feedback. Consider a geography coursework project undertaken between the ages of 14 and 16 years as part of a public examination system. The project is to be the pupils' own work, but obviously each pupil will need guidance from the teacher about the aim, scope, and nature of the project, about appropriate topics, and about suitable means of collecting and analysing data, and of how to write up the project report. At what point does the role of the teacher as instructor end and that of assessor begin? The child will gain much from the project if there is discussion, critical feedback, instruction about appearance and methods. If these are not given because of an over-emphasis on the assessment role of the teacher, the pupil will learn little on his or her own.

These formative instruments have not yet been systematically developed for use on a large scale. It is necessary that the assessment tasks developed in conjunction with the National Curriculum for pupils at the ages of 7, 11 and 14 will make a serious attempt to address this problem, and not concentrate solely on the production of tests which are essentially summative in nature.

Moderation

Moderation of assessment is necessary if it is to be fair and comparable. Consider this parable. Newly-wed Stone Age Jack and Jill set off to find a new cave in which to set up home. They come upon two empty caves set side by side in a nice south-facing low cliff. They agree to choose as their new home whichever cave is the longest. Jill, being the assertive one, suggests that they be economical of effort and that she should pace the one on the left and Jack the one on the right. This they do. However, Jill is shorter than Jack and her pace is only three-quarters of his normal pace, so they are not using the same unit of measurement.

Not only that, but Jack is biased towards caves on the right because he believes they are more lucky than those on the left; only he has not told Jill this since she may accuse him of being 'rightist'. However, this bias means that instead of taking normal paces he takes rather full paces which actually amount to twice Jill's pace.

After pacing the caves they come out and Jack announces that his came to 15 paces and Jill says that hers came to 20, so Jill's is adopted as their new home. However, a combination of their economy (each assessed by only one measurer), their lack of a standard unit of measurement (Jill's being less than Jack's), and bias in measurement (Jack being 'rightist') means that the cave chosen as best was in fact the shorter, since the right cave was actually 30 of Jill's paces long.

The same principles apply to educational assessment. Unless clearly defined units are used, with controls for bias and re-testing (or moderation), the results will not be comparable between pupils and schools, and will be misleading.

The need is not only for a clear definition, but for an increased awareness in teachers of the principles of assessment, which can only be brought about by more prominence being given to this in initial training courses and in-service education.

Uniform modes of testing versus individual styles

Put simply, much current public assessment assumes that pupils only vary on one dimension, that of knowledge. Little or no account is taken of either the pupils' learning styles or their cultural backgrounds.

The relationship between the effect of the learning style and personality of the pupil, the mode of examination and the type of assessment on performance was discussed earlier in this chapter. The effect of cultural background will be considered here.

The context in which the learning occurs or the outcomes are tested is especially important in the case of pupils whose background or experience is different from the majority of those taking a course. The traditional emphasis on the denotative aspects of a subject area in summative evaluation has to some degree compounded this problem. Where a careful attempt has been made to ensure objectivity by testing a prescribed body of content it is easy to assume that no group of learners will be put at a disadvantage, especially if all the candidates have equal access to the textbooks, etc., used on the course.

If there are discrepancies between groups, as opposed to differences in performance between individuals, areas would not be revealed by the marking schemes normally employed in summative assessment. Their presence could be detected by a statistical comparison of the grades attained by particular groups of candidates, but in practice this is rarely done. A comparison of this kind would raise the question of the compensation procedures which should be applied to the grades awarded to an individual. There is no reason to suppose that a particular group of candidates are more homogeneous than the entire group taking the course. The effect of such compensation would therefore be arbitrary in individual cases, and damage rather than restore objectivity.

The paramount consideration in public examining, however, is that no candidate or group of candidates should knowingly be placed at a disadvantage. A statistical procedure which made adjustments to grades of candidates whose true performance and potential were not being correctly represented by their original grades would ensure increased confidence in the examining process. The difficulty lies in determining the features of a candidate's educational background which should attract such compensation and in devising rules for registering candidates in this way. Many students may object that such procedures set them apart from others taking the course and that people outside the system may undervalue the grades which they are awarded. If the problems are to be tackled effectively, changes are required in the summative evaluation procedures.

There have been developments in the direction of a wider range of examination techniques to enable a greater range of skills to be assessed. In the GCSE examinations, coursework forms an important component of the final grade. Whilst the educational validity of the assessment is increased for the majority of candidates, the use of such techniques for particular groups may cause the opposite effect to occur. Traditional courses have been focused round a common resource, text books, practical classes, etc. Assignments are more open-ended in nature and can involve the use of a range of resources which the candidate is able to find outside the educational institution. Apart from books, equipment, and materials for field work, information from data bases in the public domain are in theory available to all candidates, but in practice are not. Moreover, the use of word processing and desk top publishing facilities for the production of reports may be available to some candidates, and it is idle to pretend that the quality of presentation which can be achieved in this way does not affect the judgement of examiners.

The disadvantage which these factors represent for individuals is even more serious if it occurs differentially across the groups discussed above. Particular groups, possibly ethnic groups or mature learners, will have no confidence in an examination system which, while apparently being fair and objective, is actually discriminating against them. Some groups in many, probably all, societies suffer discrimination in some form. Public examinations are an important way of mitigating such discrimination. It is therefore essential that bias, however unintentional, is avoided. The information which would enable this to be done on a sound and systematic basis could be provided by appropriate types of formative evaluation. The very nature of formative evaluation is intended to reveal information about the individual's learning history and this includes the factors discussed above. Formative evaluation is usually seen as providing information about his or her progress for the mutual benefit of the individual and the teacher. It is argued here that this knowledge must also inform the procedures adopted and judgements made by examiners. Candidates will frame and illustrate their answers in the light of their experience. This experience may be radically different from that of the examiner but, worse still, the examiner may be unaware of this and so fail to take it into account in marking an answer.

If assessment is to be fair these factors must be built in at the planning stage. It is essential that the examiners know the type and range of candidates who will be involved. The information which they need, however, can only be obtained by high-quality formative evaluation of these and similar candidates. The development of suitable procedures is a matter of urgency if educational validity is to be achieved and the confidence of the whole community assured.

CONCLUSION

Opportunities for the improvement of assessment include those related to educational initiatives, psychological research into learning and evaluation, and technological developments. Evaluation in education is also currently facing several tensions. These include: (a) reliability versus validity; (b) formative versus summative emphasis; (c) moderation; and (d) cultural background.

REFERENCES AND BIBLIOGRAPHY

Ausubel, D.P. (1985) 'Learning as constructing meaning', in N. Entwistle (ed.) *New Directions in Educational Psychology 1: Learning and Teaching*, Lewes: Falmer.

Bloom, B.S. (ed.) (1956) *Taxonomy of Educational Objectives: Cognitive domain*, London: Longman.

Riding, R.J. and Anstey, L. (1982) 'Verbal-imagery learning style and reading attainment in eight-year-old children', *Journal of Research in Reading* **5**: 57-66.

Riding, R.J. and Ashmore, J. (1980) 'Verbaliser-imager learning styles and children's recall of information presented in pictorial versus written form', *Educational Studies* **6**: 141-5.

Riding, R.J. and Calvey, I. (1981) 'The assessment of verbal-imagery learning style and their effect on the recall of concrete and abstract prose passages by eleven-year-old children', *British Journal of Psychology* **79**: 59-64.

Riding, R.J. and Cowley, J. (1986) 'Extraversion and sex differences in reading performance in eight-year-old children' *British Journal of Educational Psychology* **56**: 88-94.

Riding, R.J. and Dyer, V.A. (1980) 'The relationship between extraversion and verbal-imagery learning style in twelve-year-old children', *Personality and Individual Differences* **1**: 273-9.

INDEX